ABANDONED
PITTSBURGH
GEARS AND GHOSTS

ABANDONED PITTSBURGH
GEARS AND GHOSTS

THE HISTORIC STEEL CITY IN PICTURES

PHOTOGRAPHS BY
CHUCK BEARD

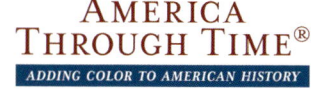

For my parents, Jerry and Joy Beard

America Through Time is an imprint of Fonthill Media LLC
www.through-time.com
office@through-time.com

Published by Arcadia Publishing by arrangement with Fonthill Media LLC
For all general information, please contact Arcadia Publishing:
Telephone: 843-853-2070
Fax: 843-853-0044
E-mail: sales@arcadiapublishing.com
For customer service and orders:
Toll-Free 1-888-313-2665

www.arcadiapublishing.com

First published 2018

Copyright © Chuck Beard 2018

ISBN 978-1-63499-046-2

All rights reserved. No part of this publication may be reproduced, stored in a retrieval system or transmitted in any form or by any means, electronic, mechanical, photocopying, recording or otherwise, without prior permission in writing from Fonthill Media LLC

Typeset in Trade Gothic 10pt on 15pt
Printed and bound by CPI Group (UK) Ltd, Croydon, CR0 4YY

CONTENTS

Introduction **7**

Foreword **9**

Connelley Trade School **11**

Engine House No. 16 **24**

Garden Theater **34**

LaSalle Electric Supply Co. **41**

Layton Bridge **50**

Mathies Coal Co. **58**

Homestead Municipal Building **66**

Wilkinsburg Train Station **72**

Carnegie Library Theater **82**

Western Penitentiary **90**

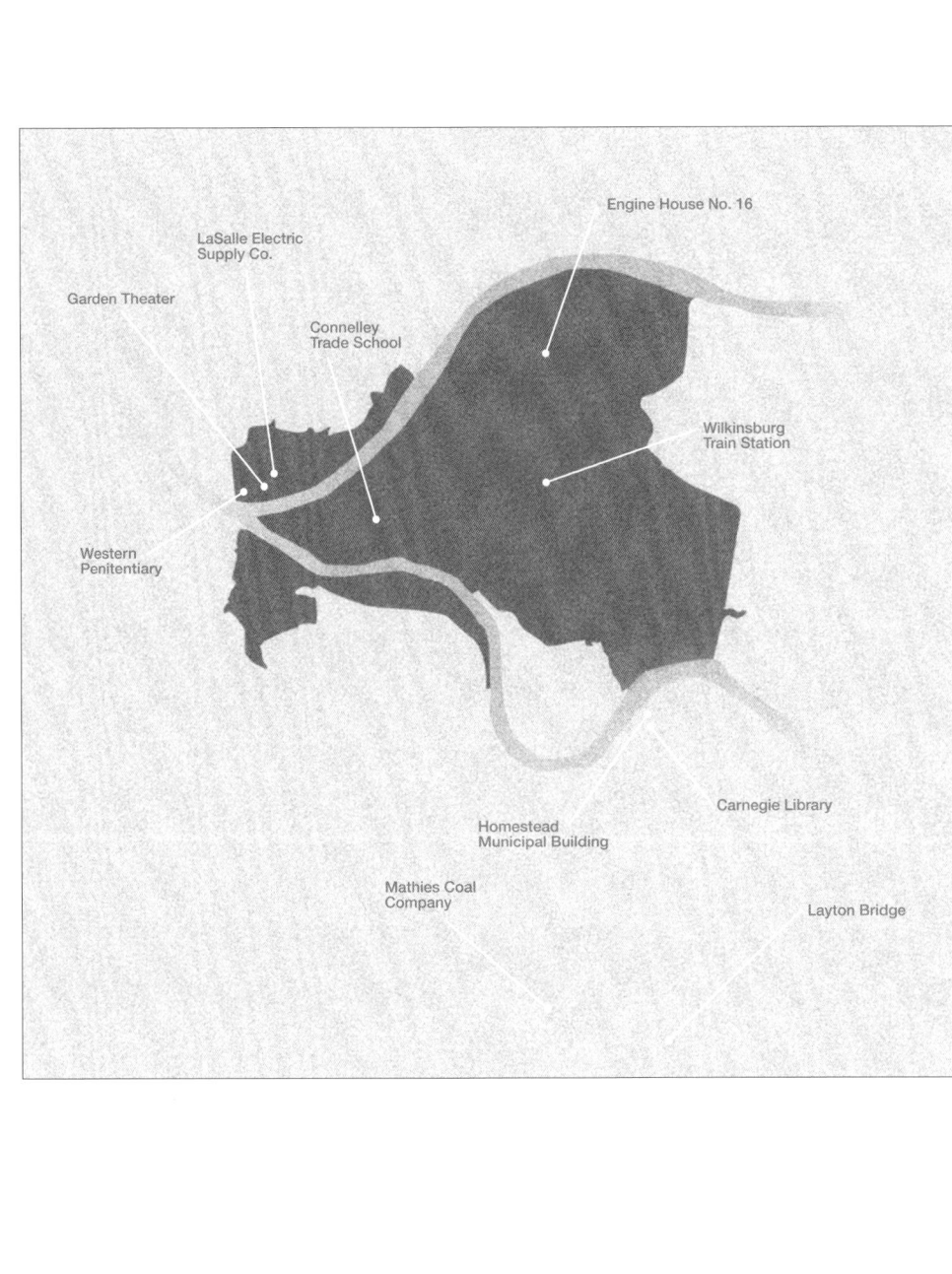

INTRODUCTION

Does a building have a soul? And once it is empty of people, does it still have a story to tell? I find an old building hidden behind tall grass and tangled vines. Its foundation is crumbling into chalky dust, and glass from shattered windows crunches under my feet. Paint peels from the door frame, curling at the ends toward the blackened roof. The door is open, but I hesitate, as always, wondering if someone is inside, if something sharp will cut me, if the blackened roof will collapse, if this is in any way a good idea. The hesitation can last for a few seconds to a few minutes. I may walk around the back of the building, then warily return to the front, hoping to gather a few shreds of information before committing myself to that tingling moment of entrance.

Inside, I freeze with a survival instinct. It's that chilling sensation of being in a place where I know I'm not supposed to be, and it's at odds with my fascination and curiosity to explore. In safe and familiar places, I don't think about the act of placing each footstep; but here — where the floor is hidden under beer bottles and lampshades and telephone wires and broken chair legs and moldy papers — each footstep is navigated slowly, heel first, then toes, then my full weight. I wish I had worn thicker boots. I wish I had a warmer coat.

Then I see that one of the moldy papers is a vacation schedule with names of people who worked here. Those people looked forward to those vacations, and they came to this building every day to make money to pay for those vacations. It's that memory of energy that still echoes in every room of this building, once alive with ambitious projects and office talk and dreams of vacations.

Taking a camera into these abandoned places has been given the denigrating moniker of ruin porn, implying that photographing these sites in their death throes is a form of exploitation. But there is beauty and spirit in the old and the new alike.

Consider two similar portraits in a different medium, side by side: one of a year-old infant, fresh-faced with newness and health and the dewy colors of possibility; the other of his great-grandfather, brow lined with furrows, eyes clouded a pale blue with cataracts, lips thin and dry from days and years and decades of grinning, scowling, laughing and grimacing in black-and-white pain.

The new face will one day be a story, but now it barely has a title and opening line. The older, broken face has an ambiguous beginning, a risky, tumultuous middle, and an uncertain ending. That is the story that I'd rather hear.

— **Chuck Beard**

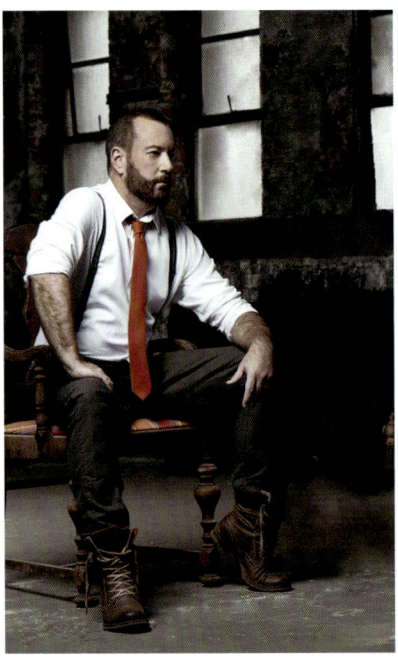

ABOUT THE AUTHOR

Photographer Chuck Beard is founder of the ongoing Abandoned Pittsburgh project, which has led to research into and exploration of twenty-plus historic locations in the Pittsburgh area. The project documents the Steel City's forgotten industrial and community sites where "beauty in decay" still exists. He is art director at Pittsburgh Magazine and a prolific photographer in artistic and journalistic media. He lives in the North Hills of Pittsburgh. Learn more at abandonedpittsburgh.com and beardfoto.com.

FOREWORD

At the beginning of the twentieth century, unusually tall buildings were under construction in New York City and these instantly captured the attention of photographers. The Flat Iron Building was unique among the rest due to its curious, yet beautiful, triangular shape. Legendary photographer Edward Steichen immortalized this iconic structure in several gum-bichromate prints, which have since become as iconic as the building itself. Along with the Shelton Hotel and Chrysler Building, skyscrapers became the subject matter for celebrated photographers from Alfred Stieglitz to Margaret Bourke-White to Berenice Abbott, and many others.

As the twentieth century came to a close, photographers became fascinated by an entirely different aspect of architecture: its decay. In North America, from East Coast to West, there has been widespread attention focused on the physical appearance of post-industrialization. One gifted photographer from Western Pennsylvania who combs the regional landscape for visible traces of our industrial heritage is Chuck Beard. This volume of his Abandoned Pittsburgh project provides yet another compelling installment of his portraits of the Steel City's forgotten past.

The vantage point chosen by Beard for his images is illustrative of the respect that he has for these broken buildings. These hoppers, meal bins, vats, conveyors, grates, sinkholes, tunnels and funnels are so mysterious to us that we can only read them as fascinating studies of tonal gradations, enjoying the way light falls on form. In this way they become what has recently been termed ruin porn. We are indeed seduced by the visual richness but feel slightly guilty about luxuriating in what is really a view of decline.

Recognizing the past is a first step toward respecting it, and Beard participates in that effort with each abandoned site around Pittsburgh that attracts his focus. He recognizes that these once-vibrant sites have stories to tell, and we are grateful to him for his dedication in translating them for present and future generations.

— Linda Benedict-Jones
(Linda Benedict-Jones is former Curator of Photography at the Carnegie Museum of Art, Pittsburgh)

CONNELLEY TRADE SCHOOL

At the time of its opening in 1929, the Clifford B. Connelley Trade School was one of the largest and most modern schools of its kind, offering classes in carpentry, plumbing, automotive mechanics and more to over 1,500 students. The Classical Revival and Art Deco building in the Hill District, over 170,000 square feet, housed a cafeteria, gymnasium, auditorium and below-ground swimming pool. After severe budget cuts in the 1990s and a sharp decline in enrollment, the school closed but was given new life as the Energy Innovation Center. Renovation of the auditorium, shown here, will begin soon.

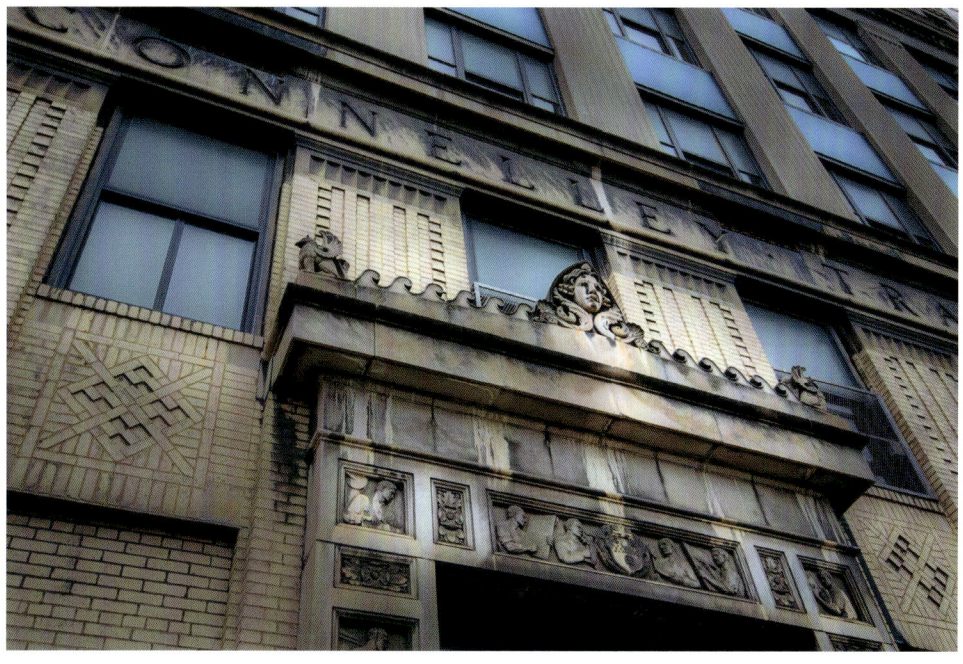

Facade

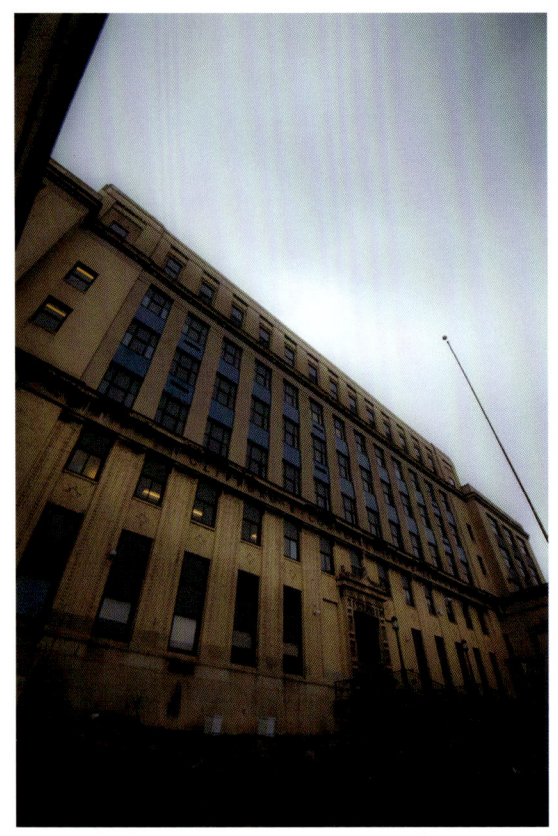

Exterior

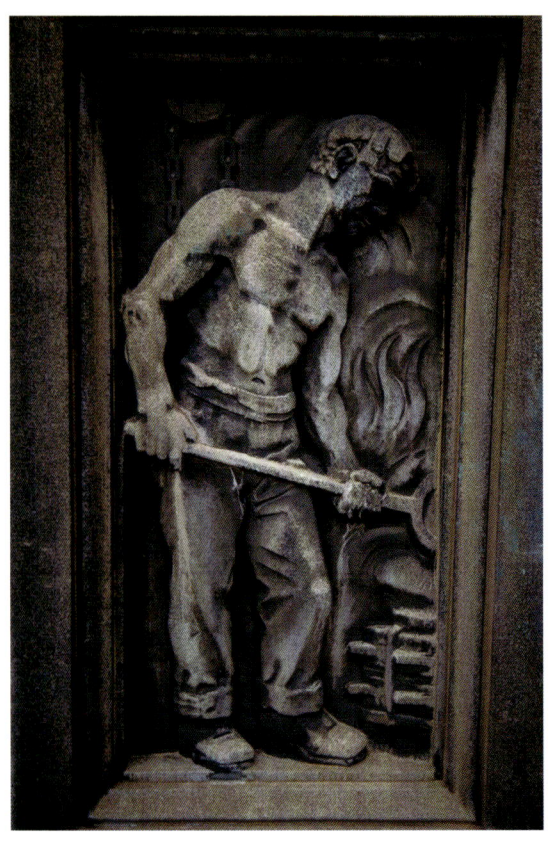

Shovel

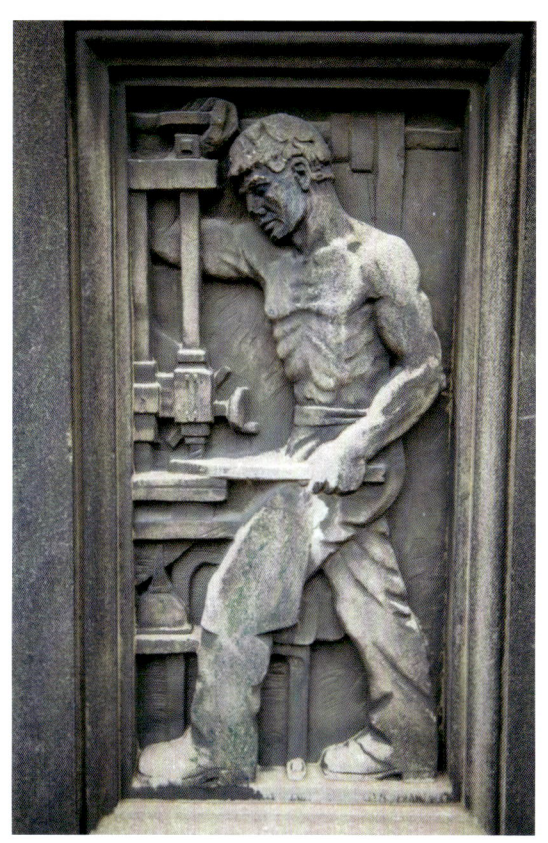

Vice

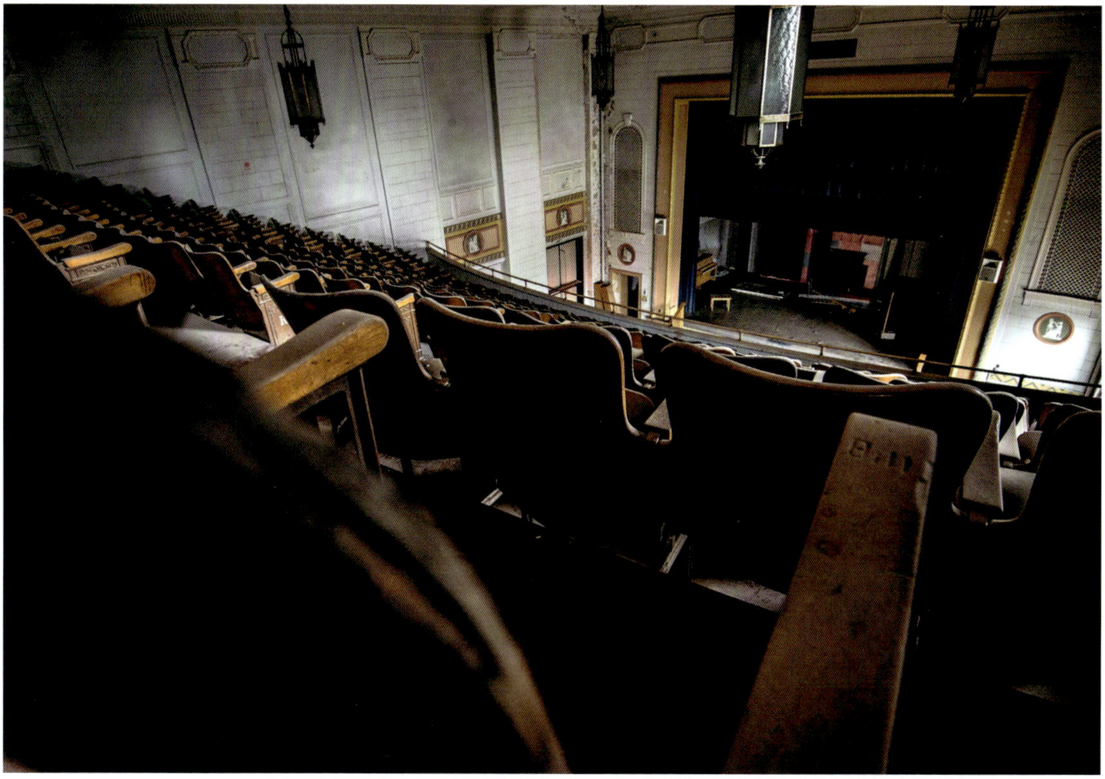

Balcony Angle

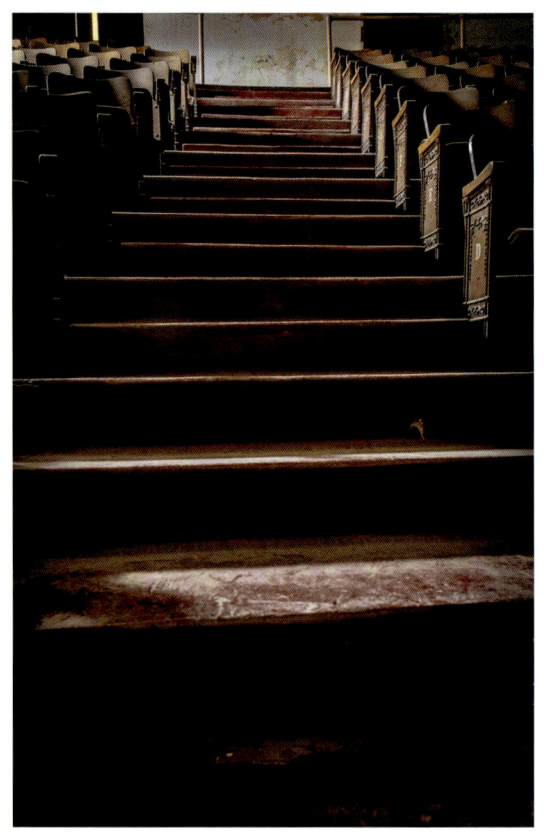

Steps

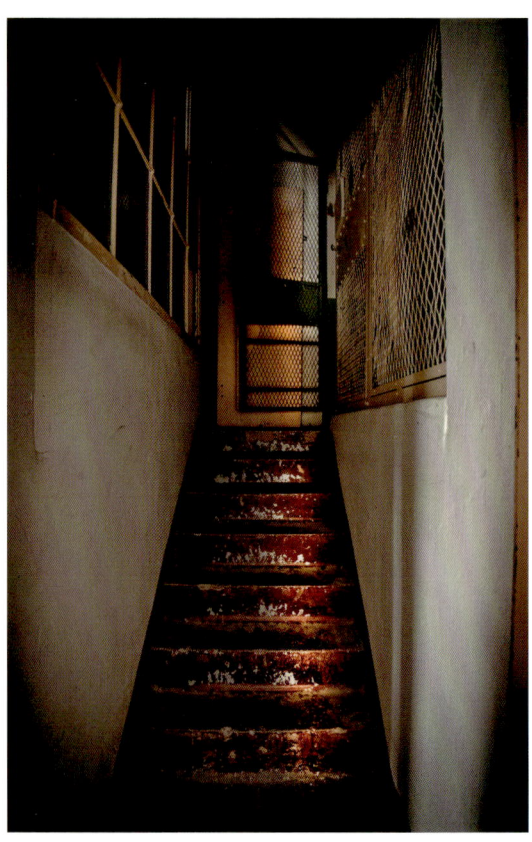

Loft Cage

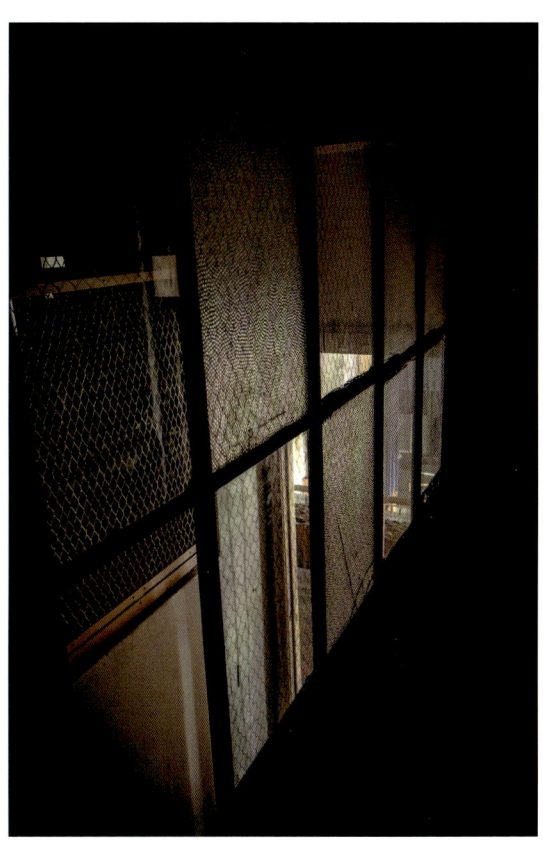

Projector Room

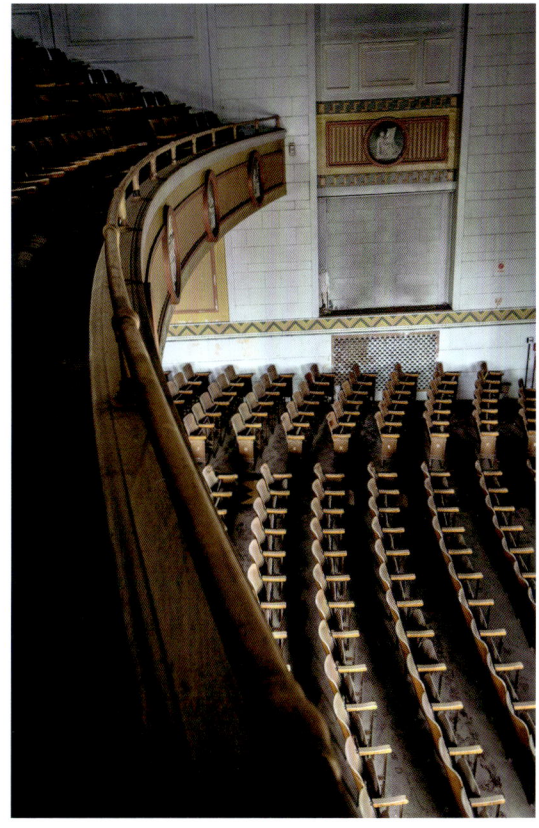

Balcony Shadow

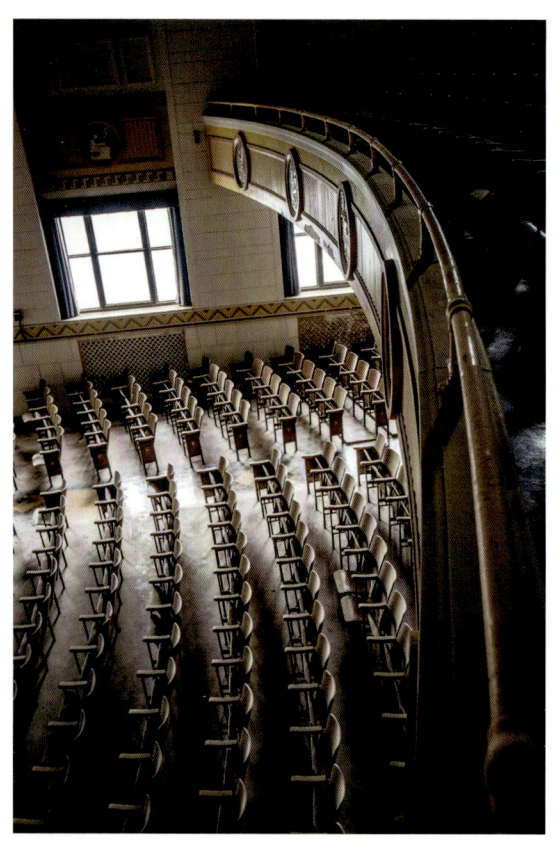

Balcony Light

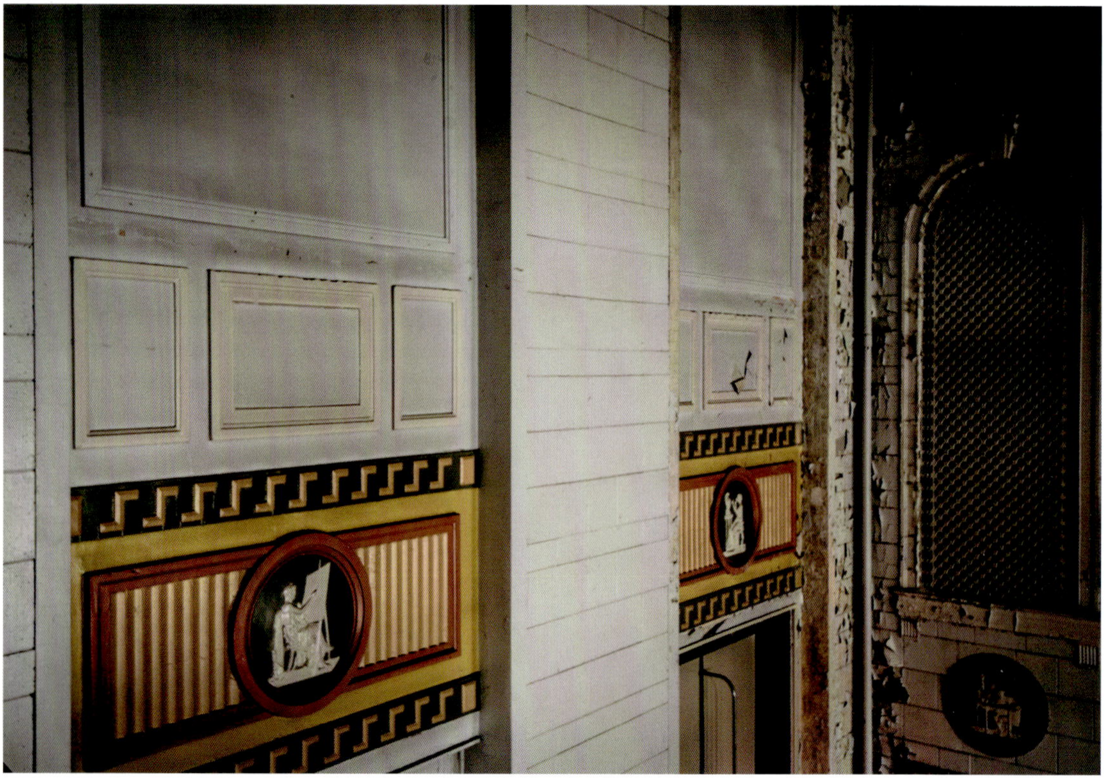

Arts

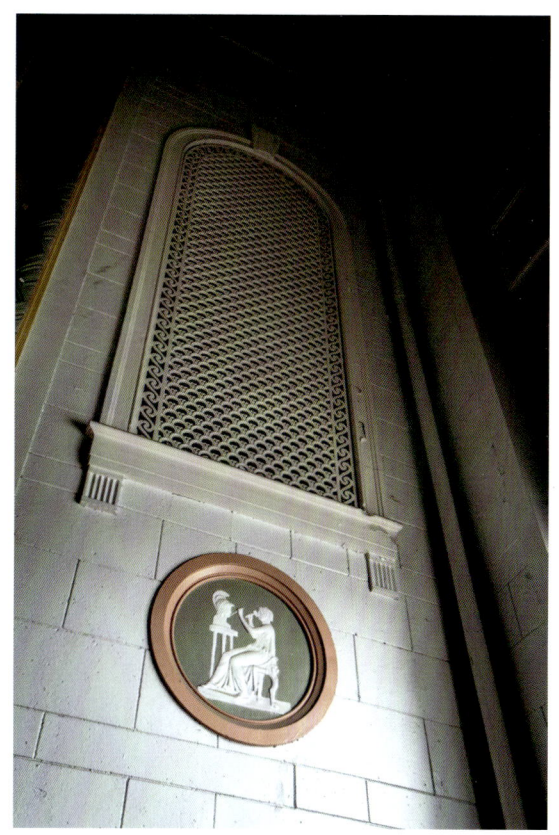
Medallion

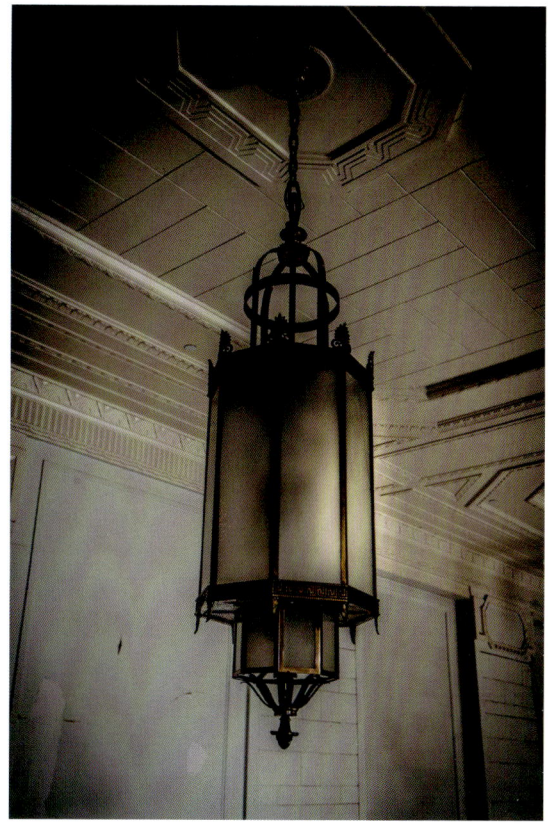
Hanging Light

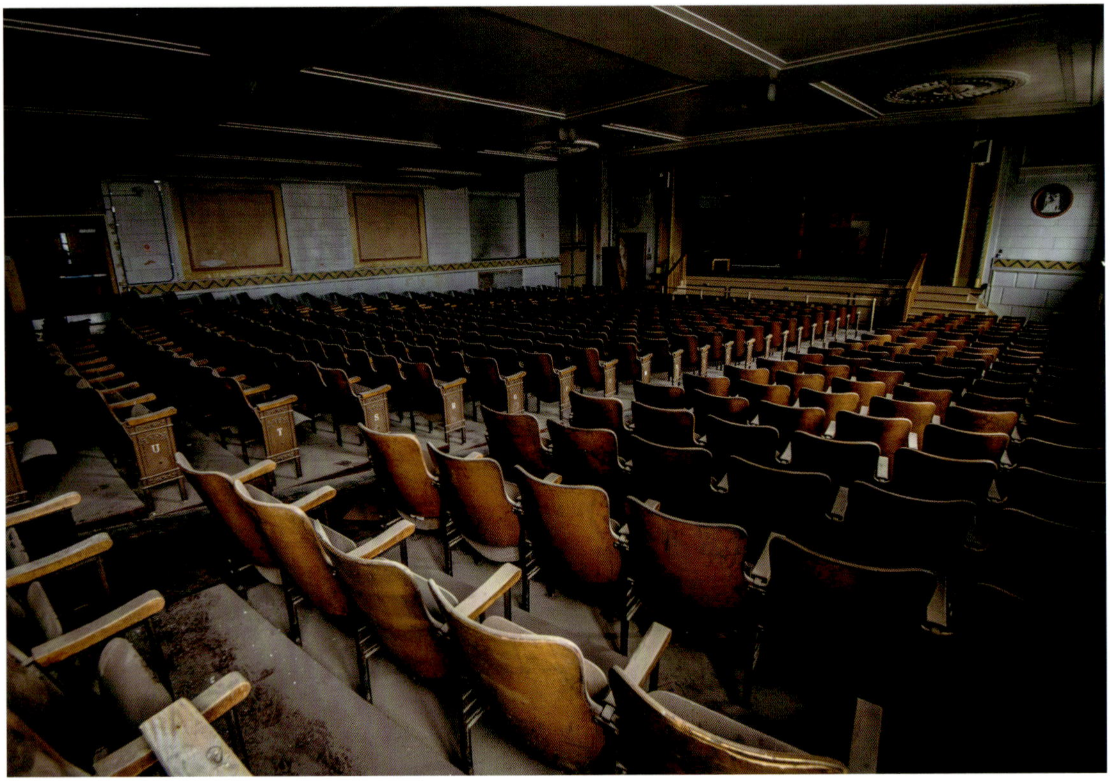

Main Floor

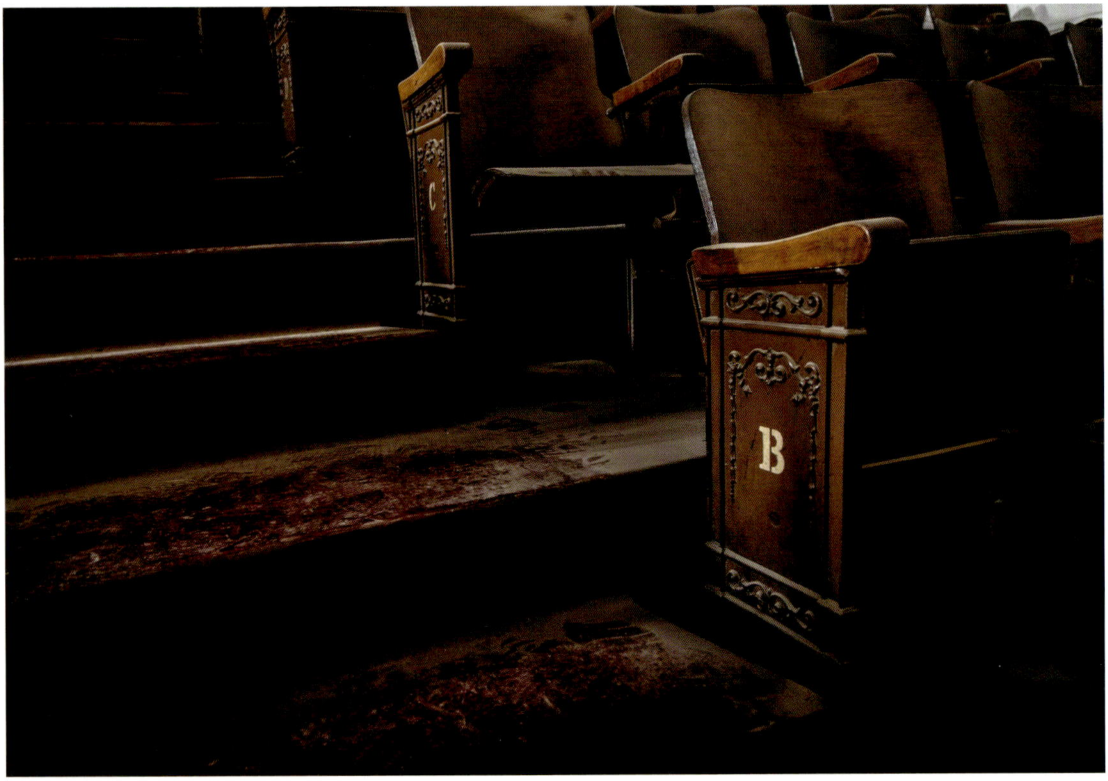

Chair BC

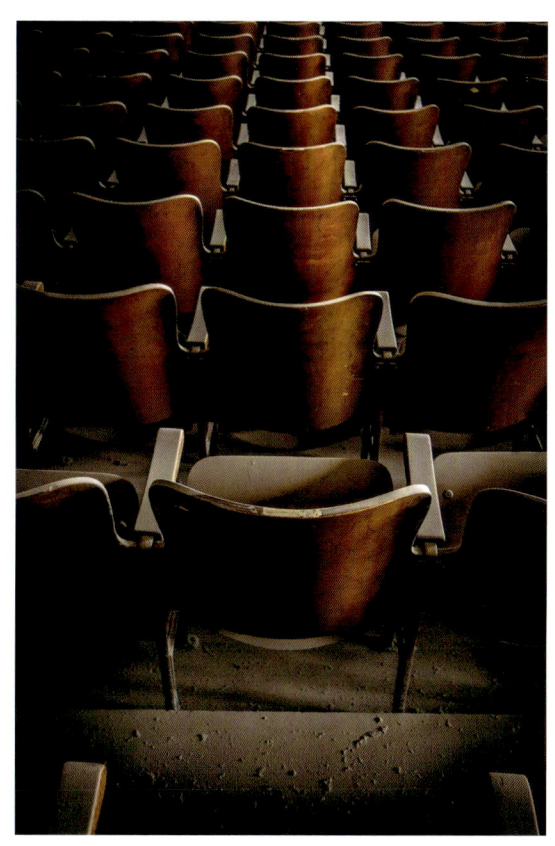

Standing Room Only (vertical)

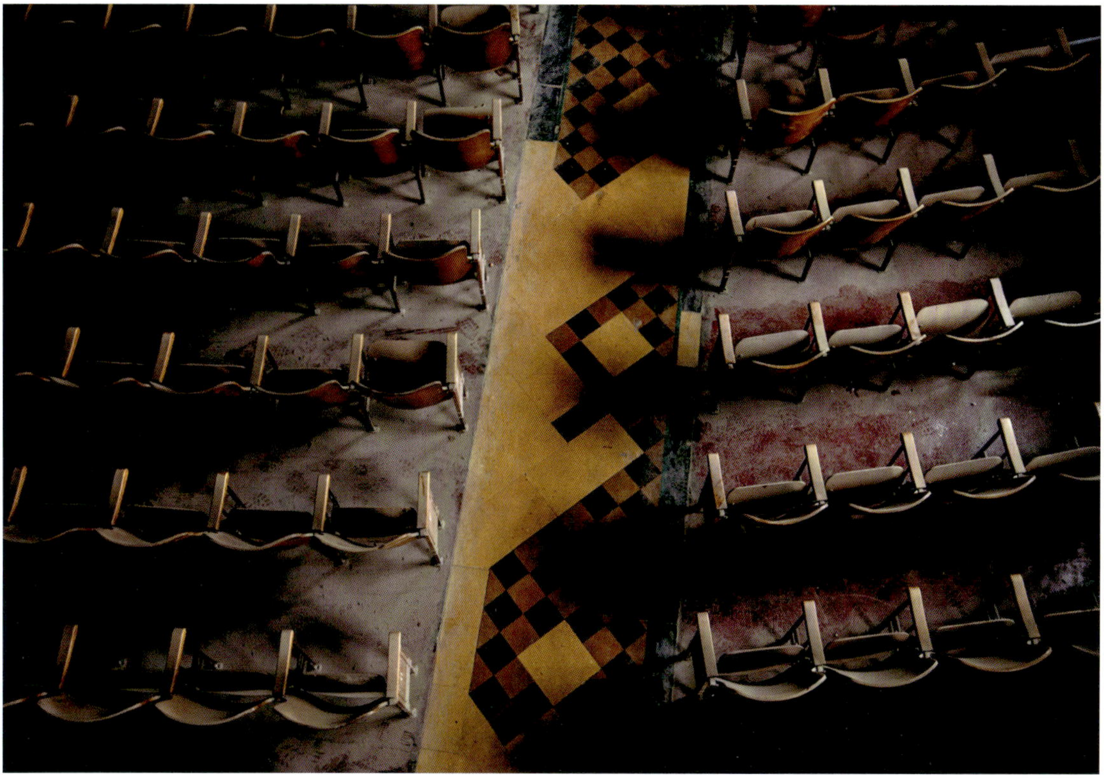

Standing Room Only (horizontal)

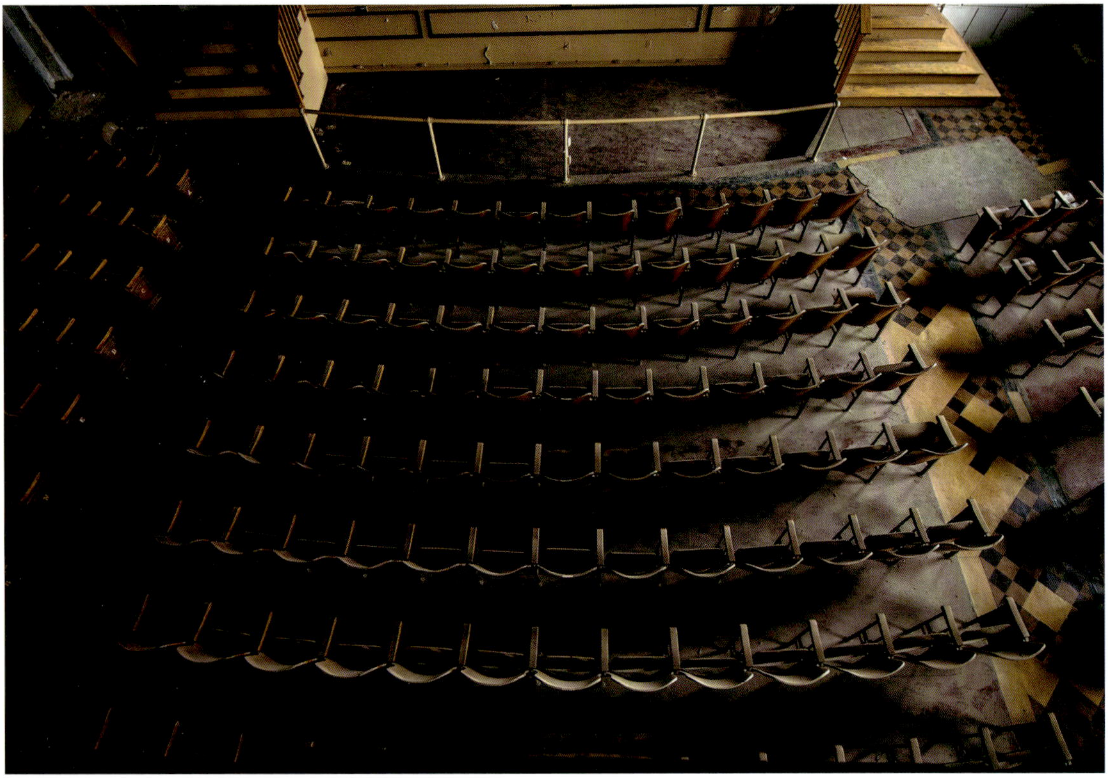

Bird's Eye

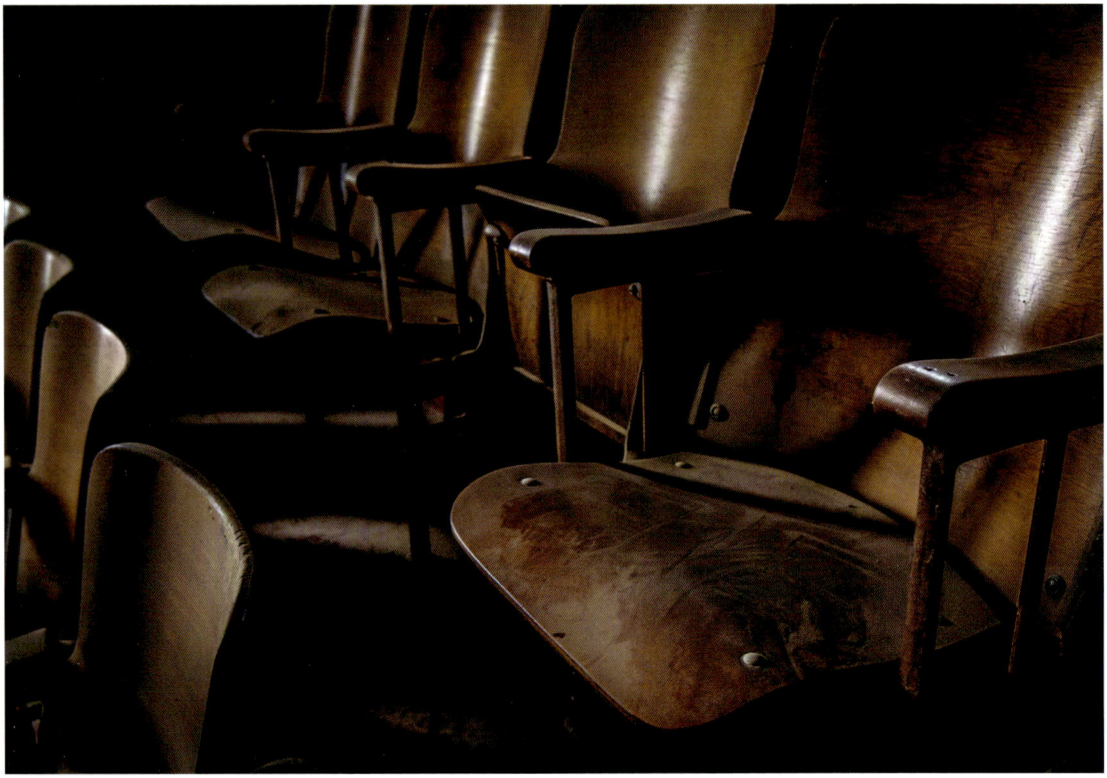

Empty Seats

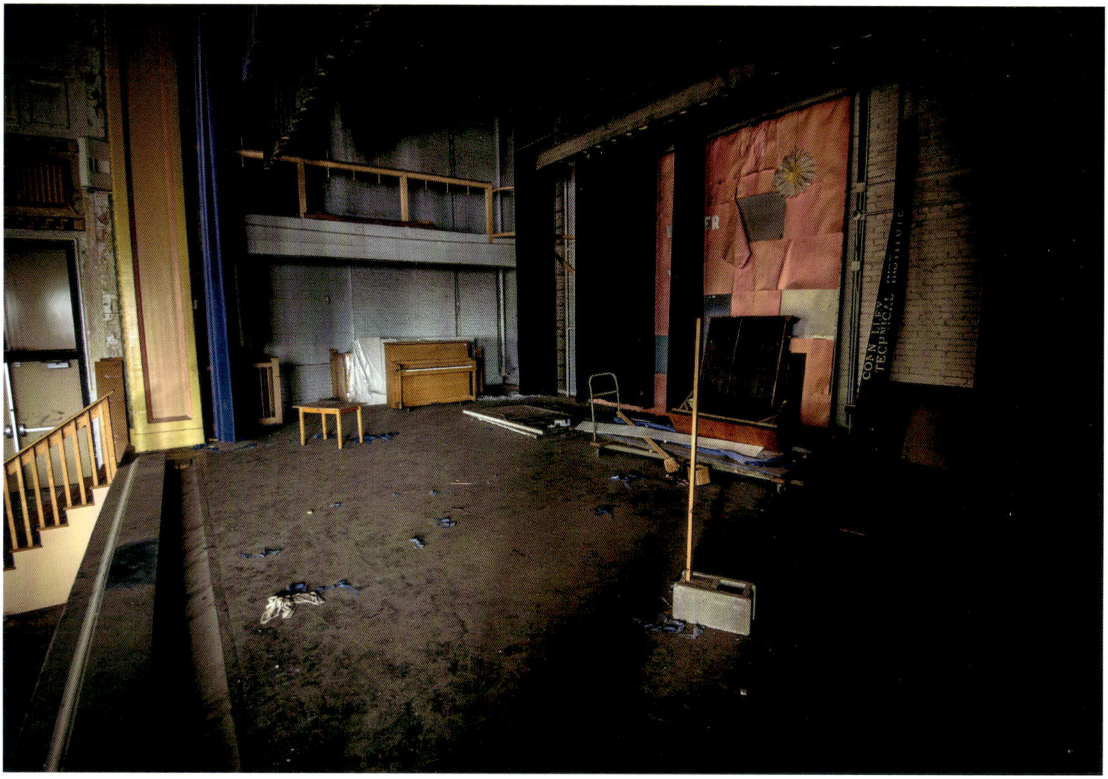

Stage Left

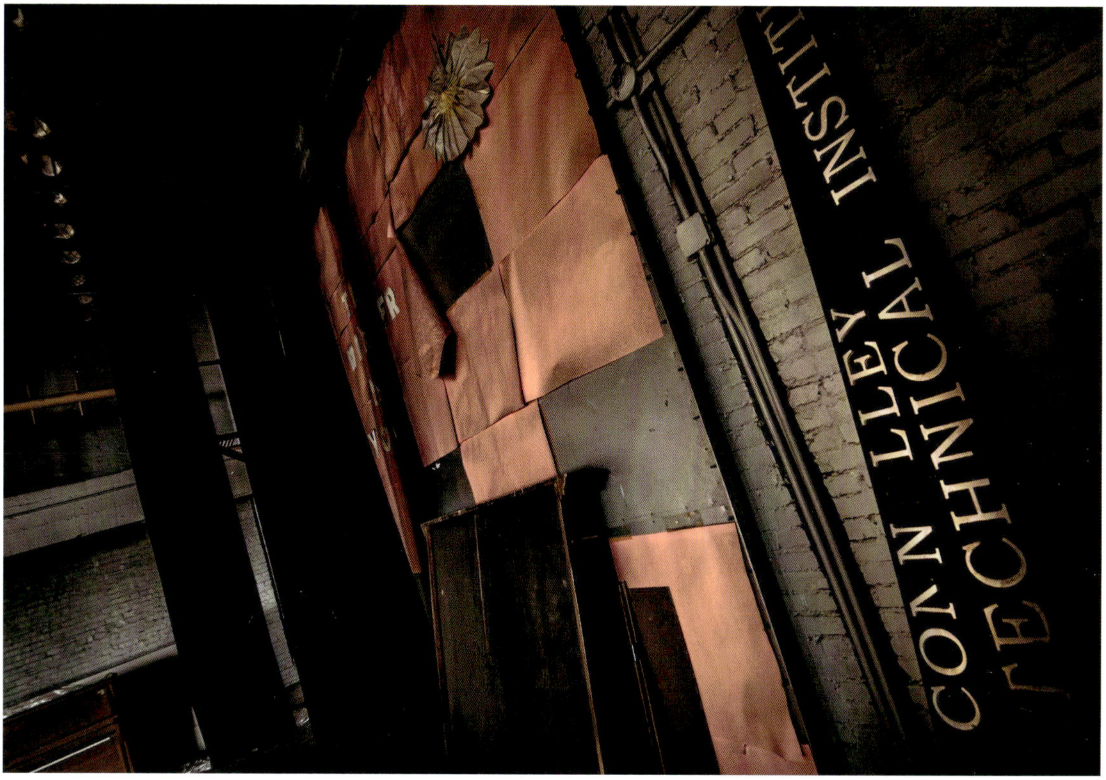

Connelley Banner

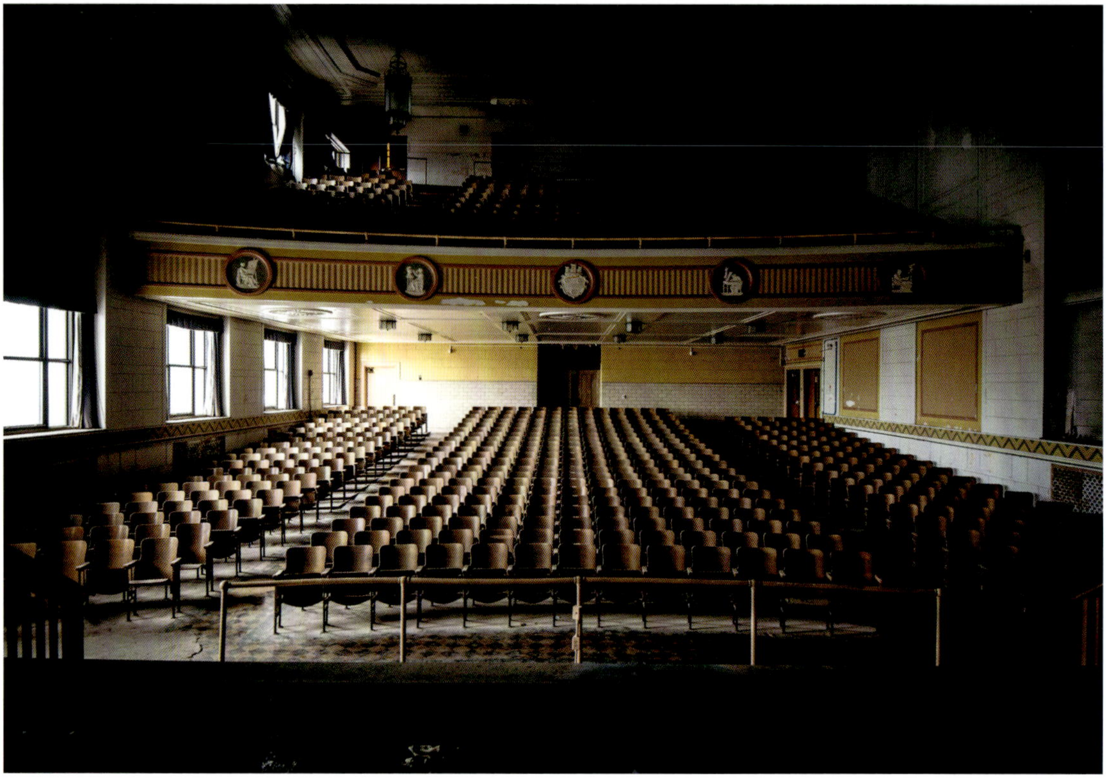

Stage

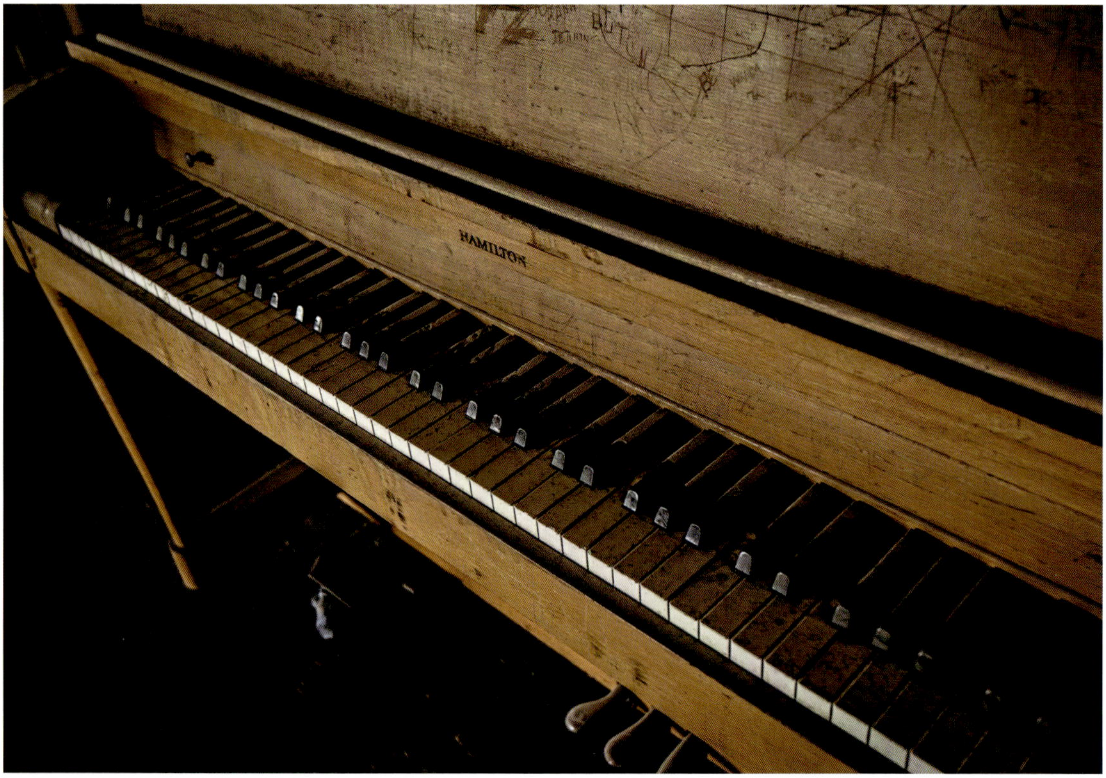

Piano

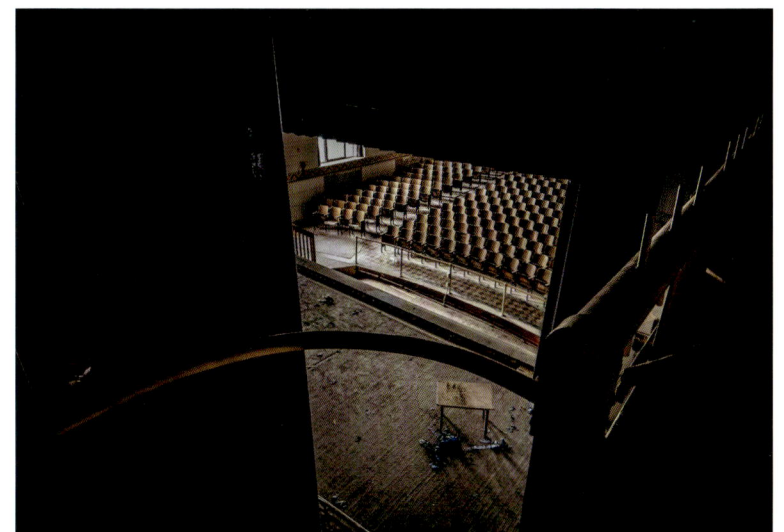

Wings

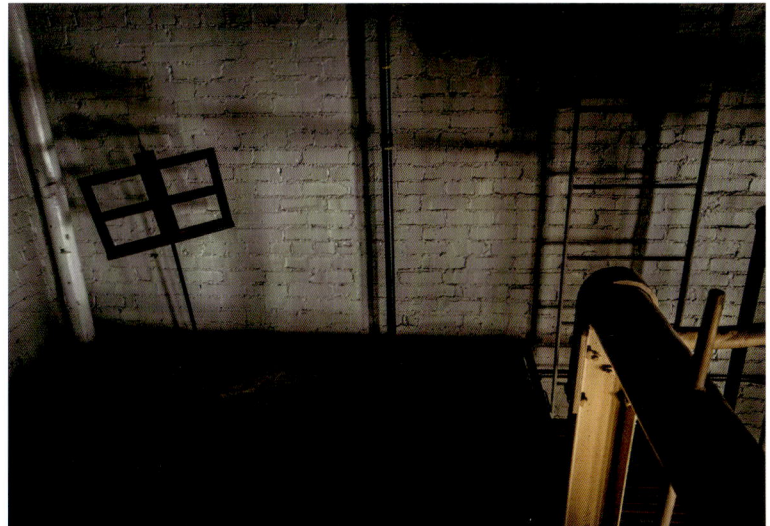

Music Stand

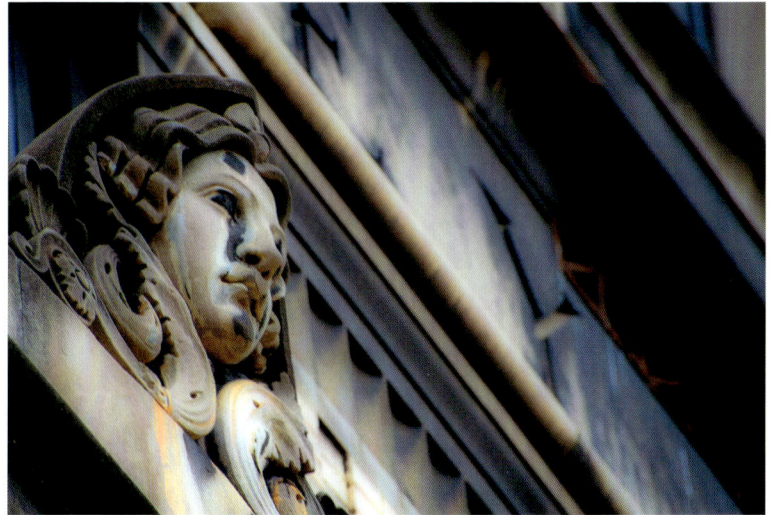

Goddess

ENGINE HOUSE NO. 16

Engine House No. 16 was built in 1889 and featured two large front bays that opened for horse-drawn fire engines. The city of Pittsburgh used the building as a fire station until the late 1980s; the former basement shower shown here was used as an armory. The building has been renovated as the new home of one of the city's most successful design firms.

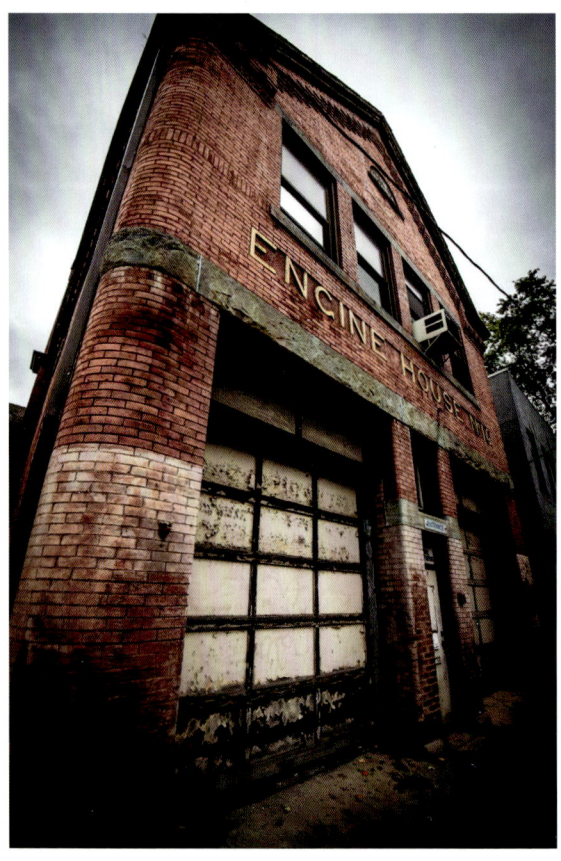

Facade

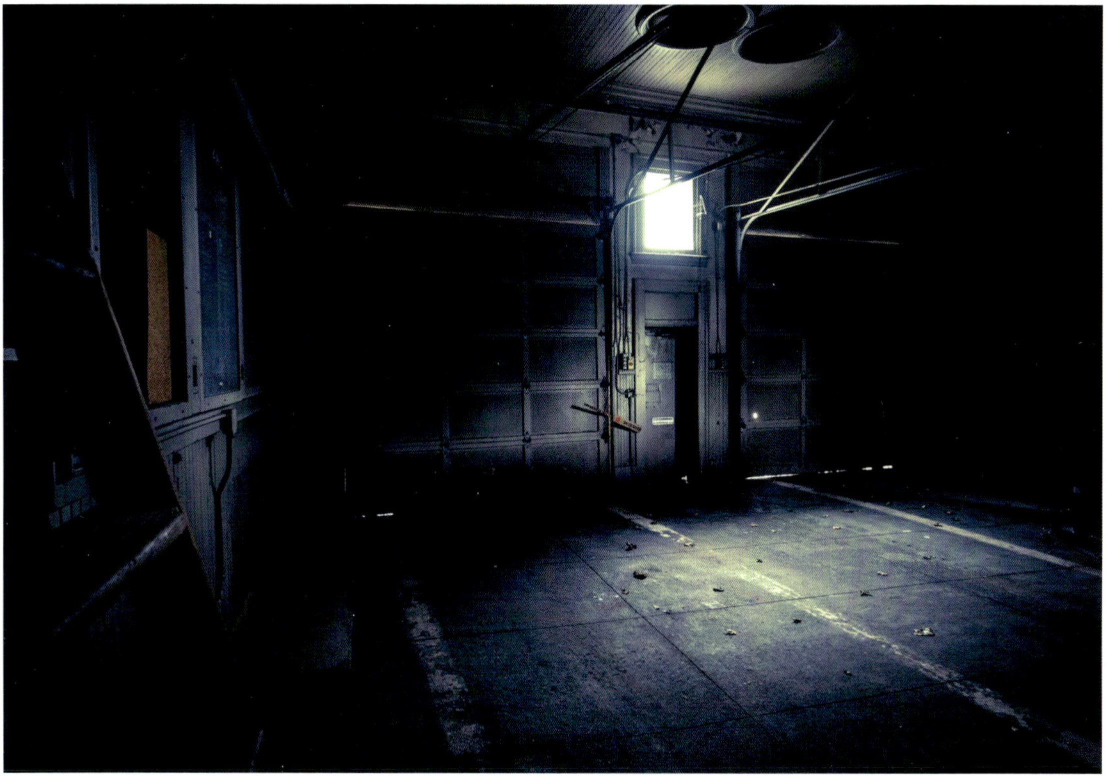

Fire Hall

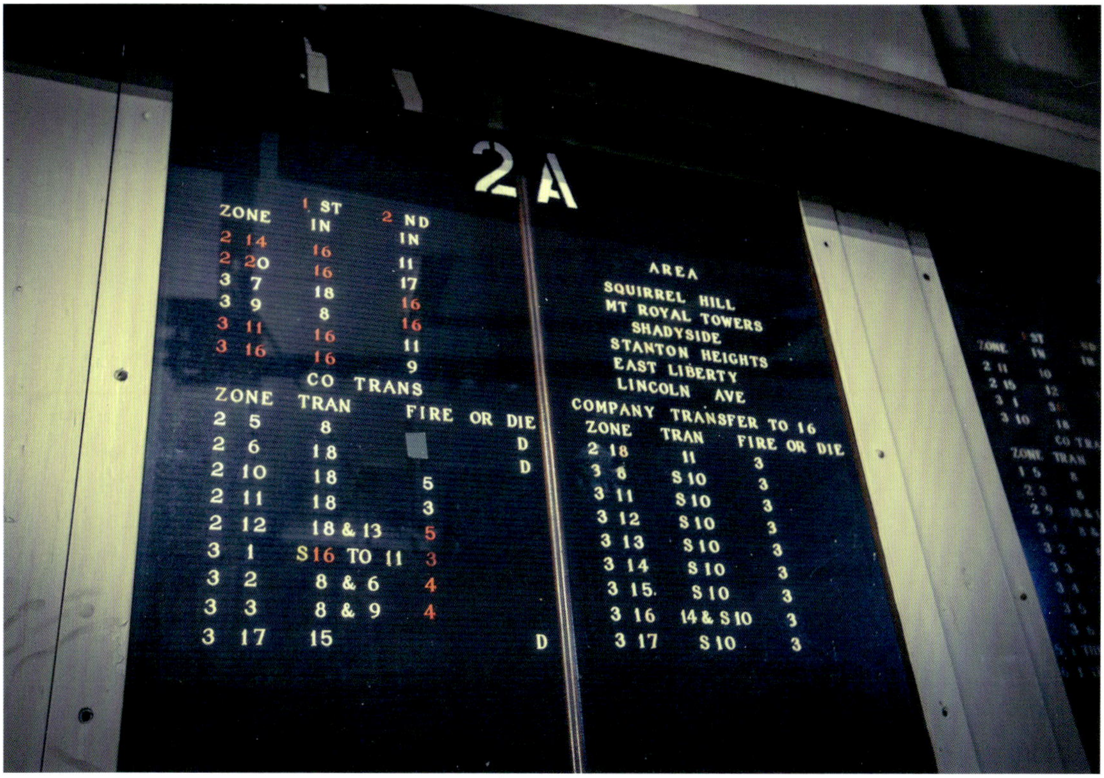

2A

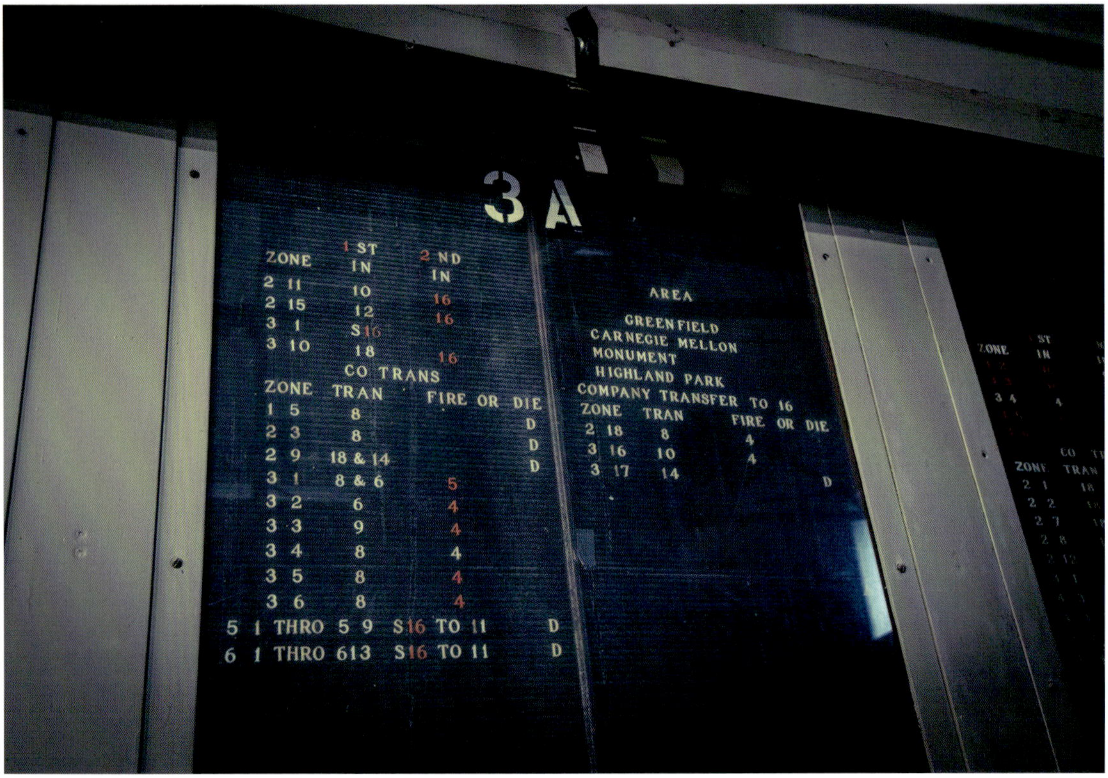

3A

ZONE	1ST IN	2ND IN
2 11	10	16
2 15	12	16
3 1	S16	
3 10	18	16

CO TRANS

ZONE	TRAN	FIRE OR DIE
1 5	8	D
2 3	8	D
2 9	18 & 14	D
3 1	8 & 6	5
3 2	6	4
3 3	9	4
3 4	8	4
3 5	8	4
3 6	8	4
5 1 THRO 5 9	S16 TO 11	D
6 1 THRO 613	S16 TO 11	D

AREA
GREENFIELD
CARNEGIE MELLON
MONUMENT
HIGHLAND PARK

COMPANY TRANSFER TO 16

ZONE	TRAN	FIRE OR DIE
2 18	8	4
3 16	10	4
3 17	14	D

3A

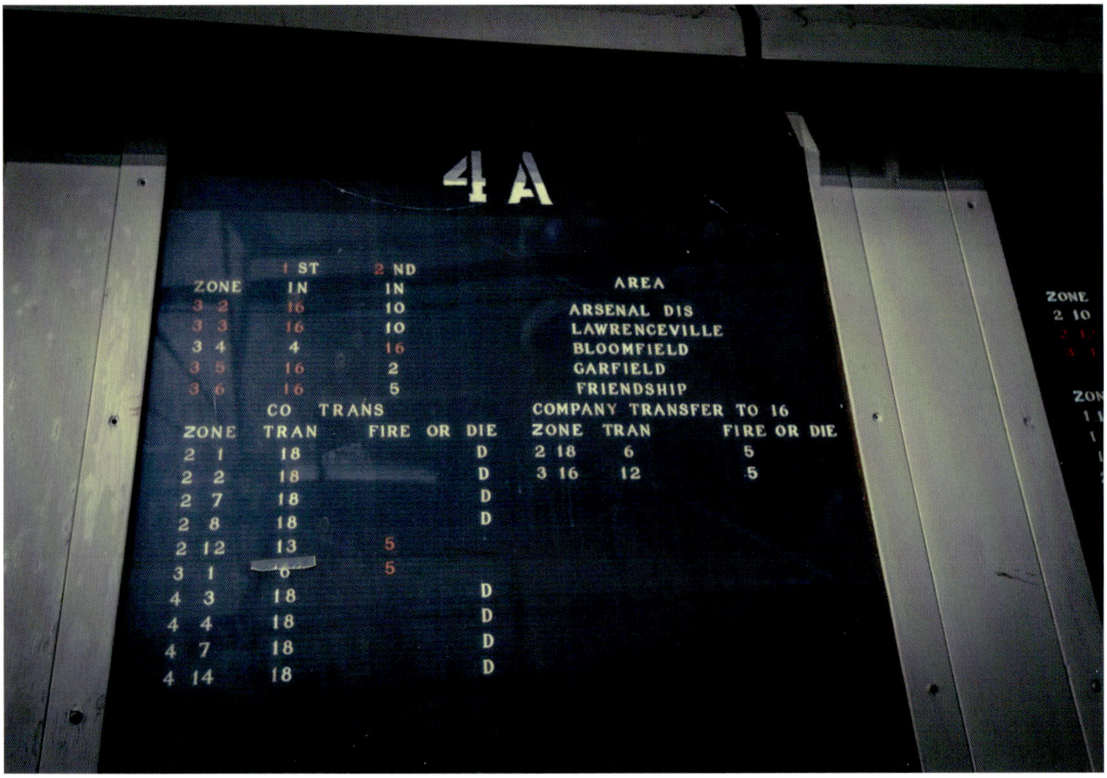

4A

ZONE	1ST IN	2ND IN
3 2	16	10
3 3	16	10
3 4	4	16
3 5	16	2
3 6	16	5

CO TRANS

ZONE	TRAN	FIRE OR DIE
2 1	18	D
2 2	18	D
2 7	18	D
2 8	18	D
2 12	13	5
3 1	6	5
4 3	18	D
4 4	18	D
4 7	18	D
4 14	18	D

AREA
ARSENAL DIS
LAWRENCEVILLE
BLOOMFIELD
GARFIELD
FRIENDSHIP

COMPANY TRANSFER TO 16

ZONE	TRAN	FIRE OR DIE
2 18	6	5
3 16	12	5

4A

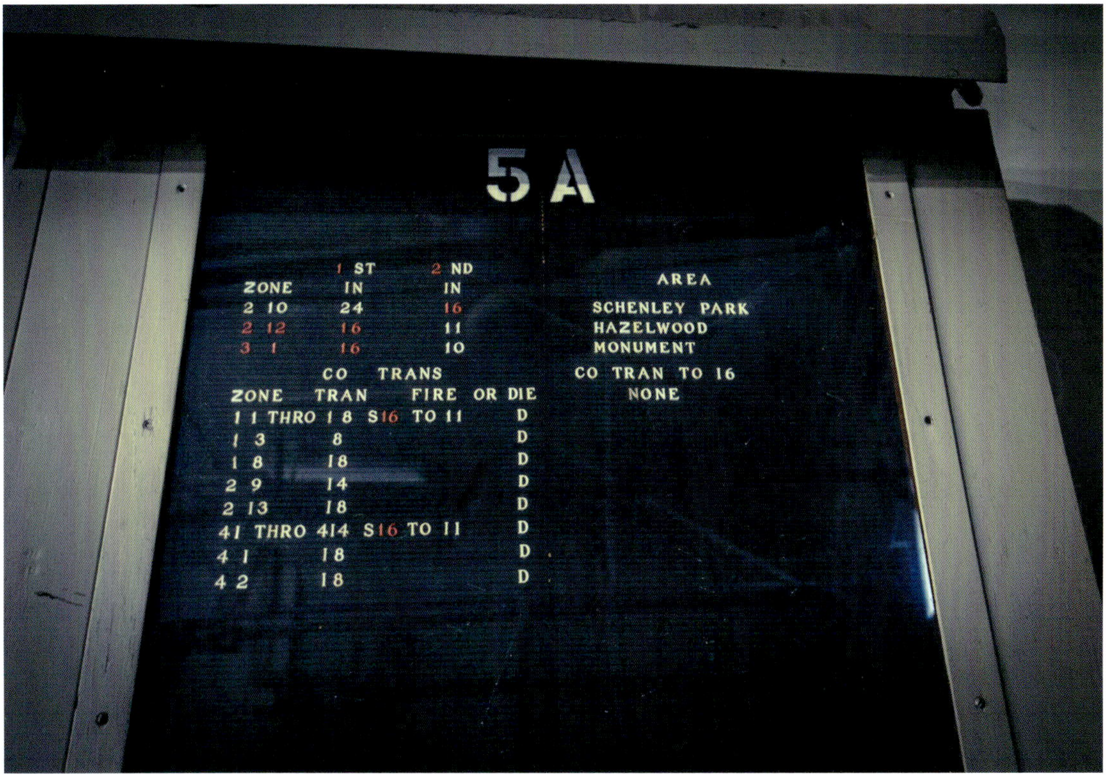

5A

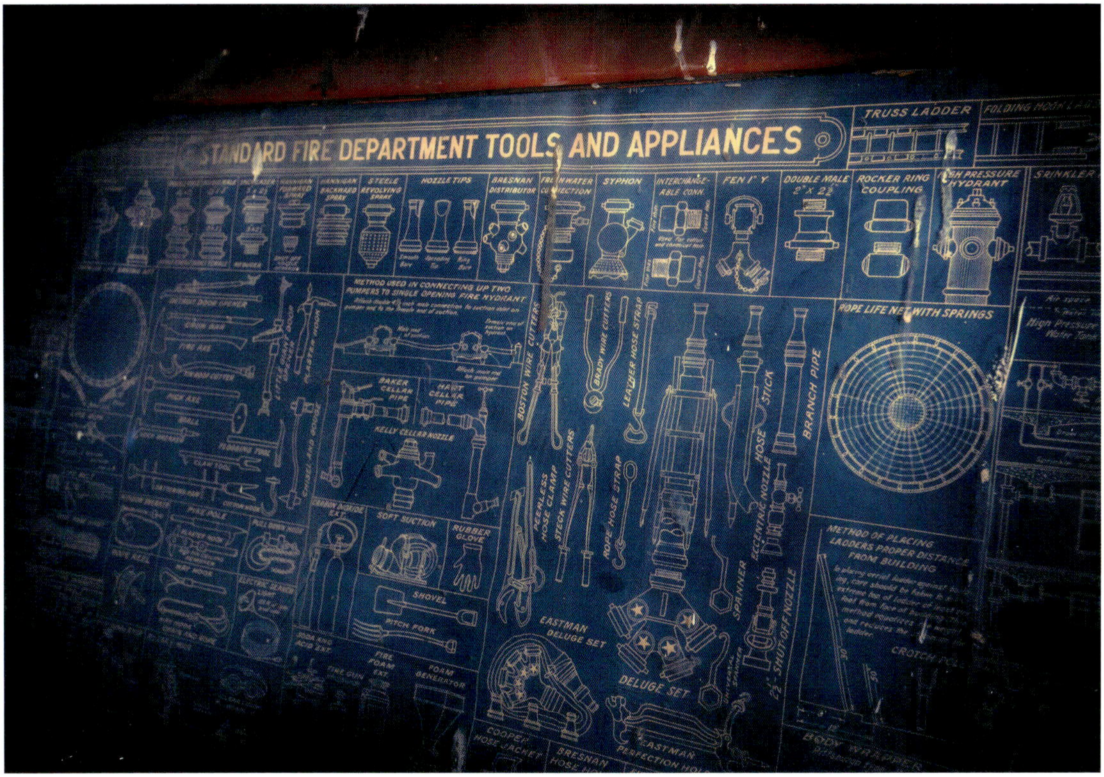

ZONE	1 ST IN	2 ND IN	AREA
2 10	24	16	SCHENLEY PARK
2 12	16	11	HAZELWOOD
3 1	16	10	MONUMENT

	CO	TRANS	CO TRAN TO 16
ZONE	TRAN	FIRE OR DIE	NONE
1 1 THRO 1 8	S 16 TO 11		D
1 3	8		D
1 8	18		D
2 9	14		D
2 13	18		D
4 1 THRO 4 14	S 16 TO 11		D
4 1	18		D
4 2	18		D

5A

Tools and Appliances

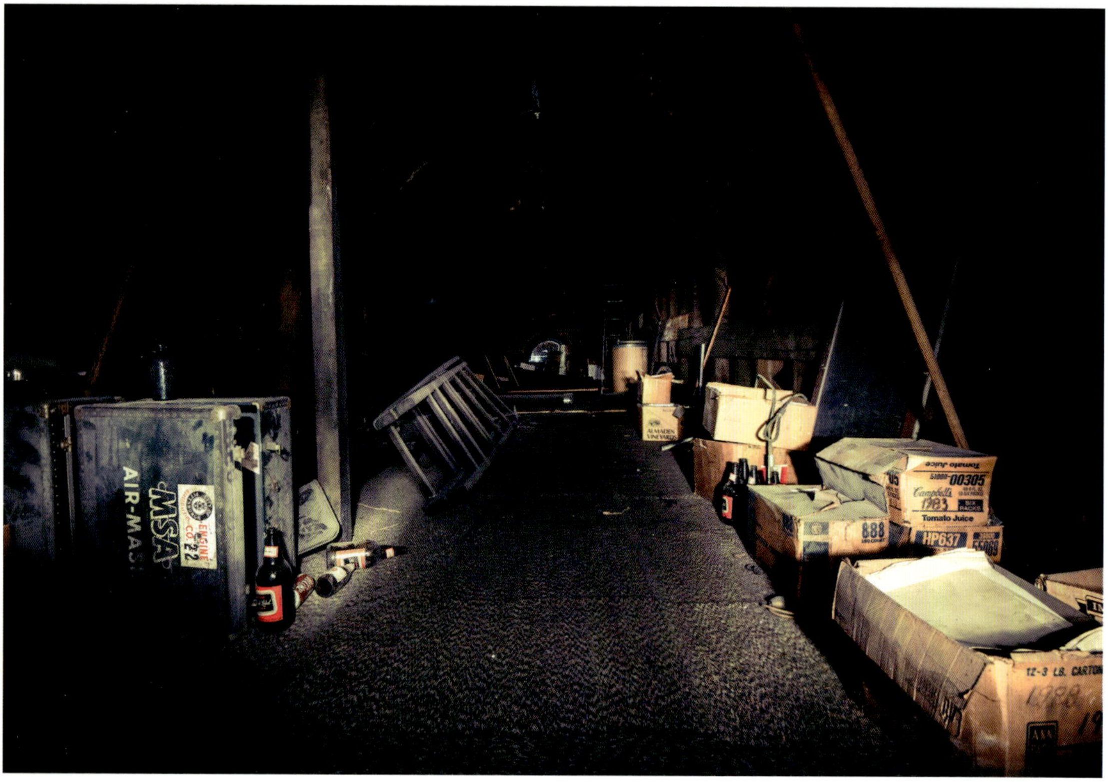

Attic

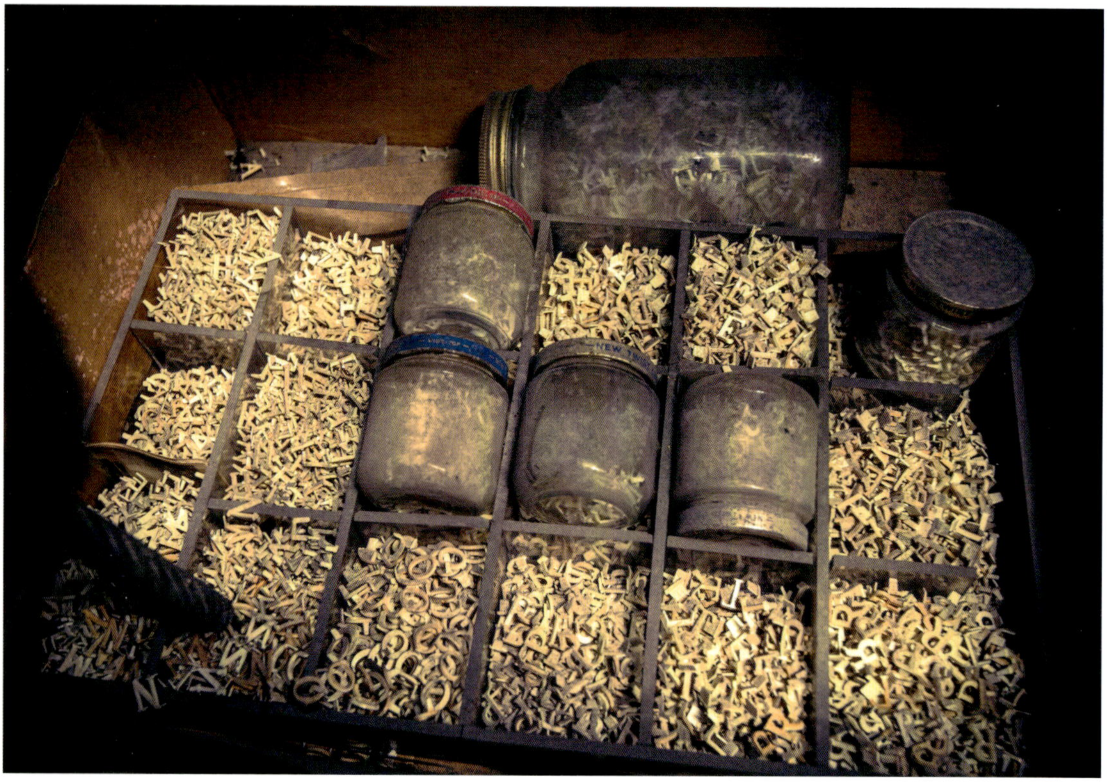

Letter Bin

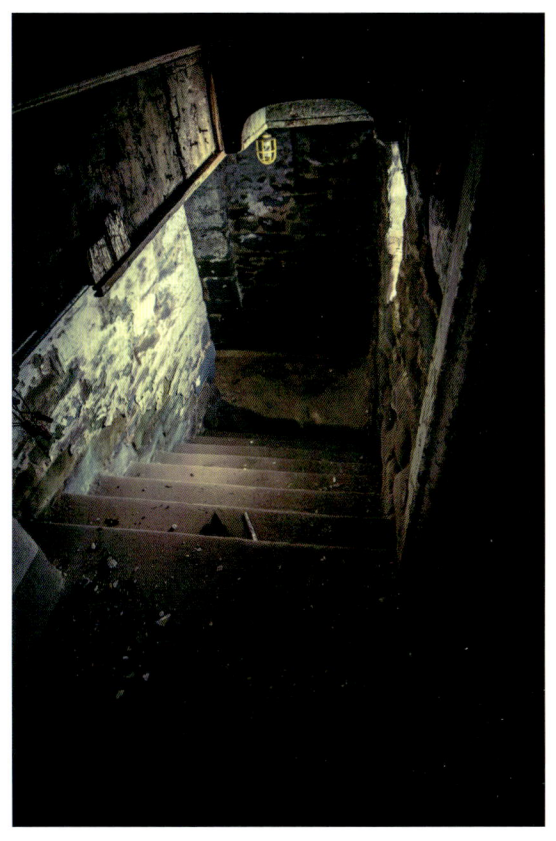

Basement

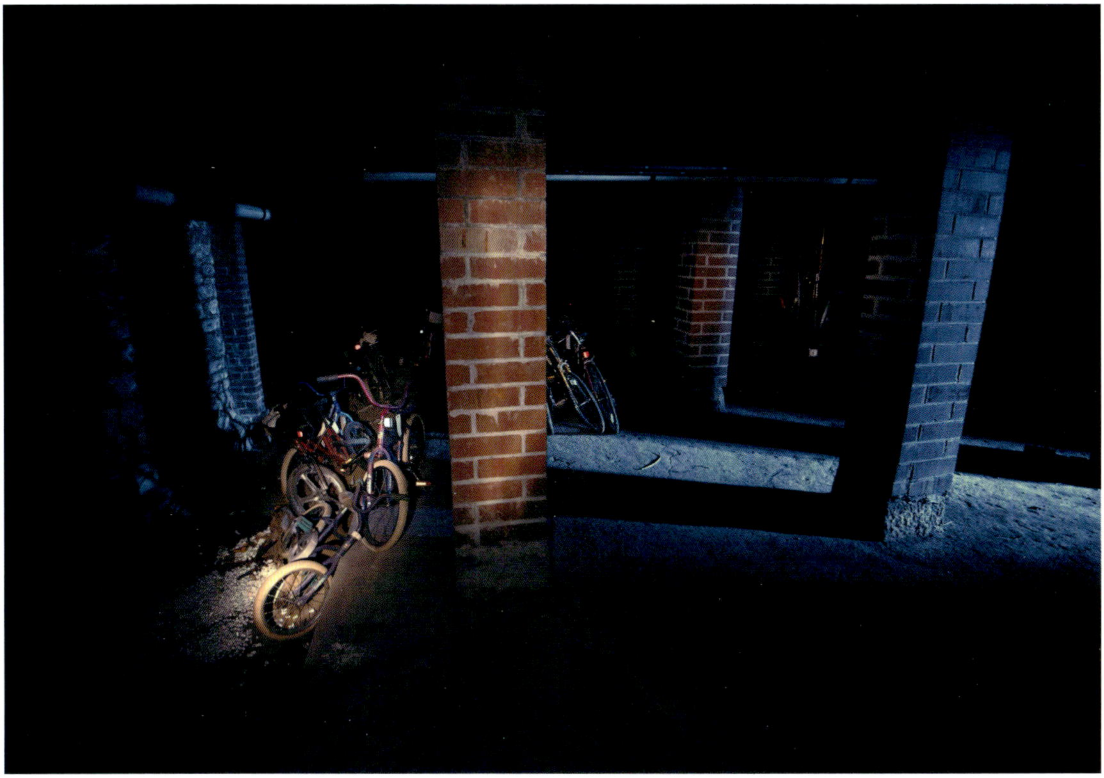

Abandoned Bicycles

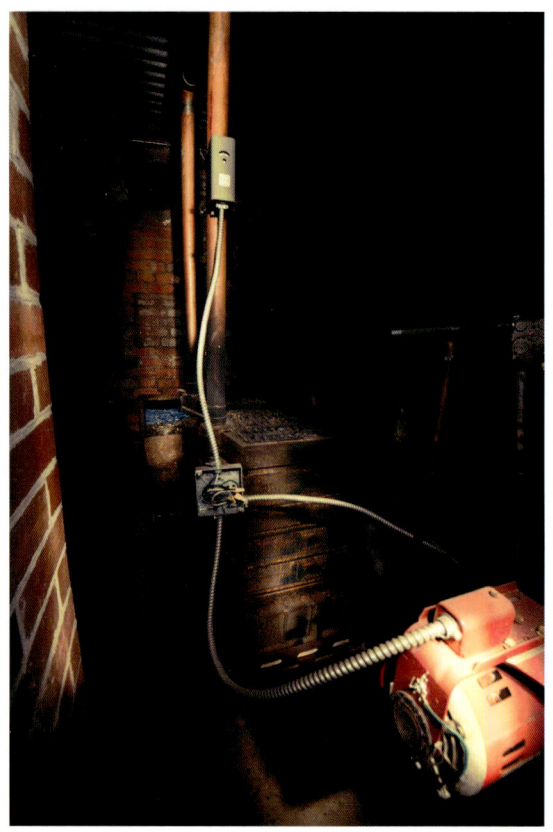

Circuit

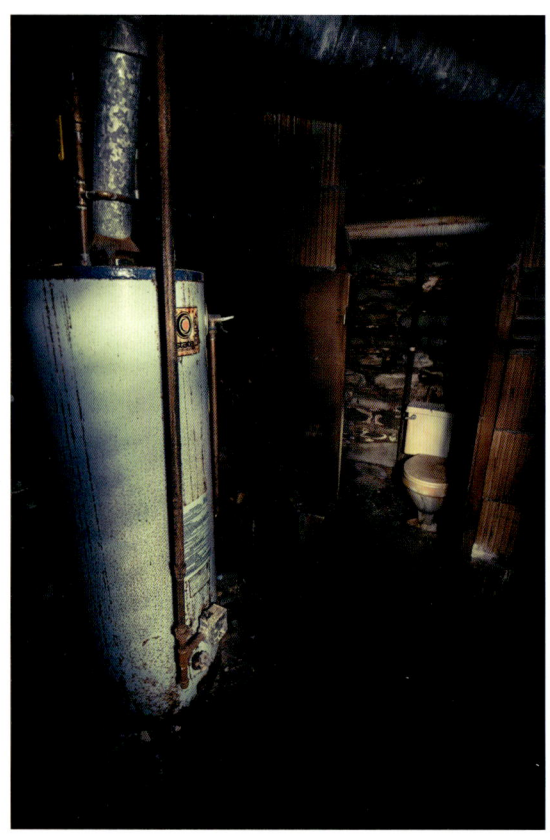

Toilet

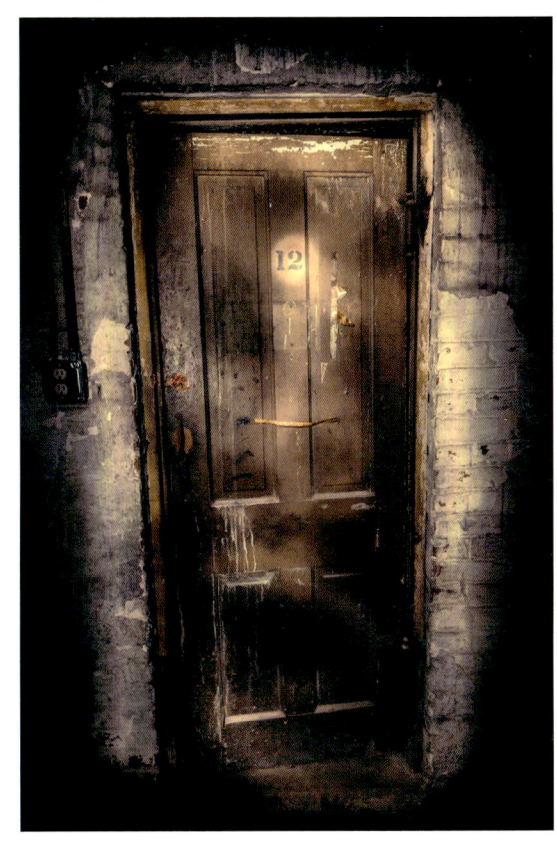

Door 12

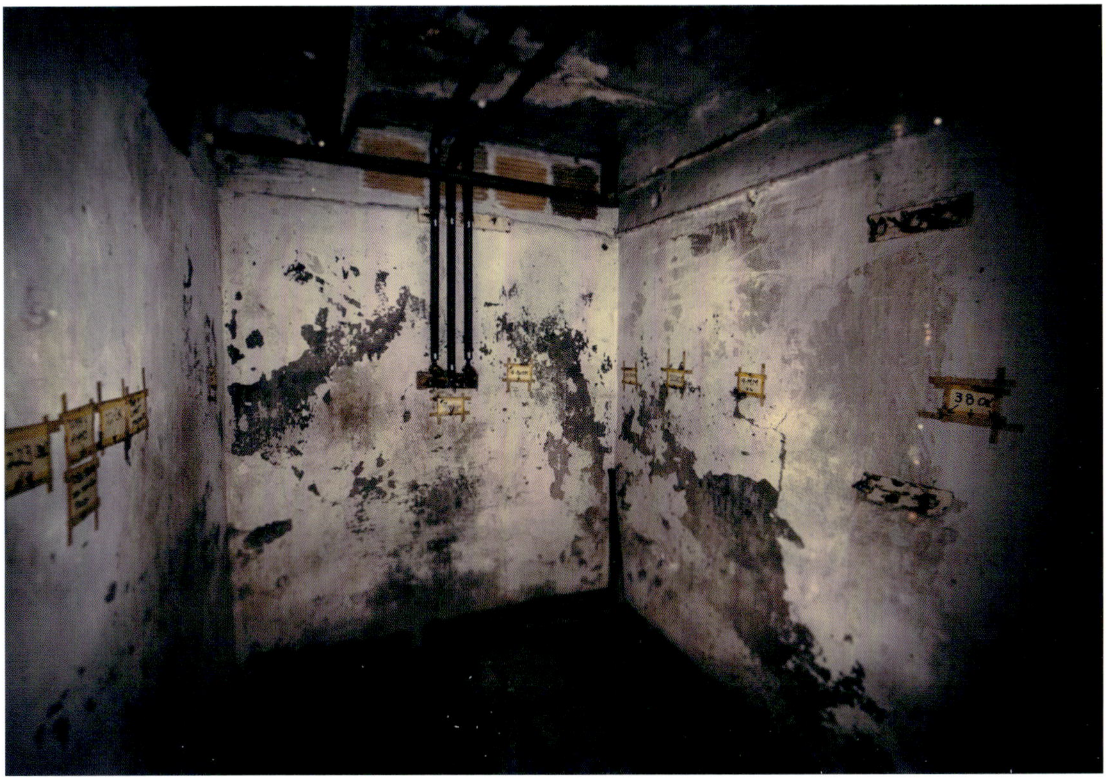

Shower

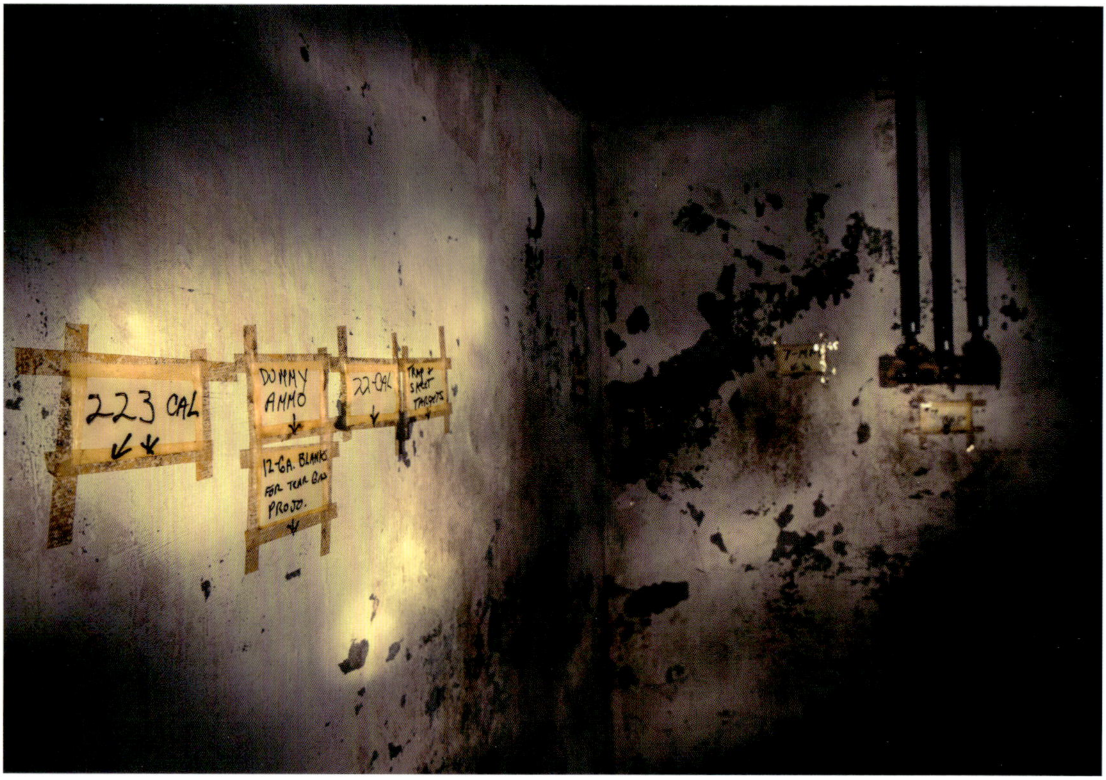

Ammo

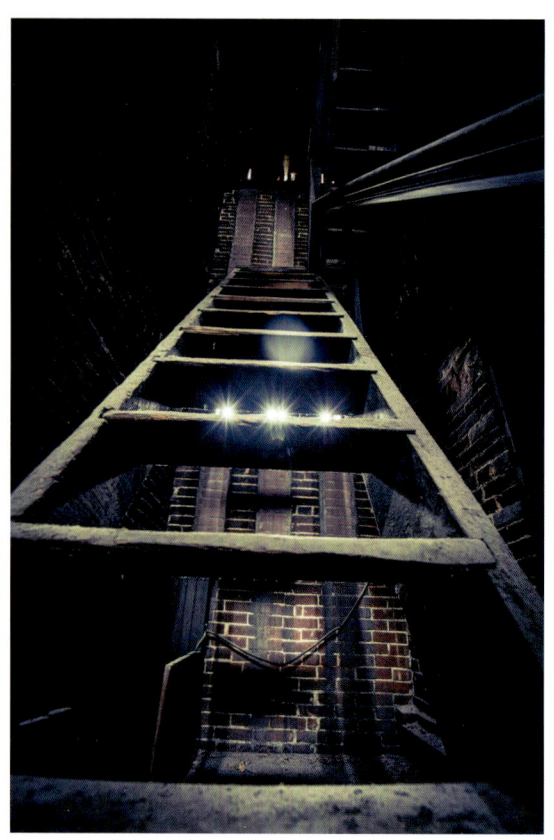

Ladder

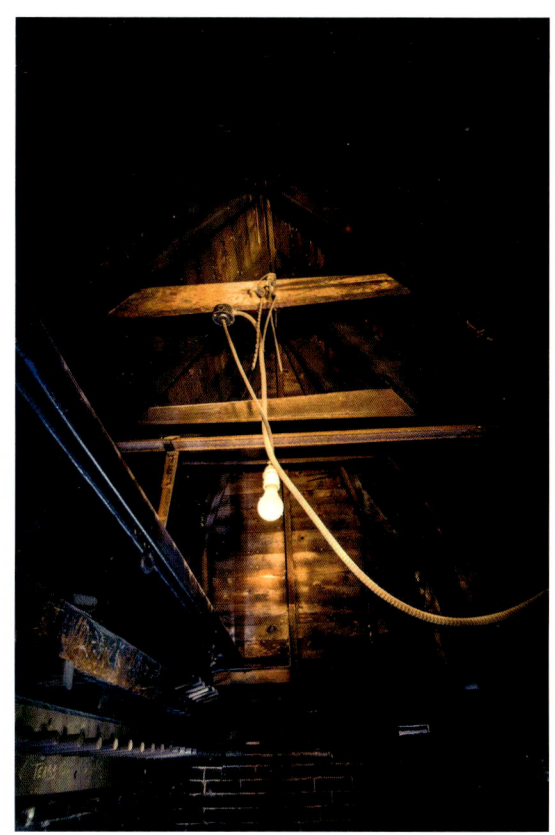

Attic Light

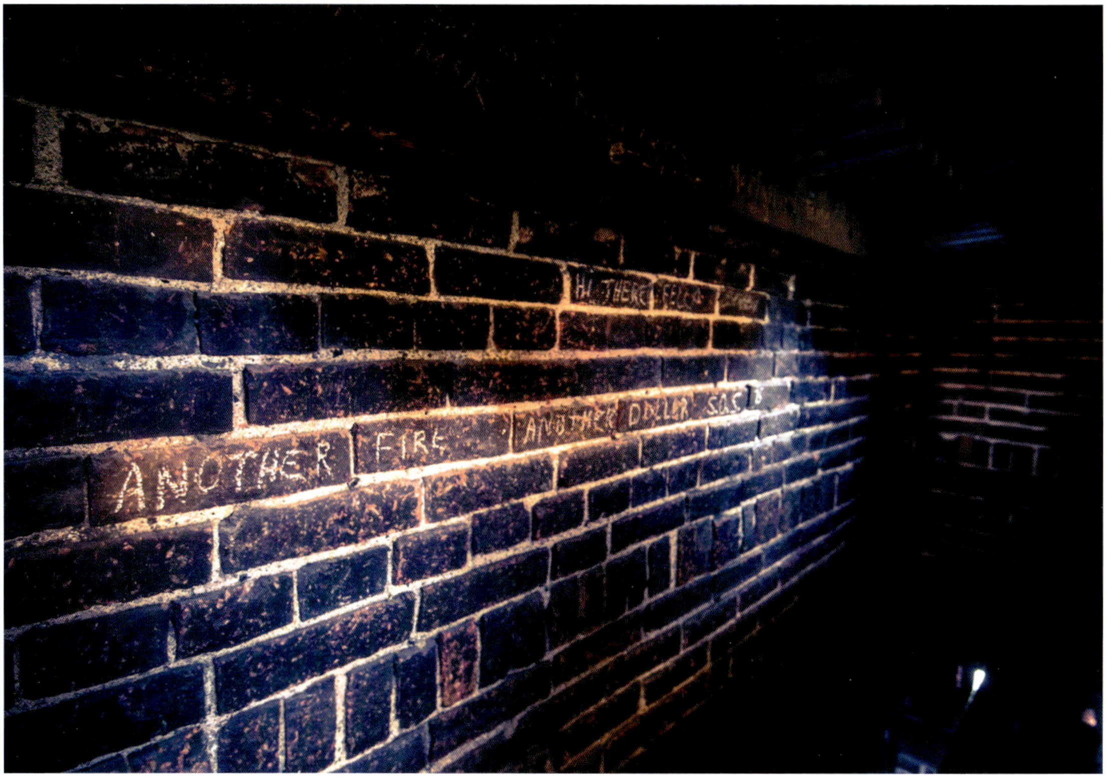

Another Fire, Another Dollar

GARDEN THEATER

Built in 1915 on Pittsburgh's North Side, the Garden Theater was a 1,000-seat movie theater built in the Beaux Arts style by architect Thomas H. Scott. Quite popular for showing mainstream films in the decades of its heyday, the theater became known as an adult-film venue after showing the pornographic film *Deep Throat* in 1973. It closed in 2007 and was placed on the list of City of Pittsburgh historic designations in 2008. It is now being renovated as an upscale restaurant space.

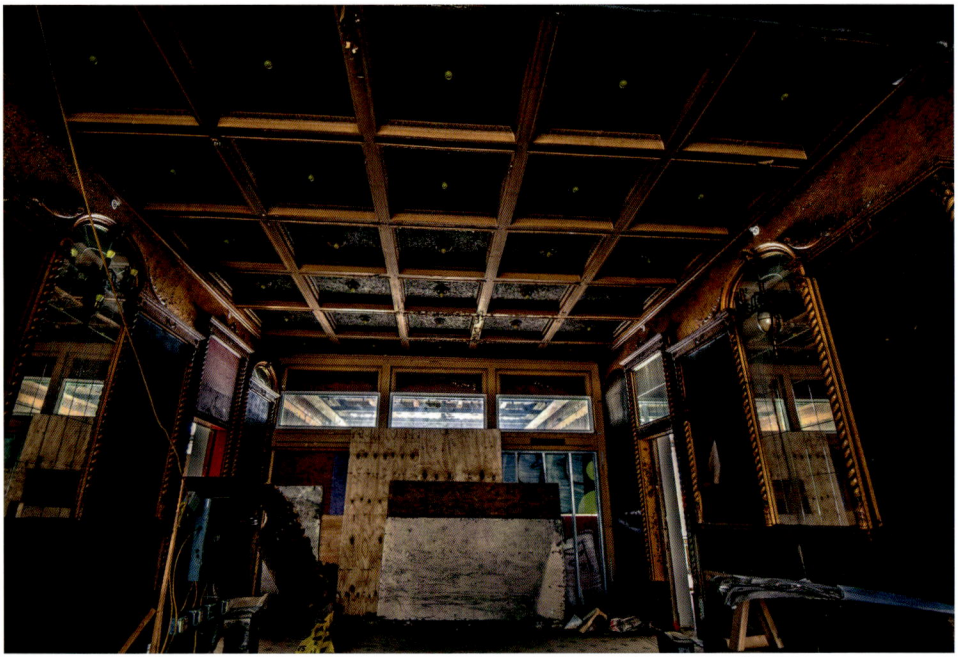

Theater Lobby

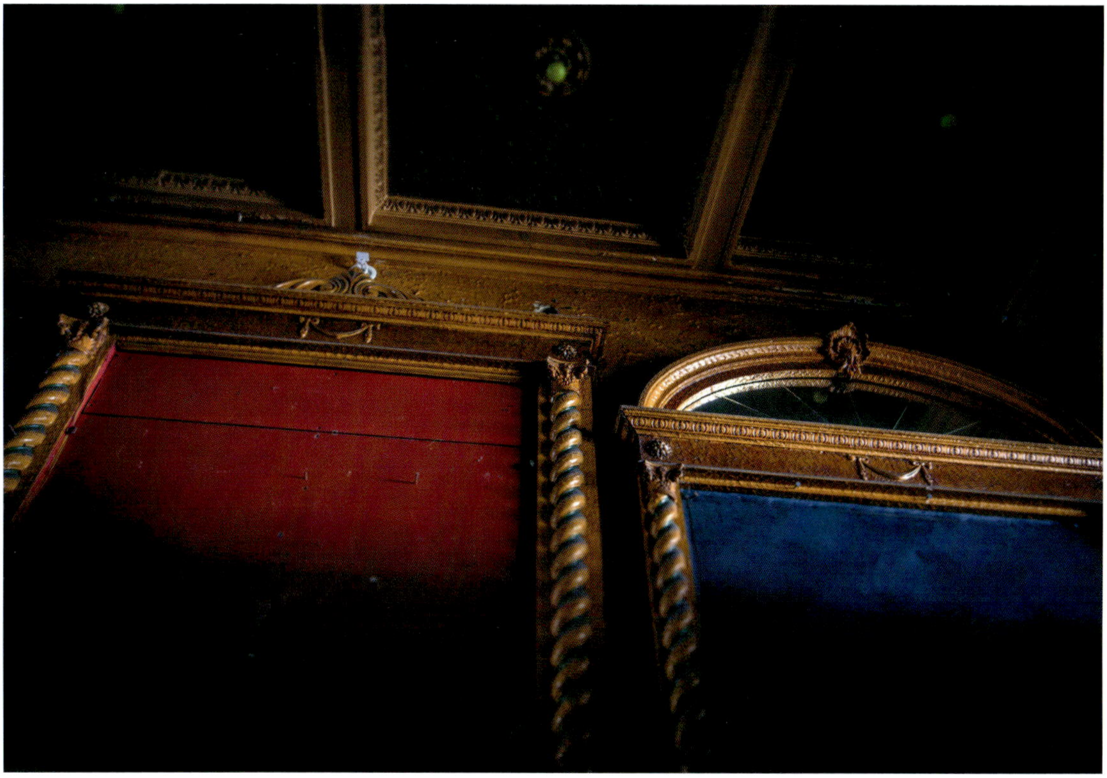

Now Showing

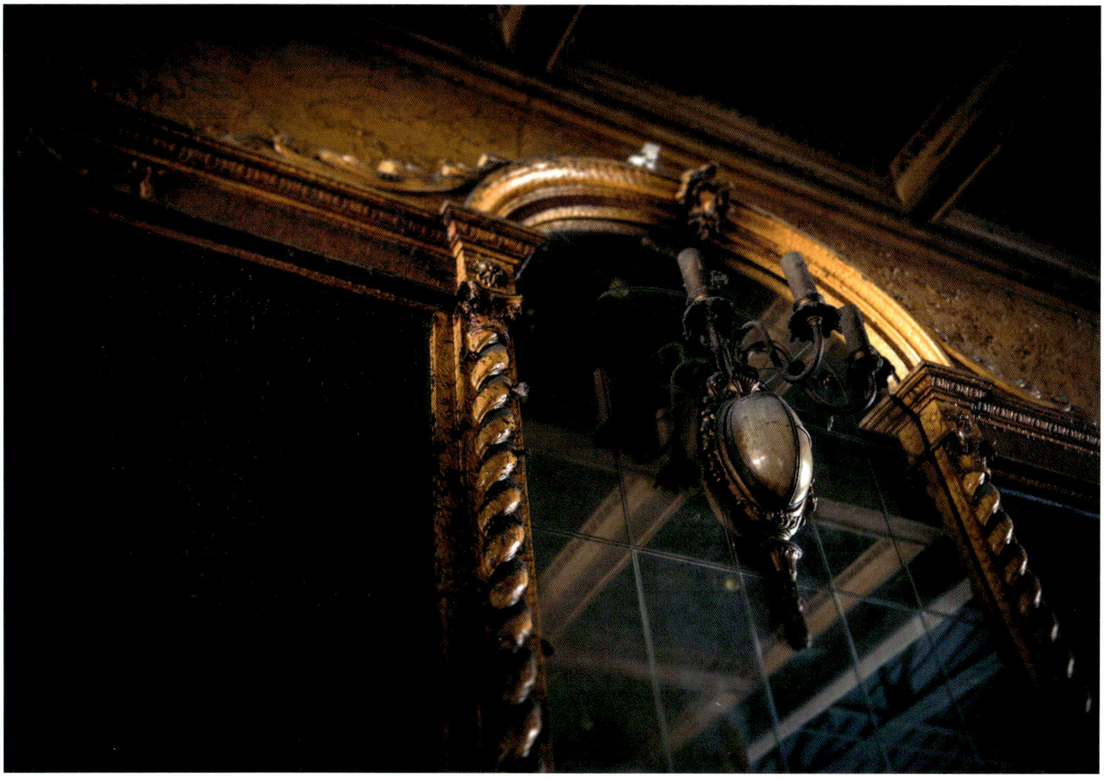

Sconce

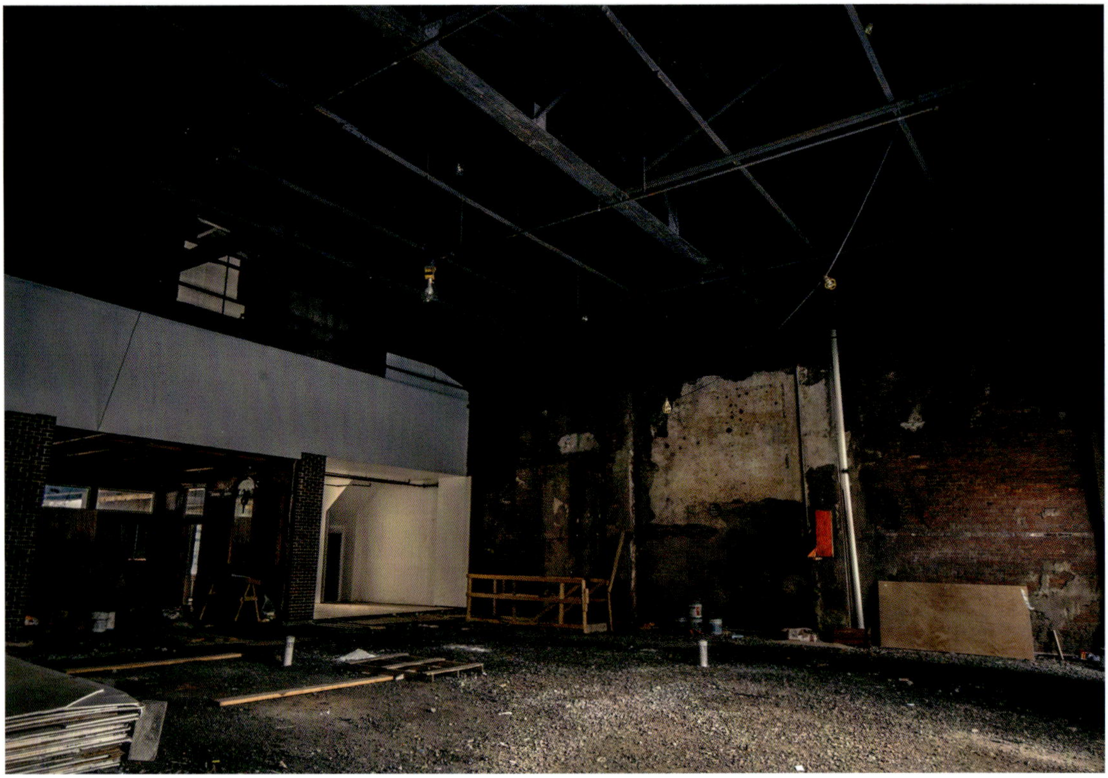

Theater

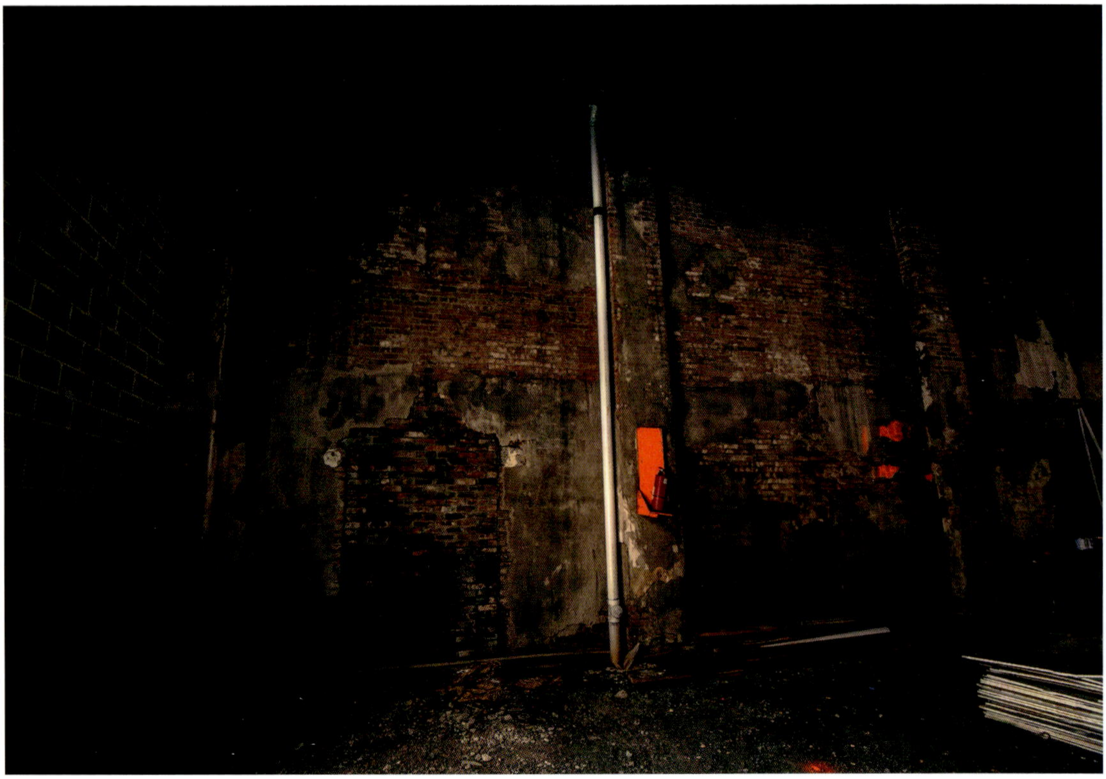

Orange

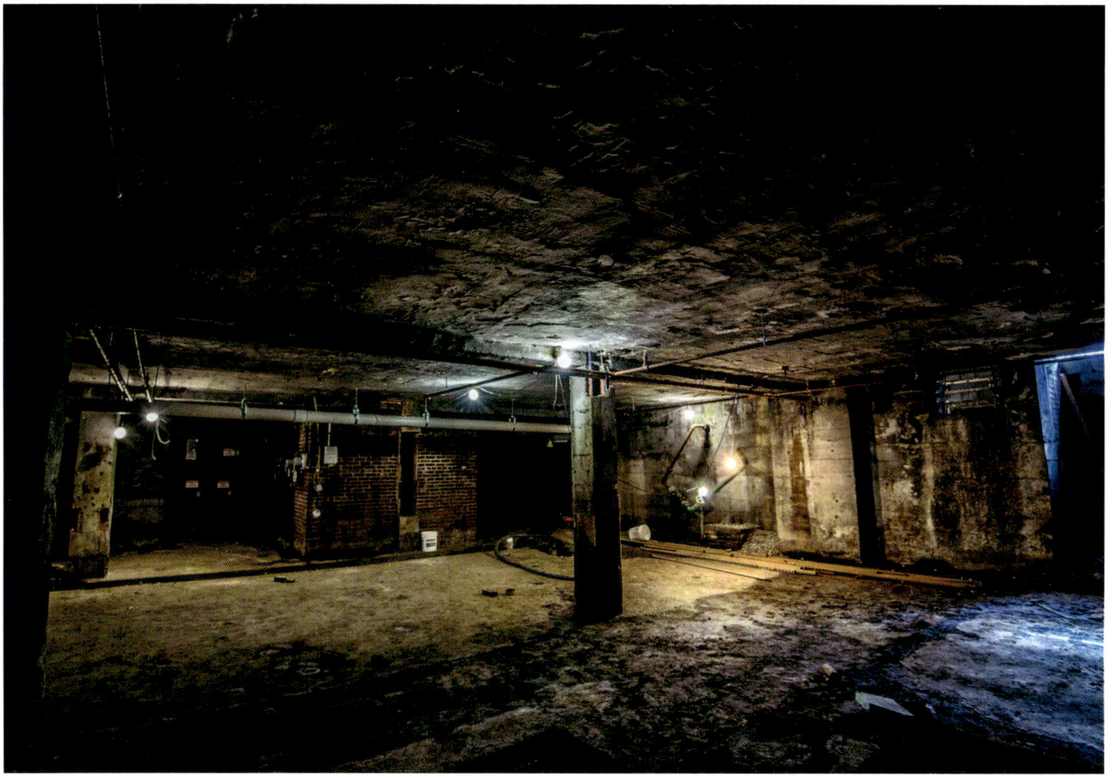

Basement

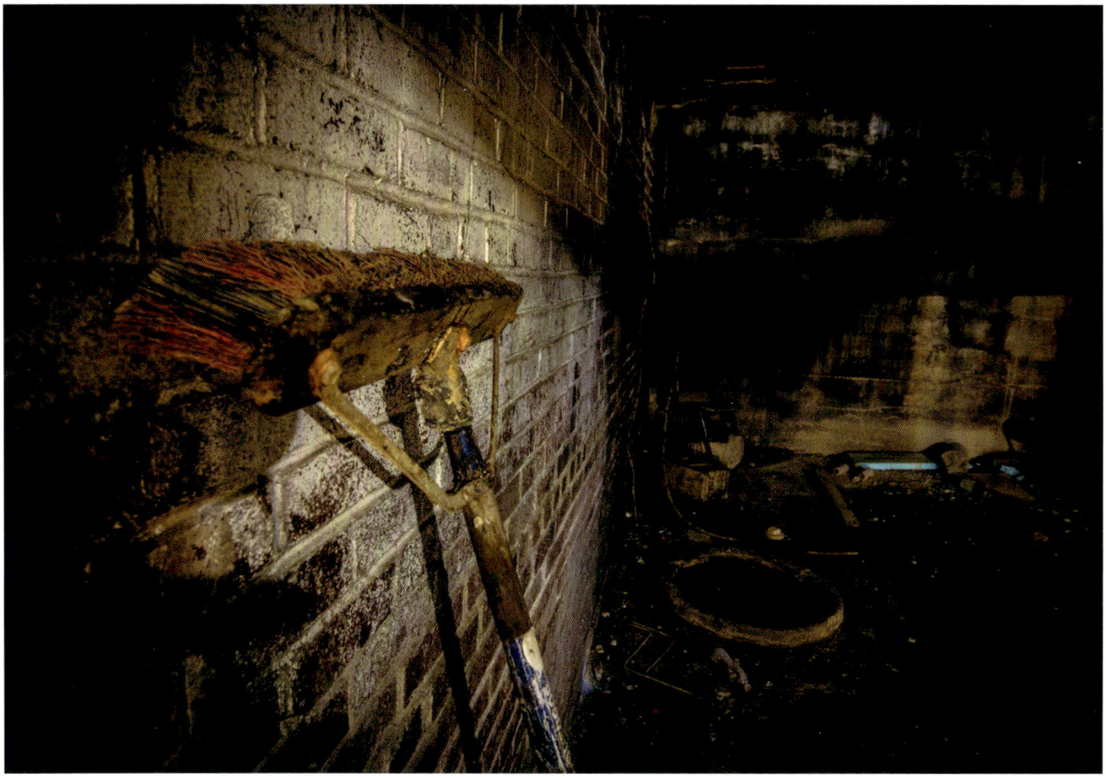

Broom

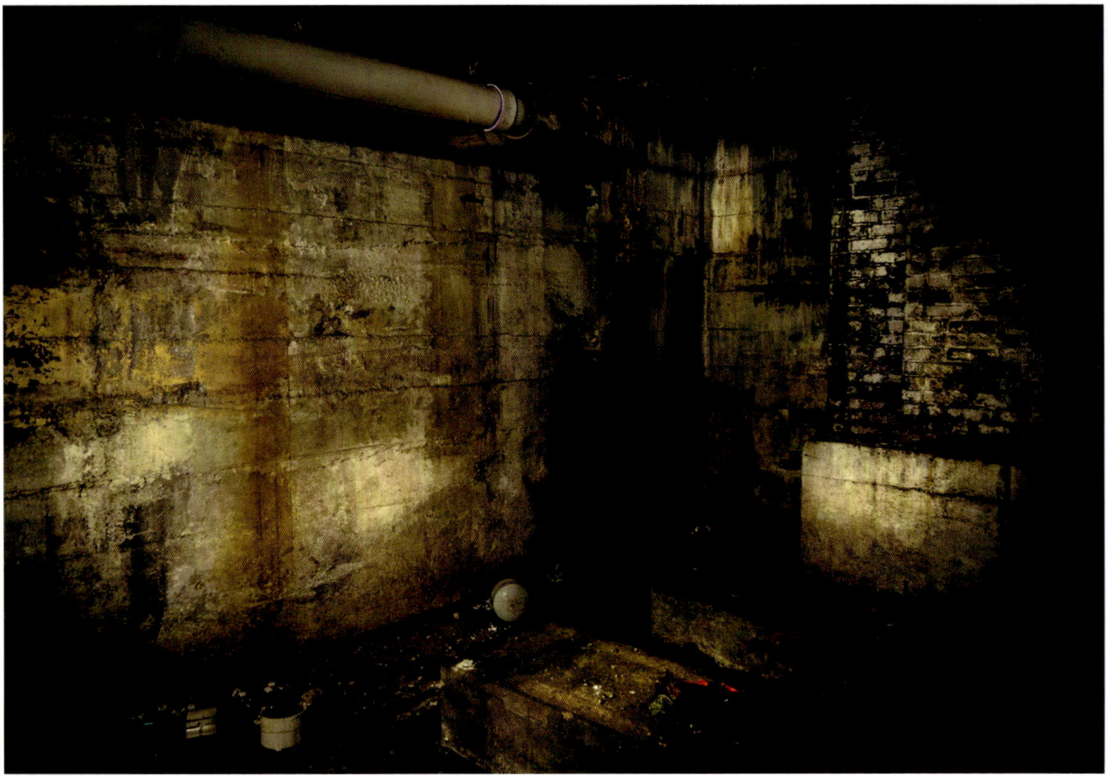

Corner

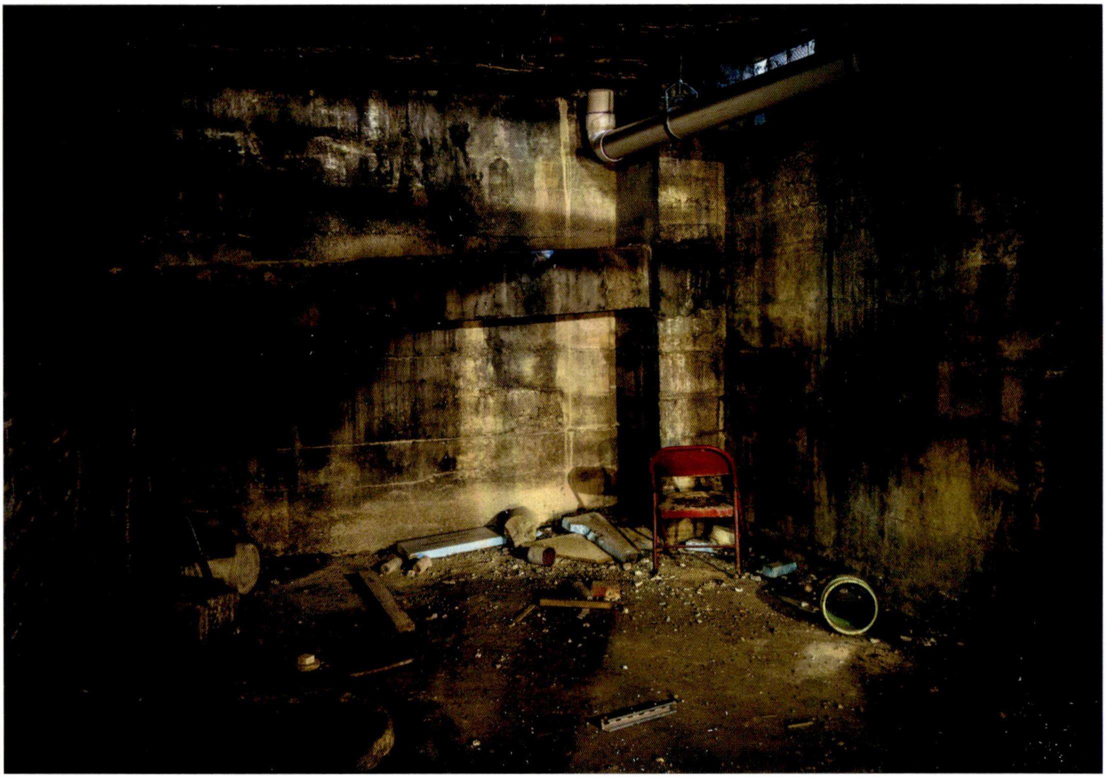

Red Chair

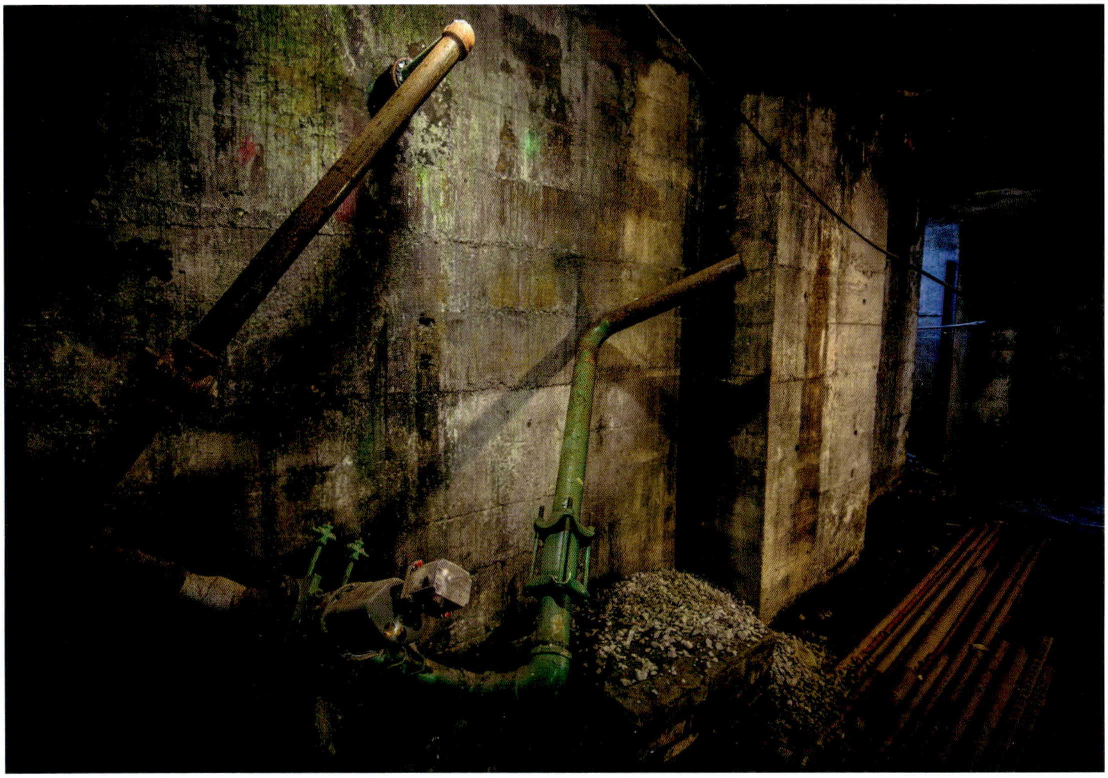

Basement Pipes

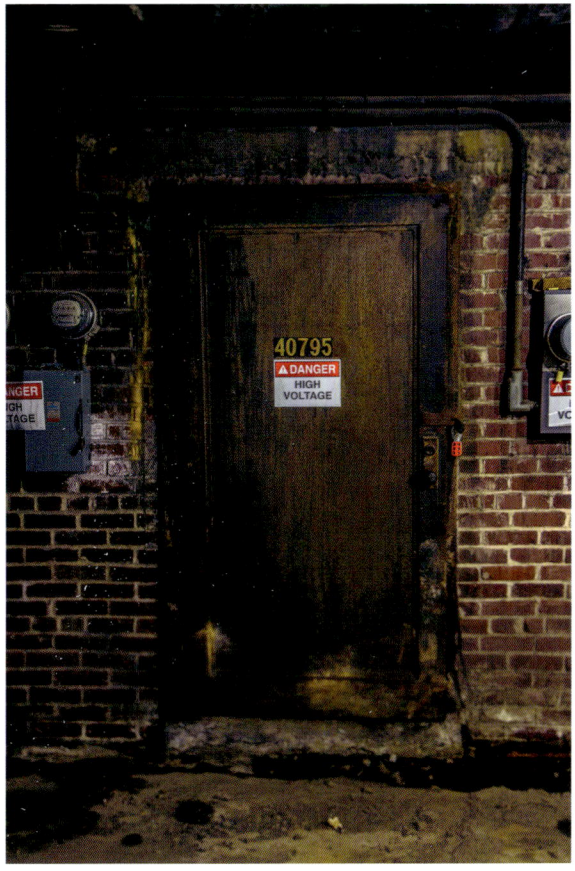

Danger: High Voltage

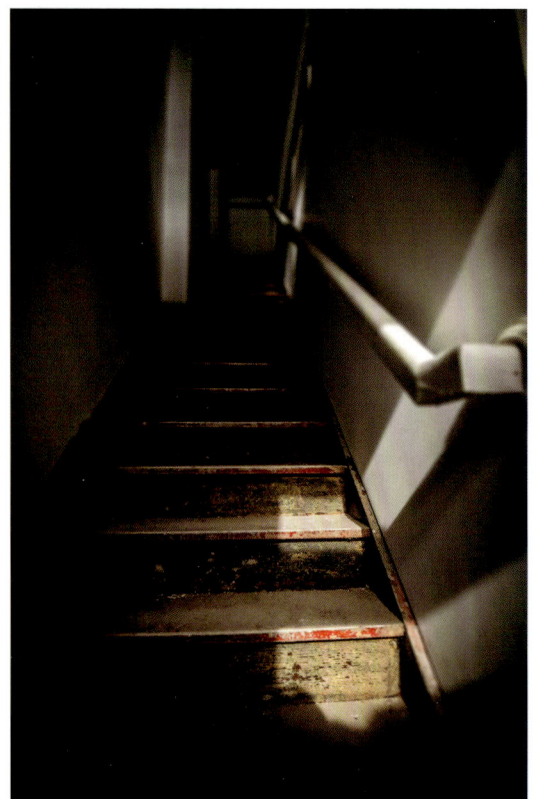

Stairs

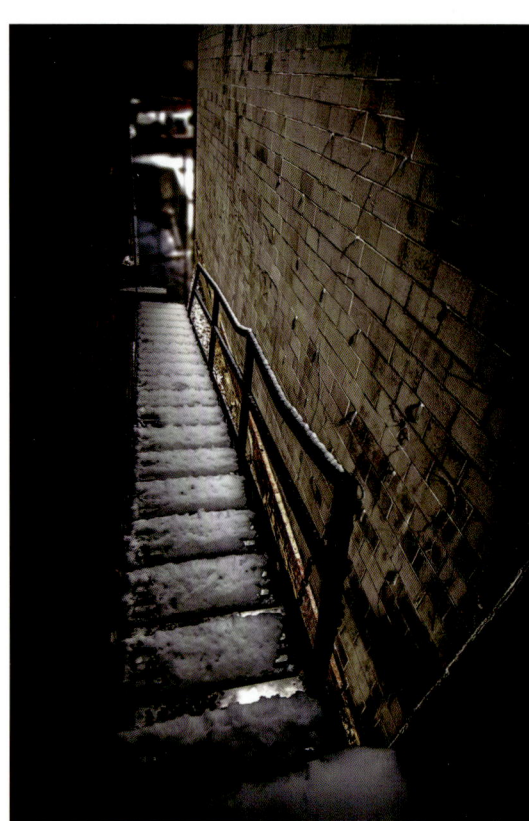

Escape

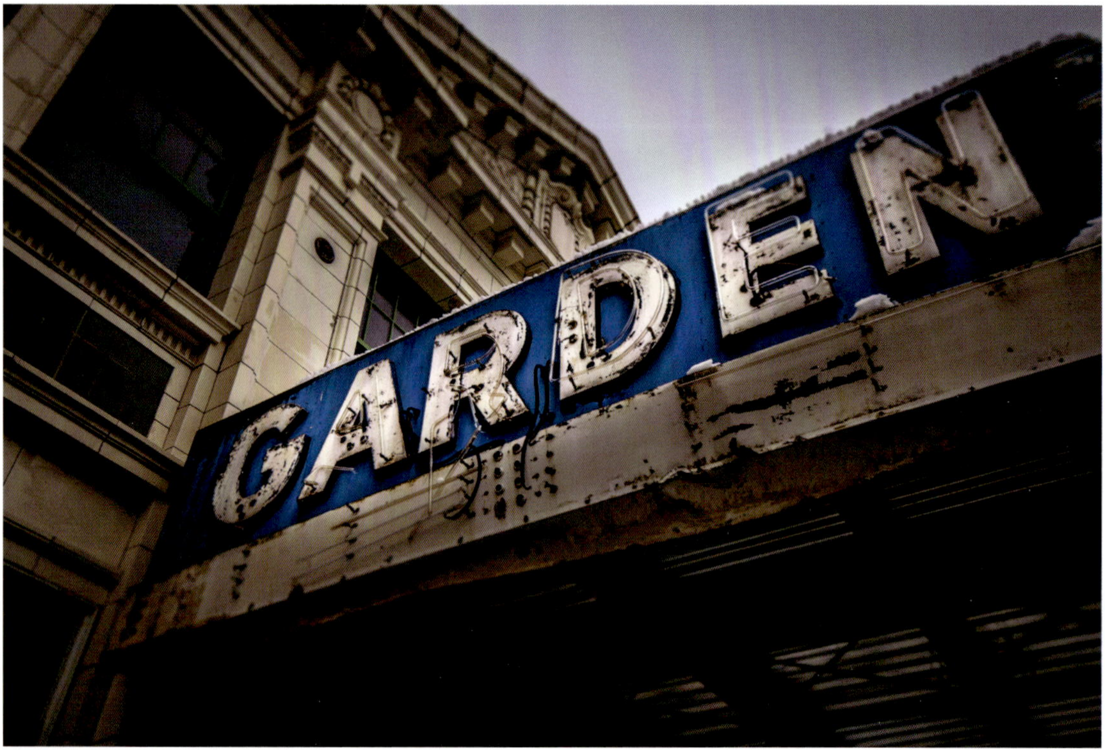

Marquee

LASALLE ELECTRIC SUPPLY CO.

I saw the LaSalle Electric Supply Co. building on a cold and wet January morning. Of all the abandoned sites I have explored, I had never felt so uneasy as I did here. I found a dark stairwell and climbed all the way up to the fifth floor, and then back down to the basement and then an inky sub-basement. I was alone but living quarters had been set up by homeless inhabitants — mirrors, mattresses, clothes lines, easy chairs — even a sacred space for religious readings.

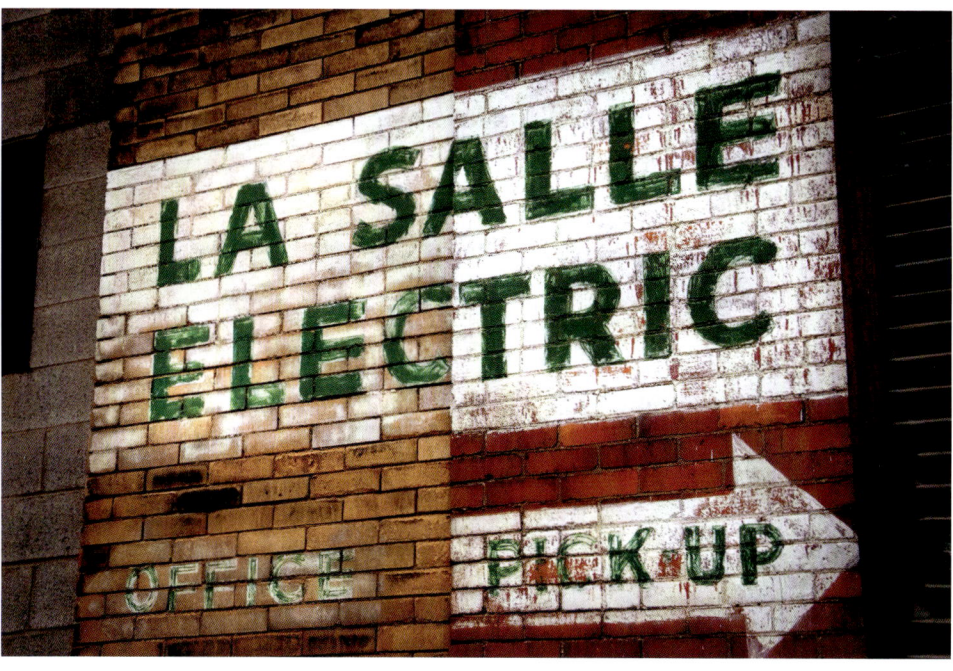

Pick-Up

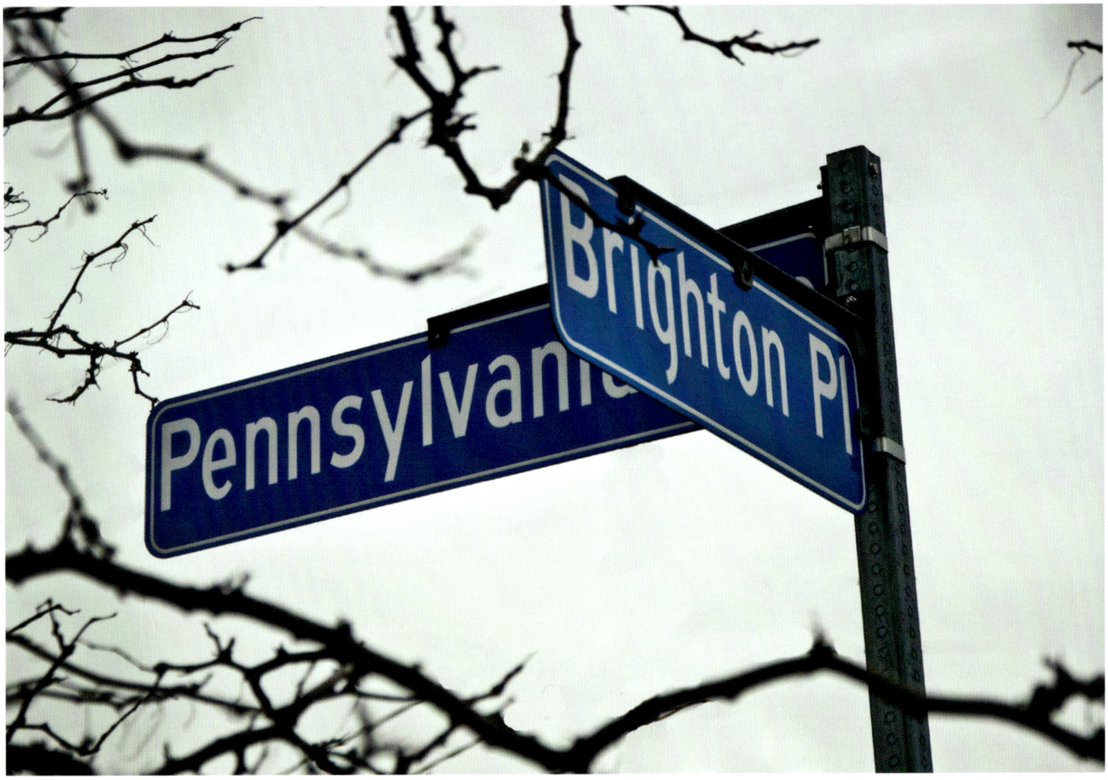

Pennsylvania & Brighton

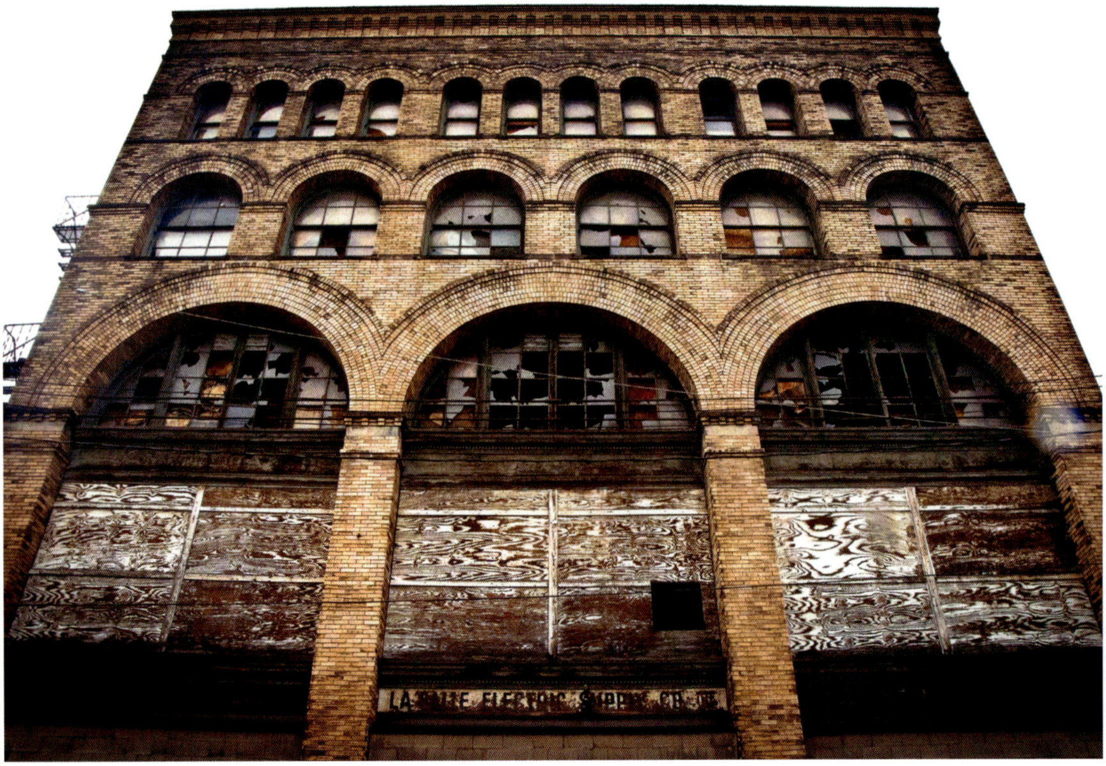

Perspective

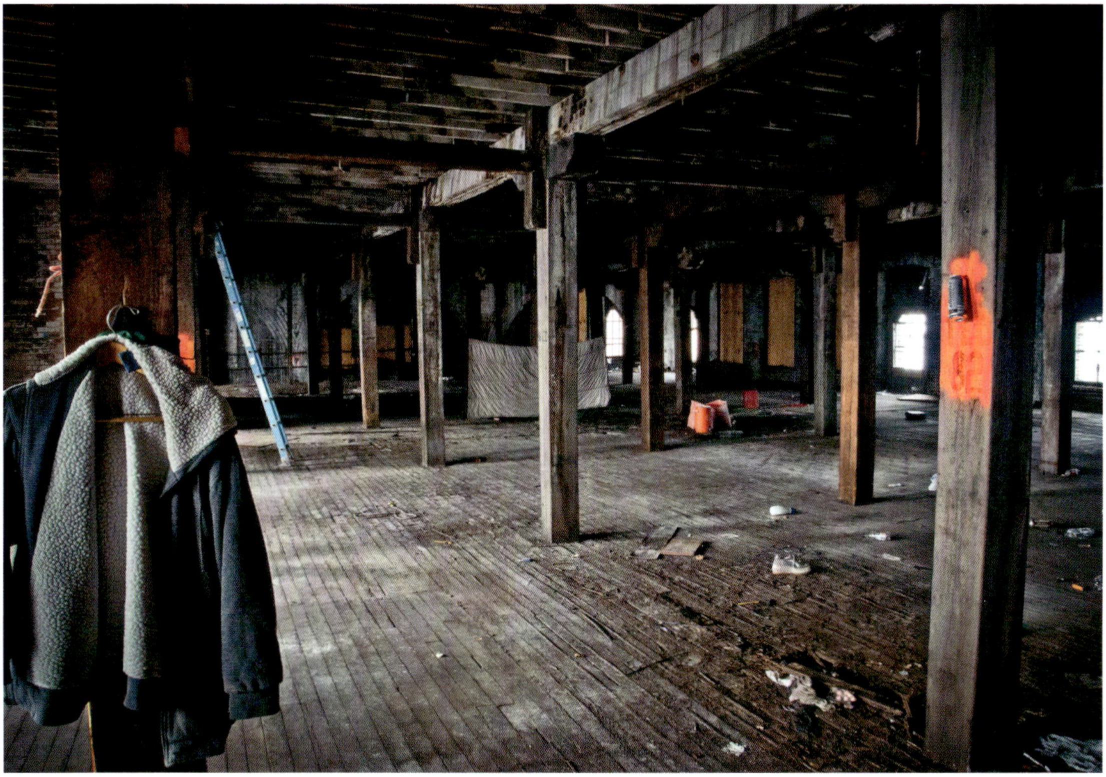

Coat

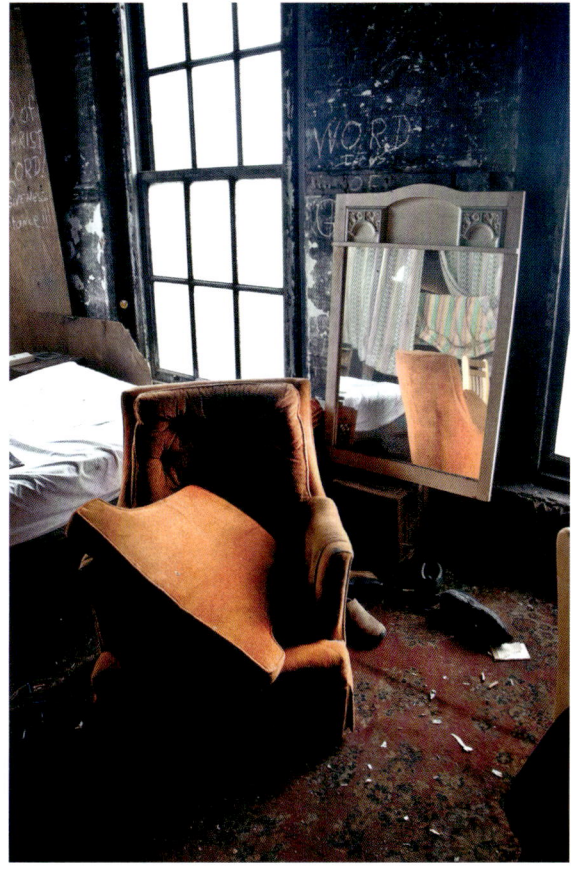

Comfortable Chair

Preach!

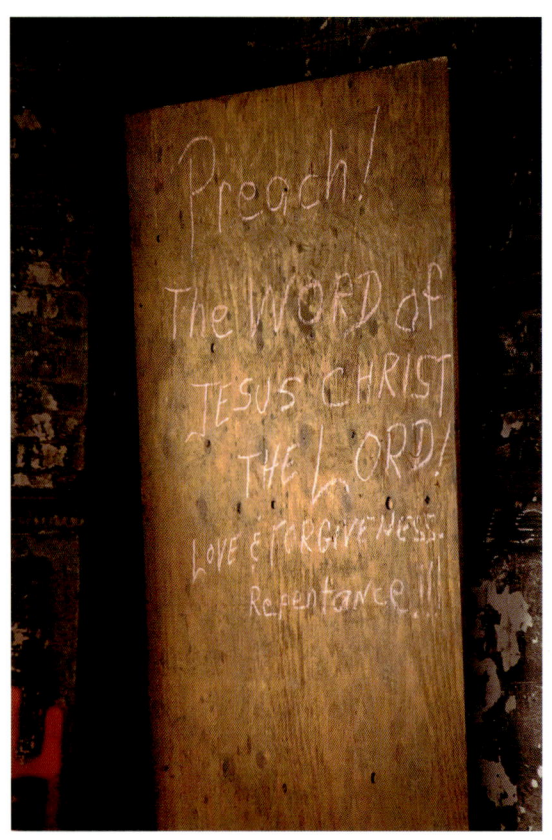

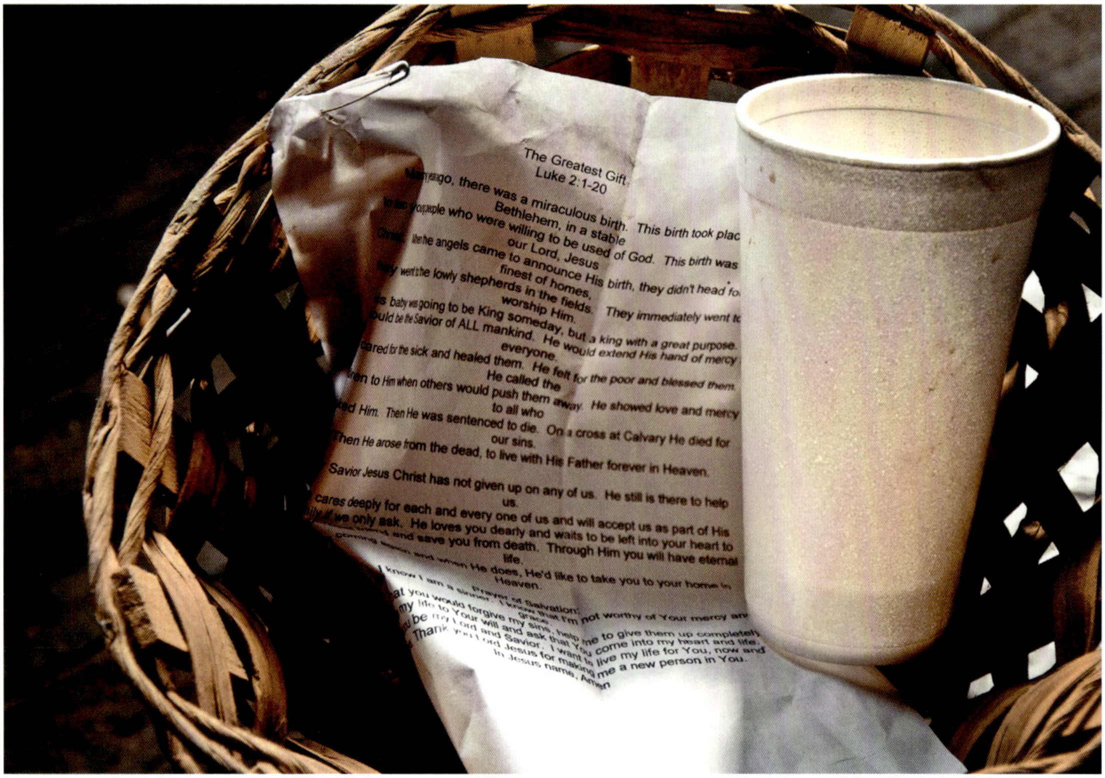

The Greatest Gift

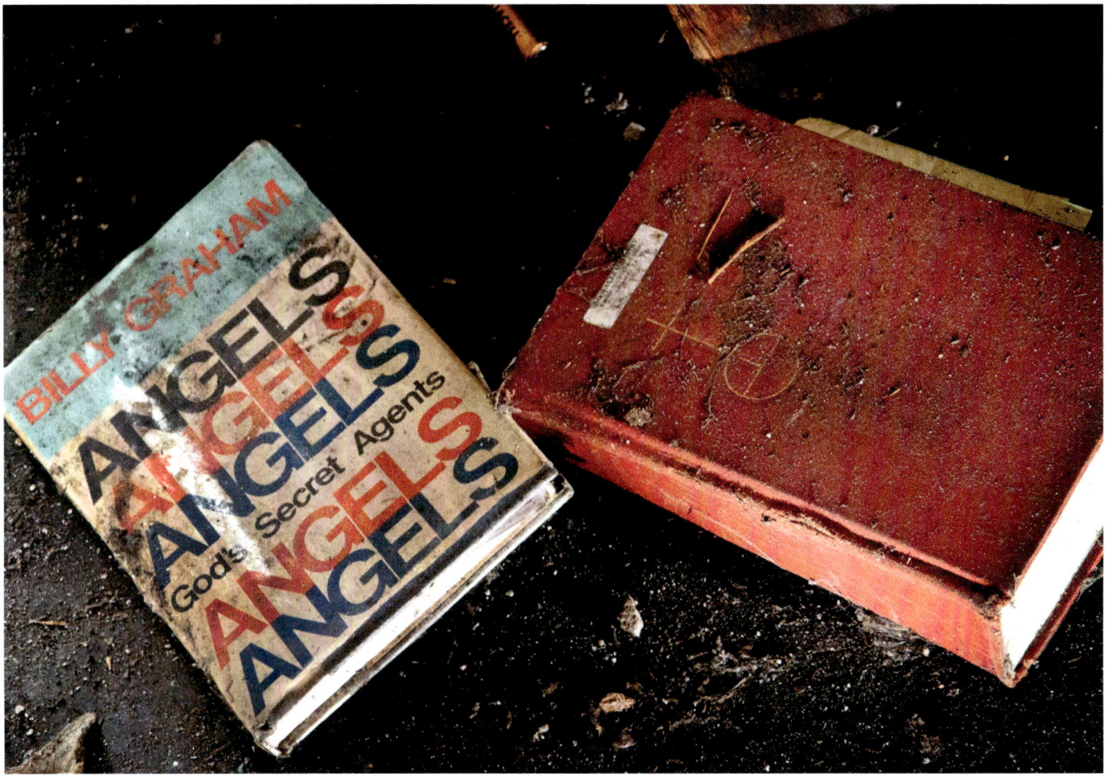

God's Secret Agents

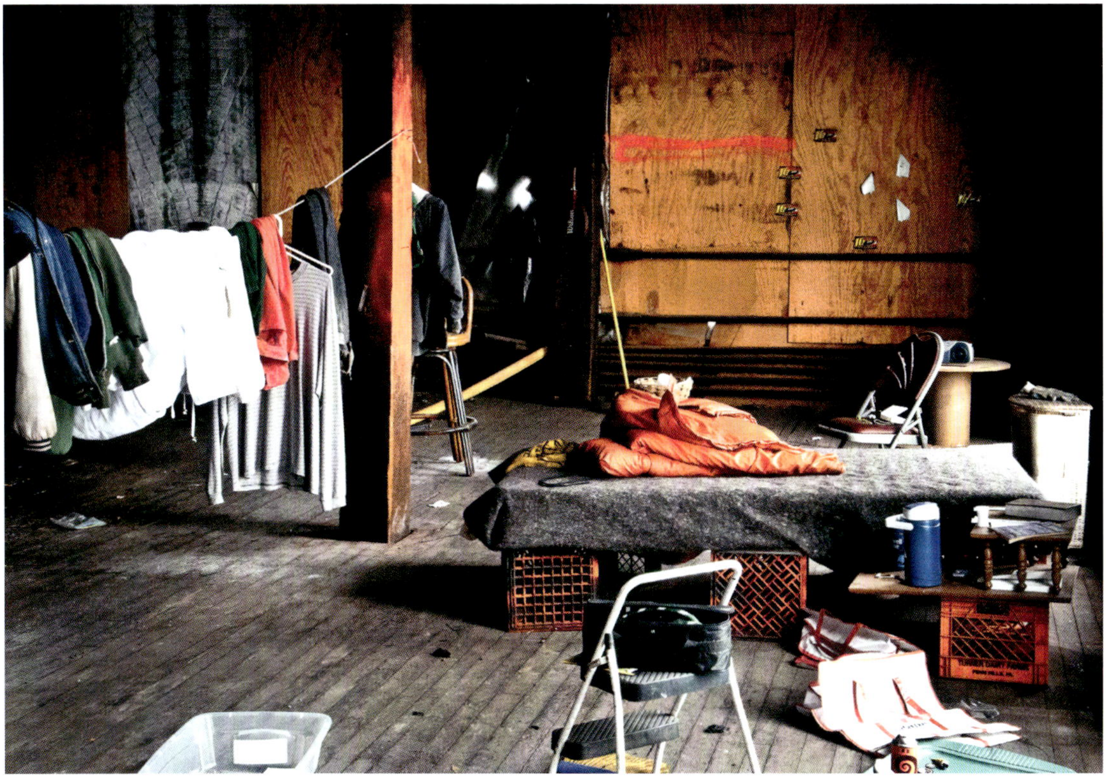

Bed

45

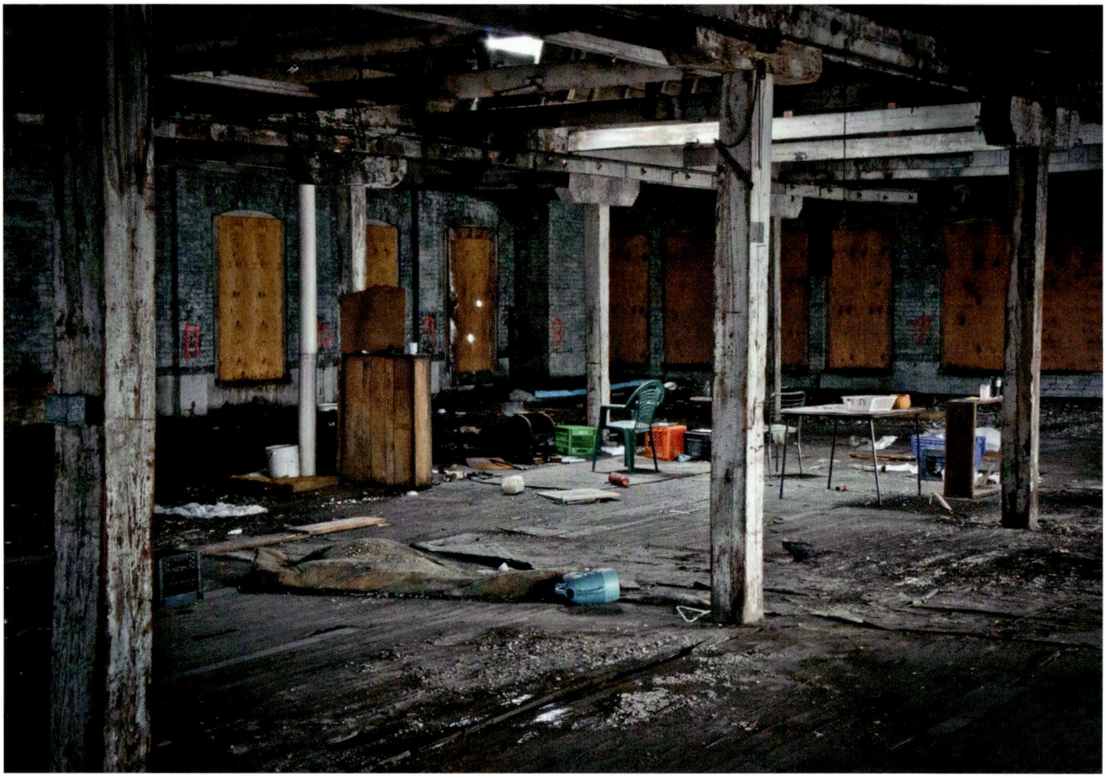

5th Floor

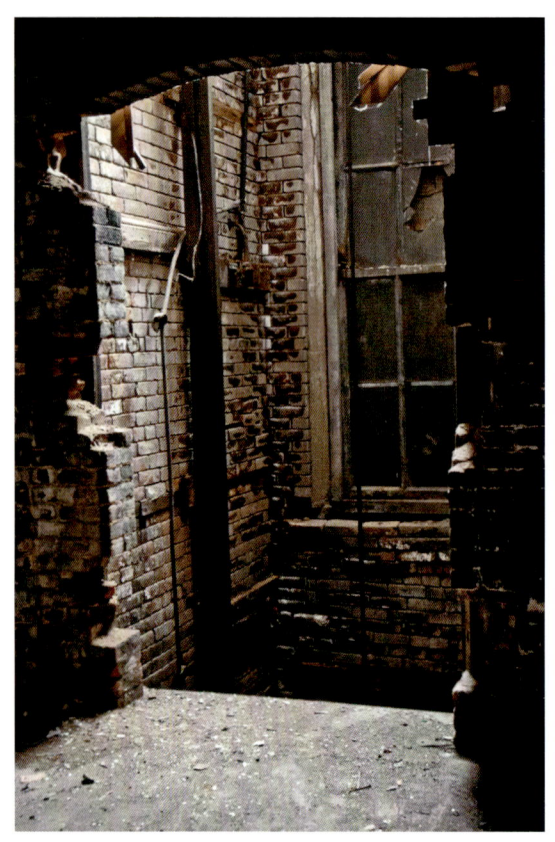

Elevator

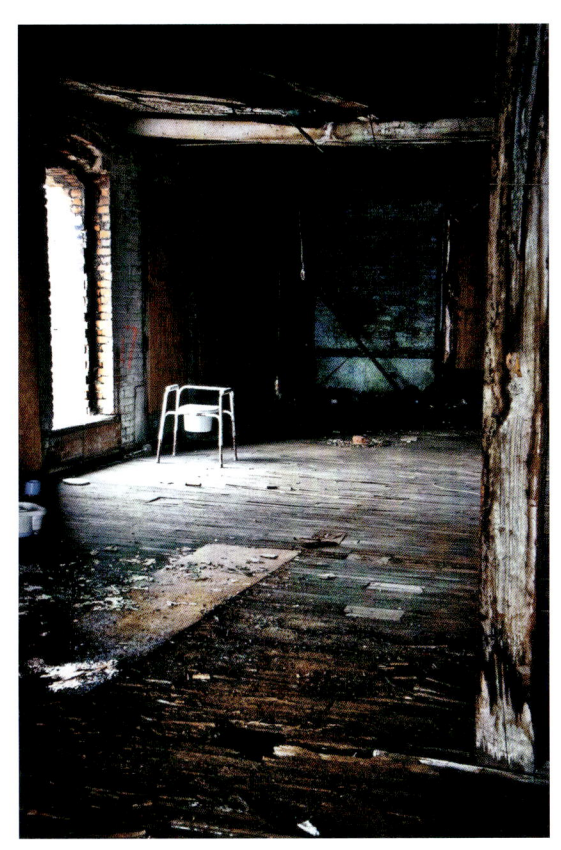

Restroom With a View

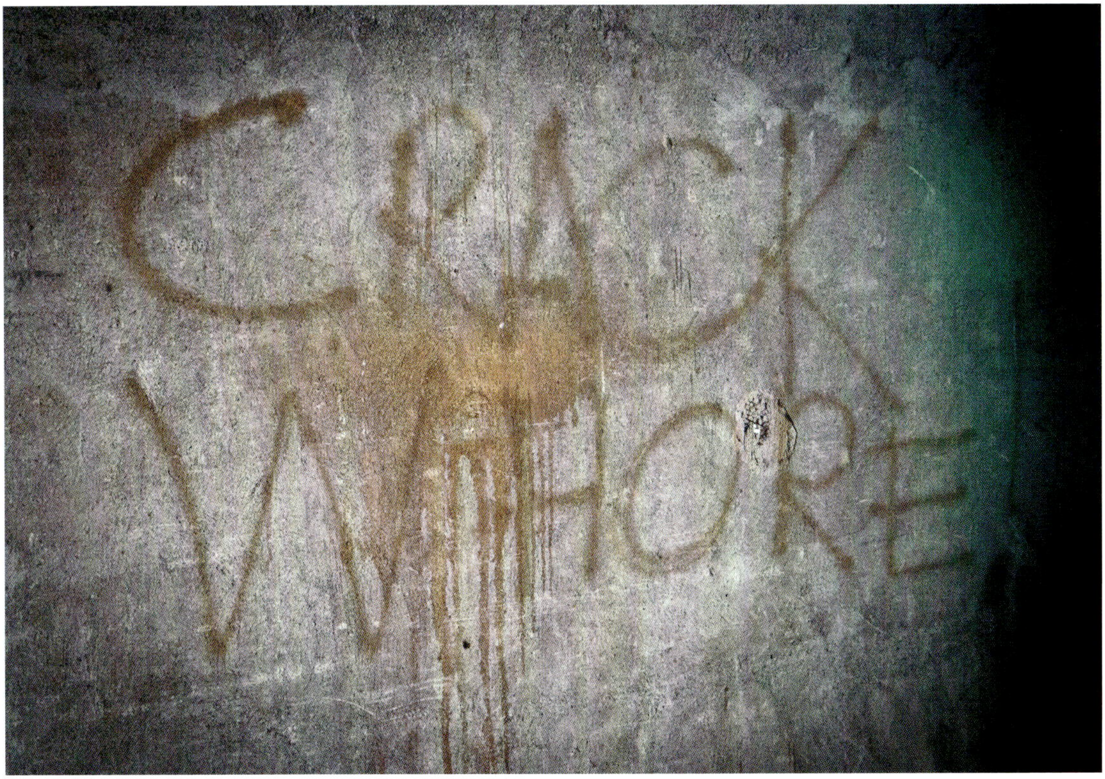

Crack Whore

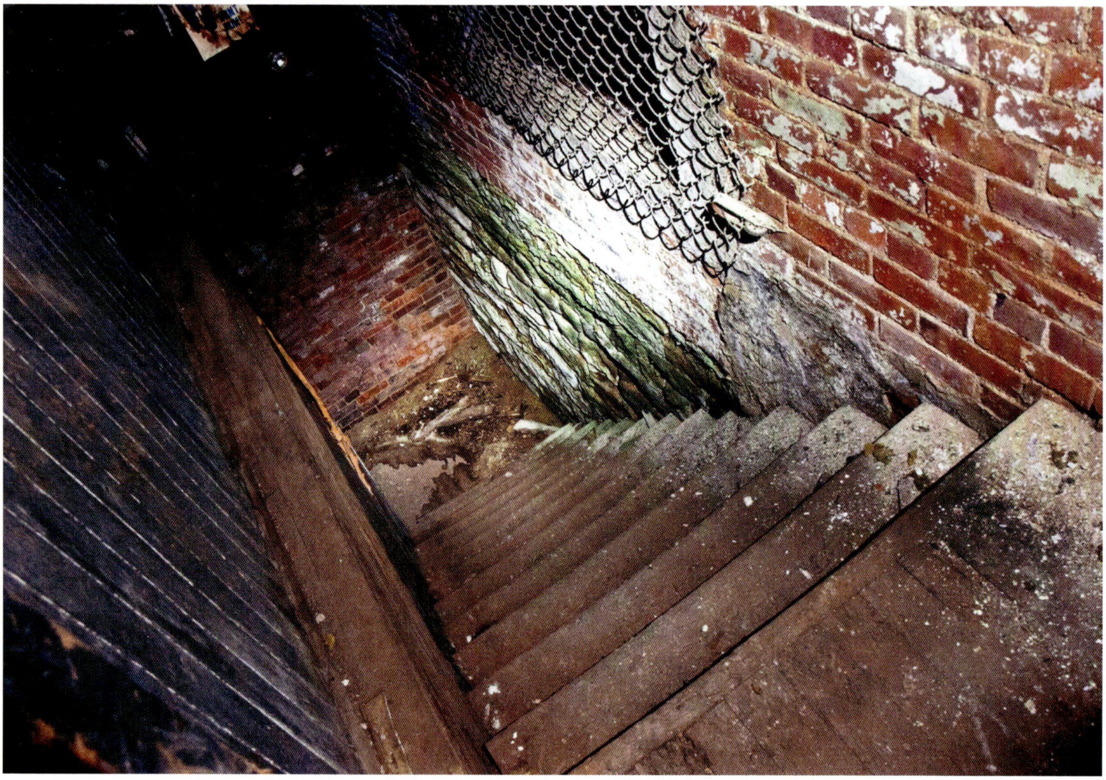

Basement Steps

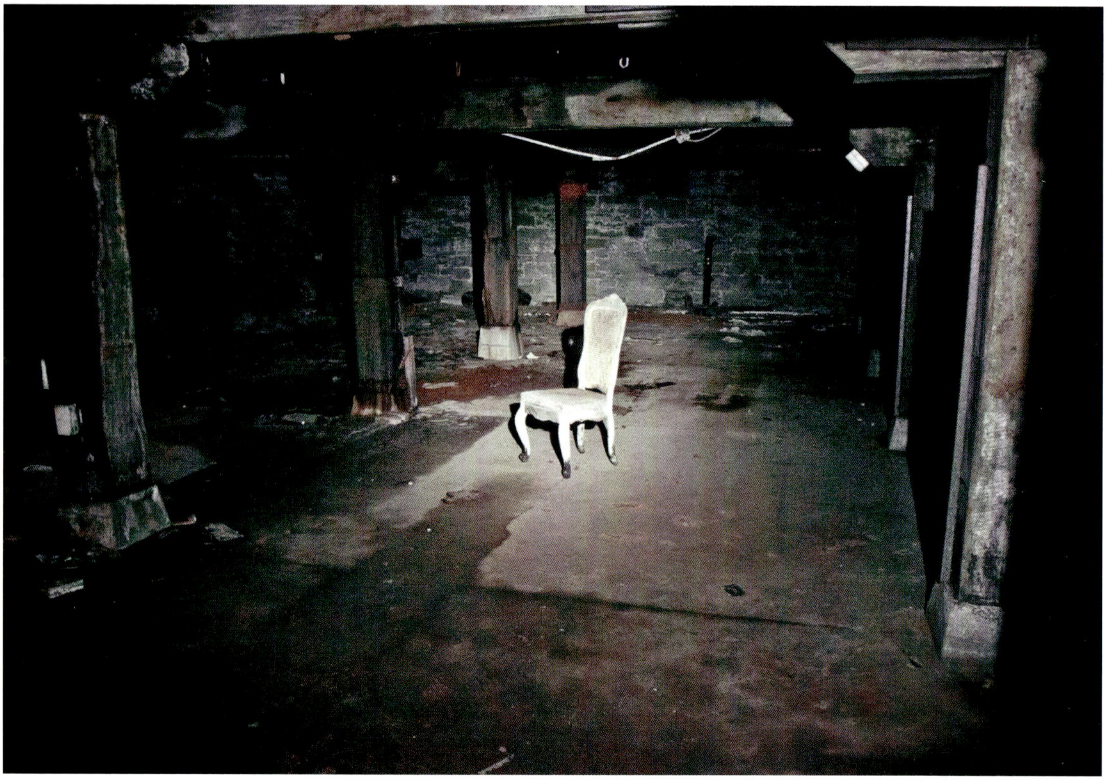

Basement Chair

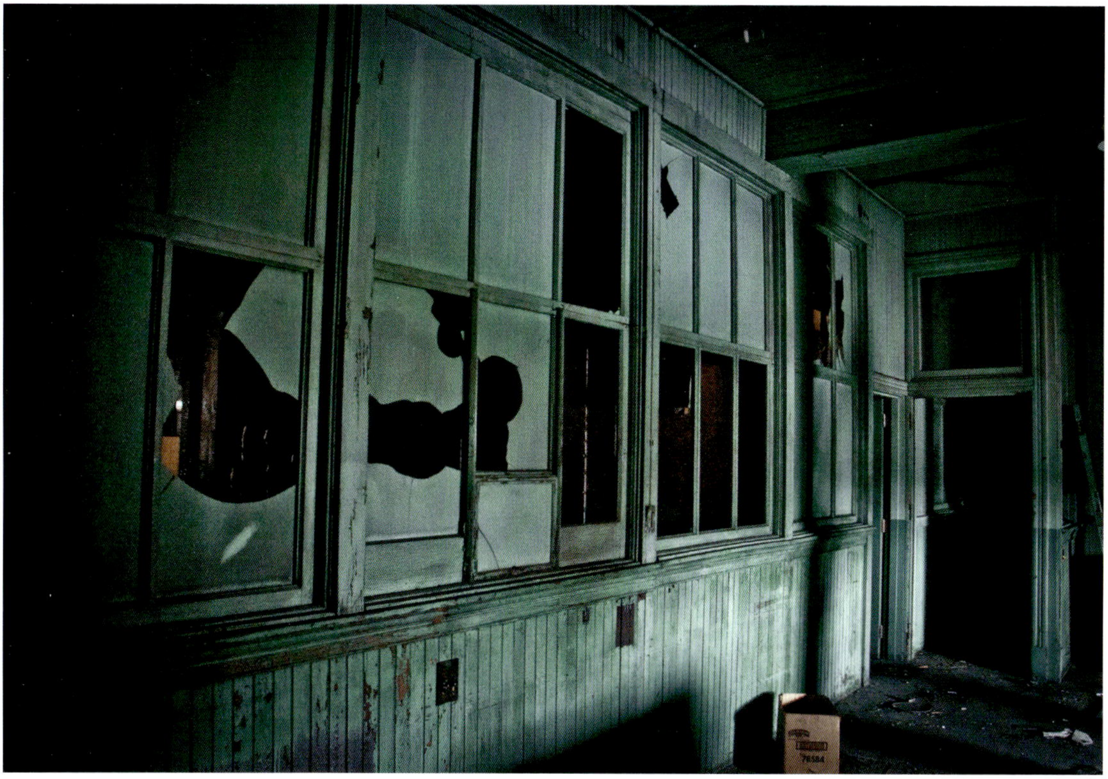

Green Room

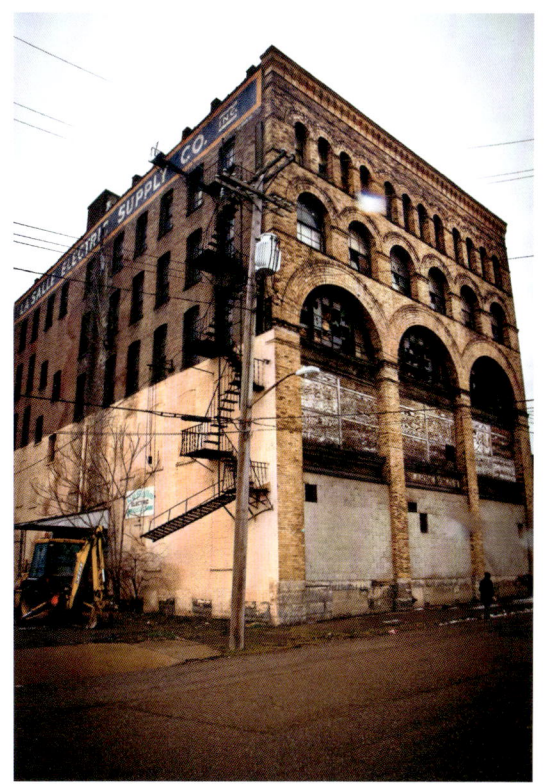

Fire Escape

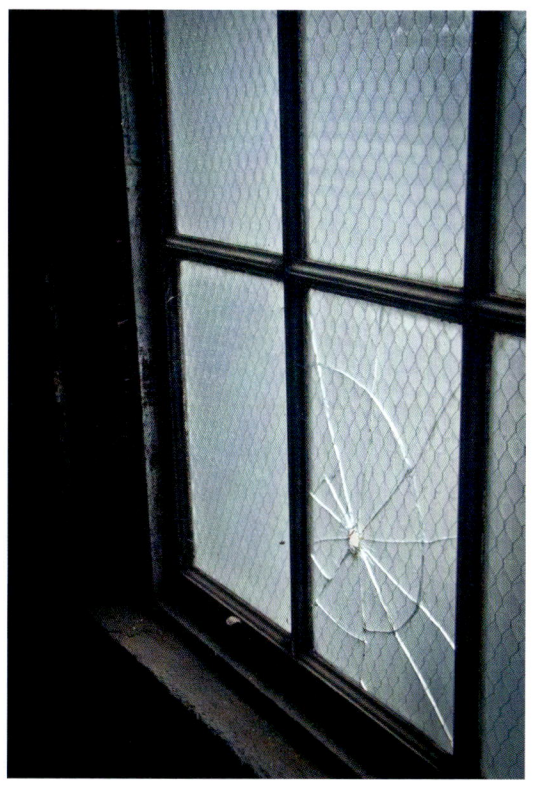

Window Web

LAYTON BRIDGE

The Layton Bridge stretches over the Youghiogheny River, connecting Layton and Perryopolis via a one-lane tunnel. Construction began in 1893 and was completed in 1899. It was originally built for the Washington Run Railroad; the last train crossed in 1931, and the span was converted to automotive use in 1933. It's believed that the historic Spark's Fort was built nearby, as early as 1774. Key scenes of the 1991 movie *Silence of the Lambs* were filmed at a nearby house.

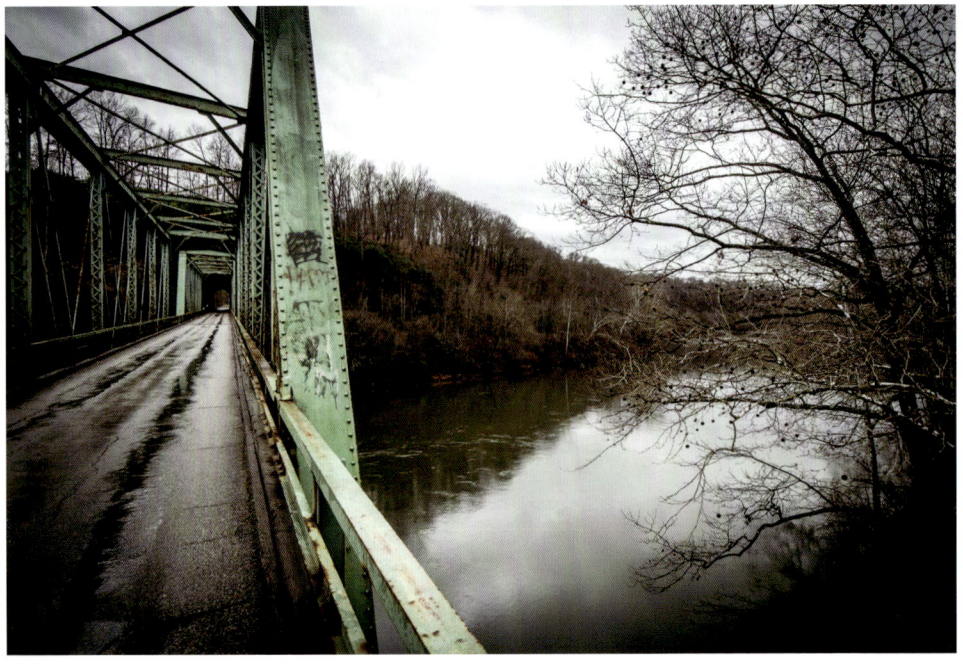

River

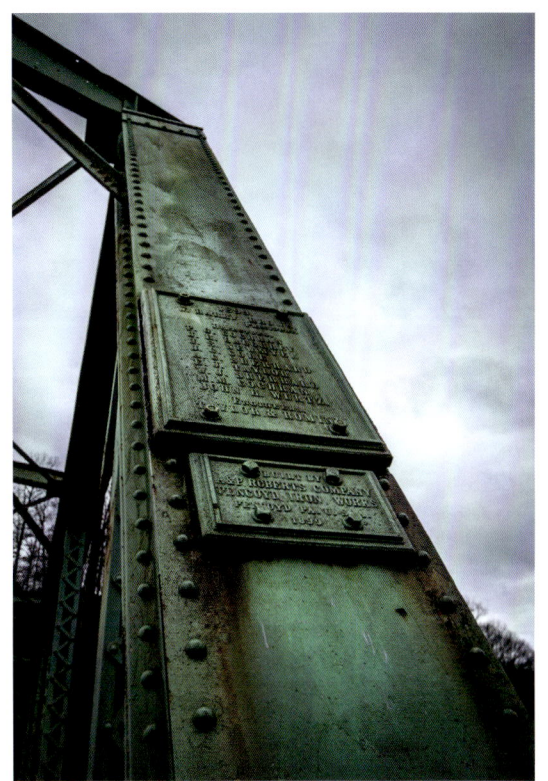
Pencoyd Iron Works, 1899

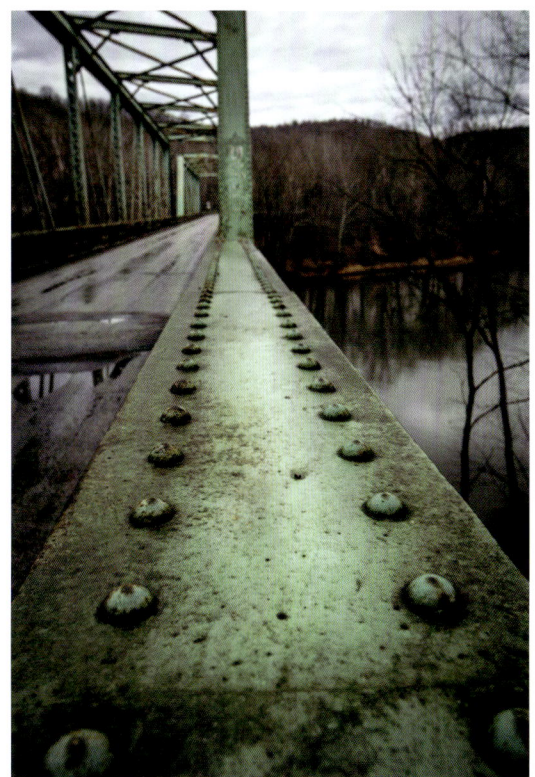
Bolts

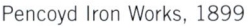
Girders

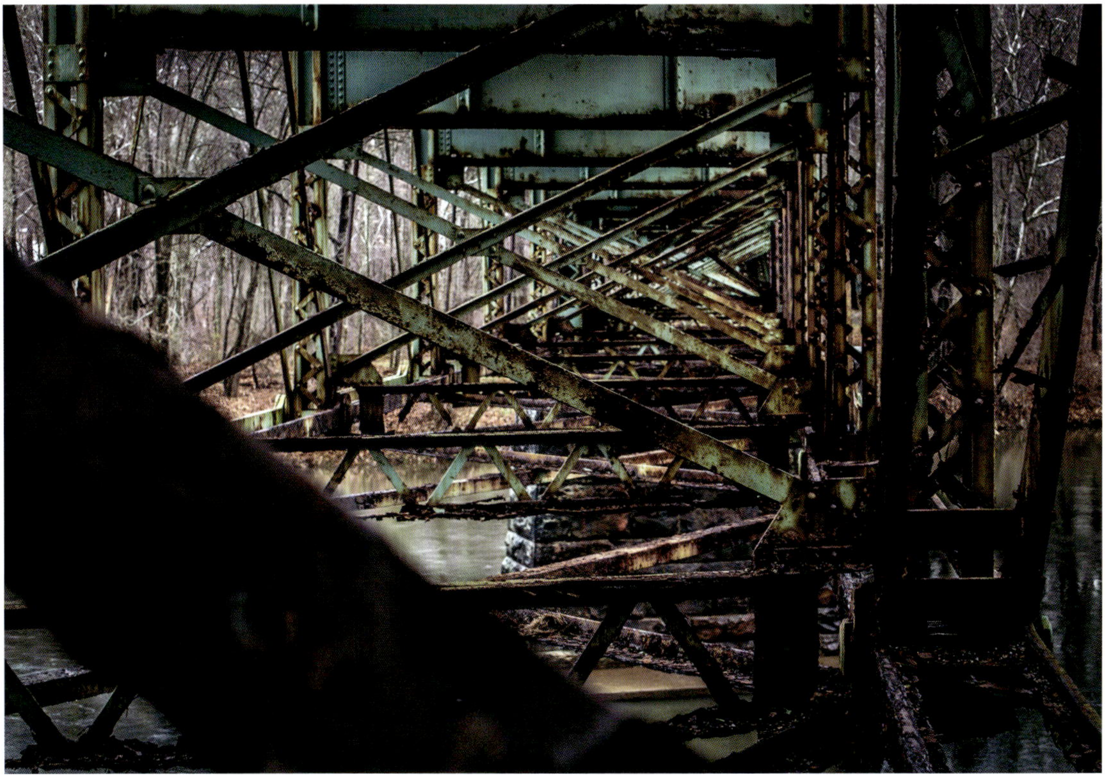

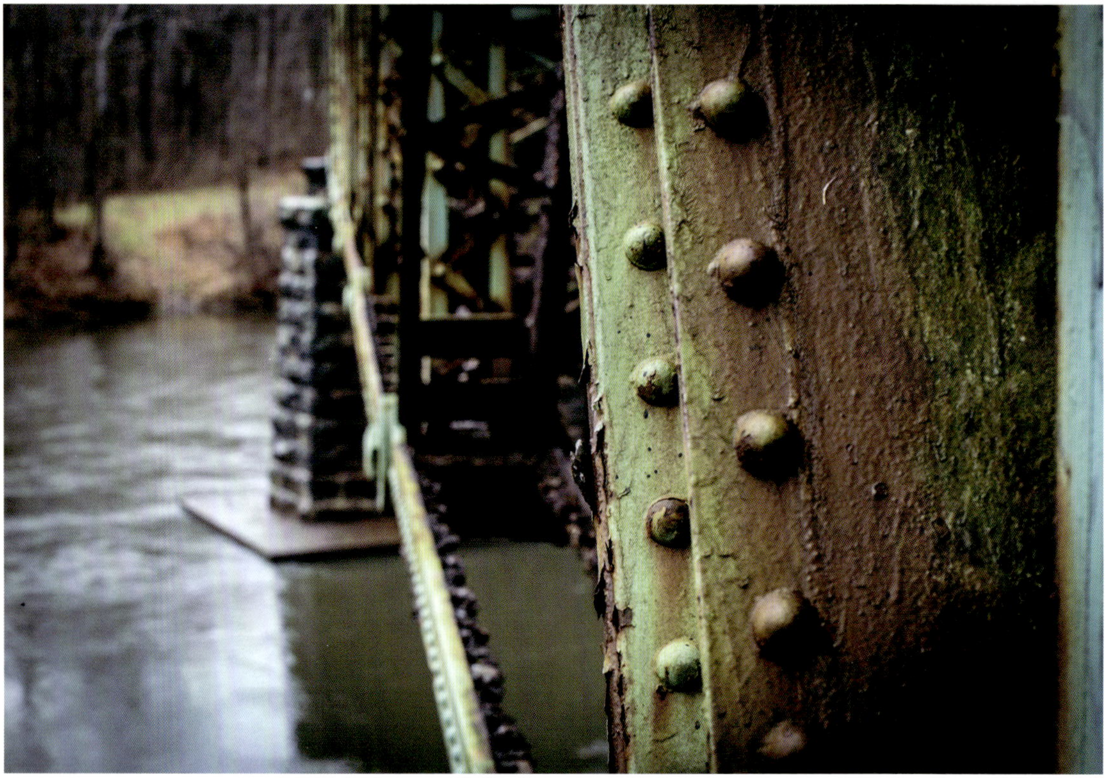

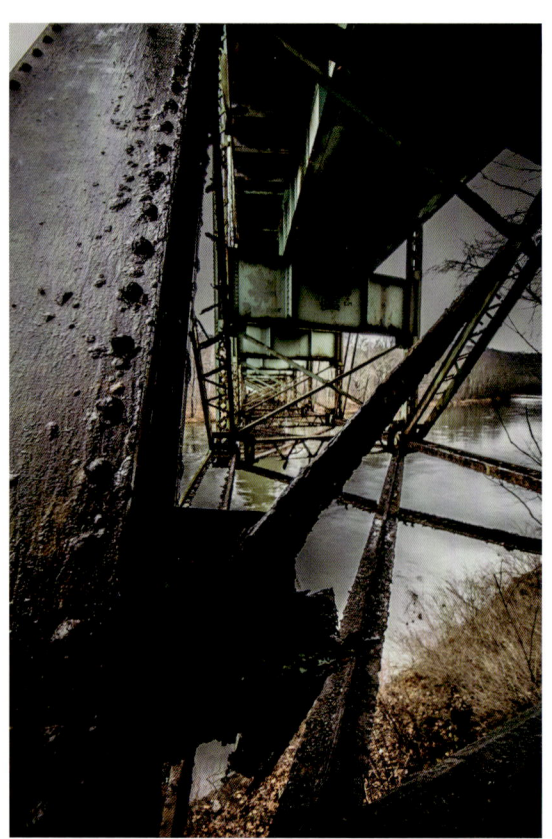

Algae

Rust

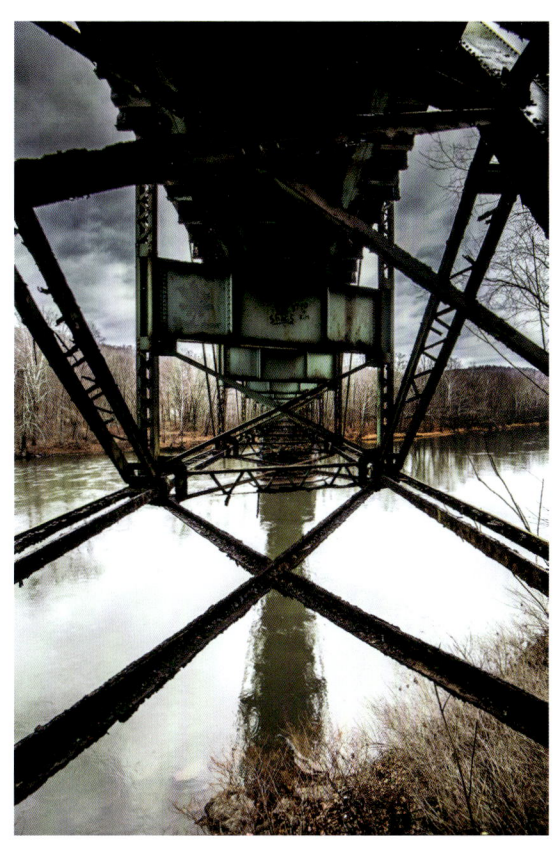
Spider

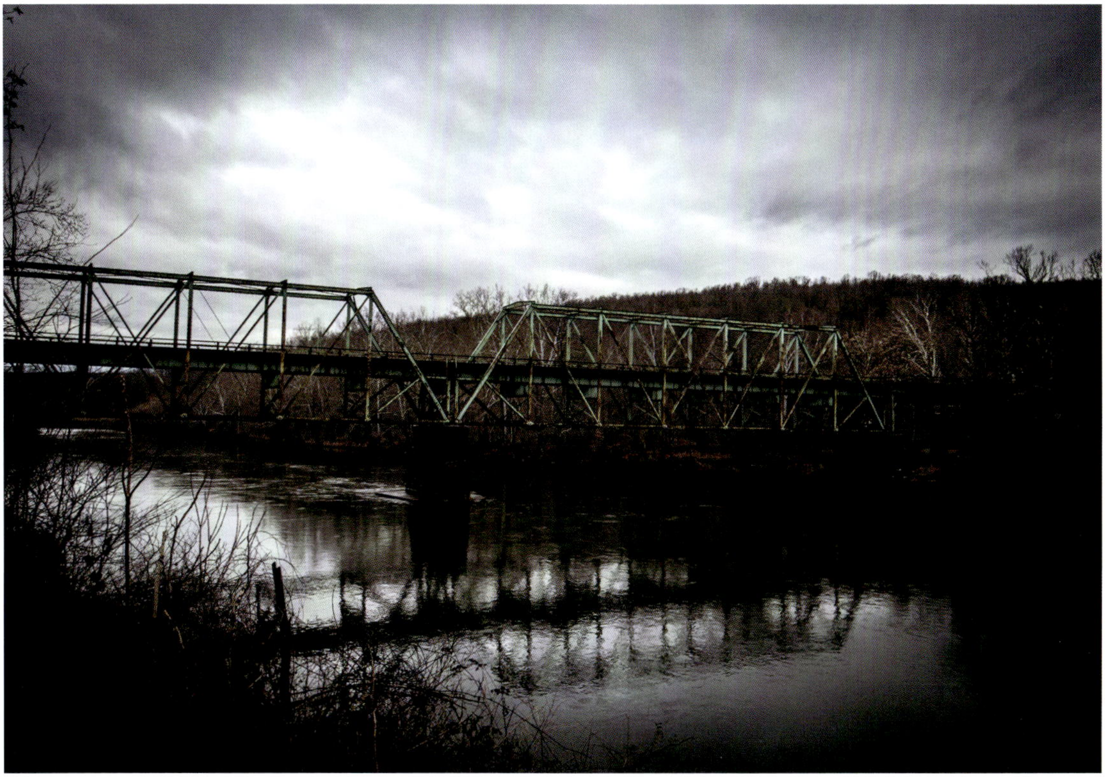

Layton Bridge

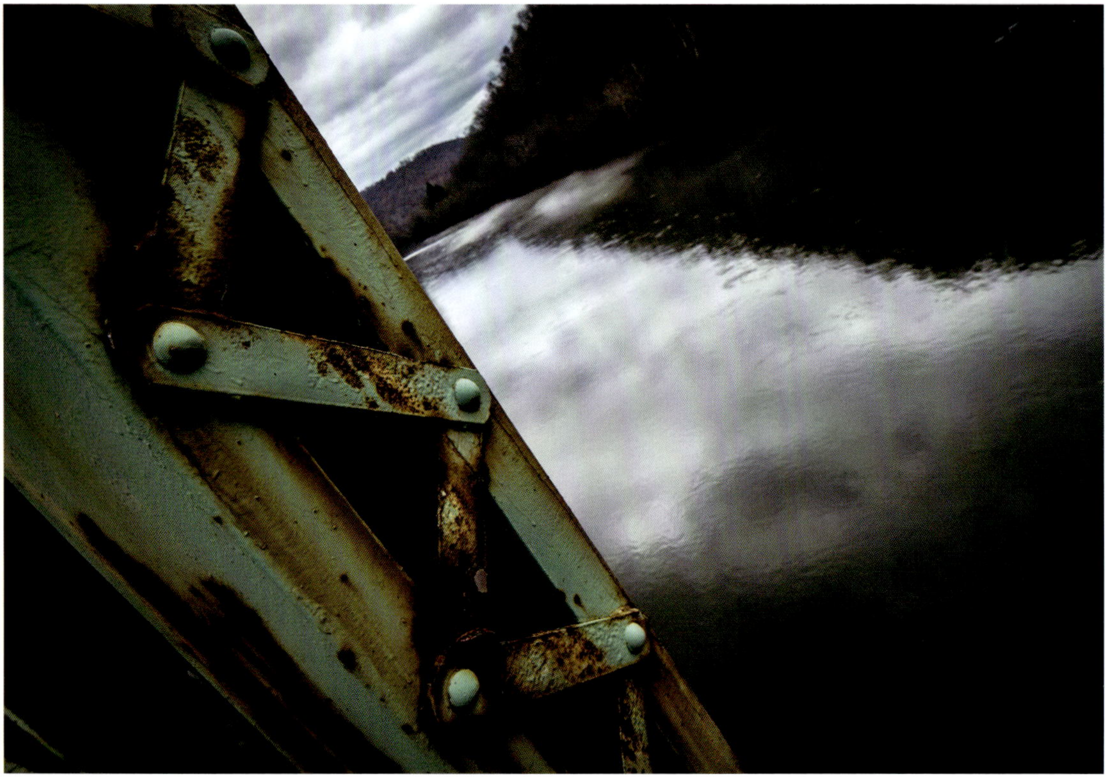

Mist

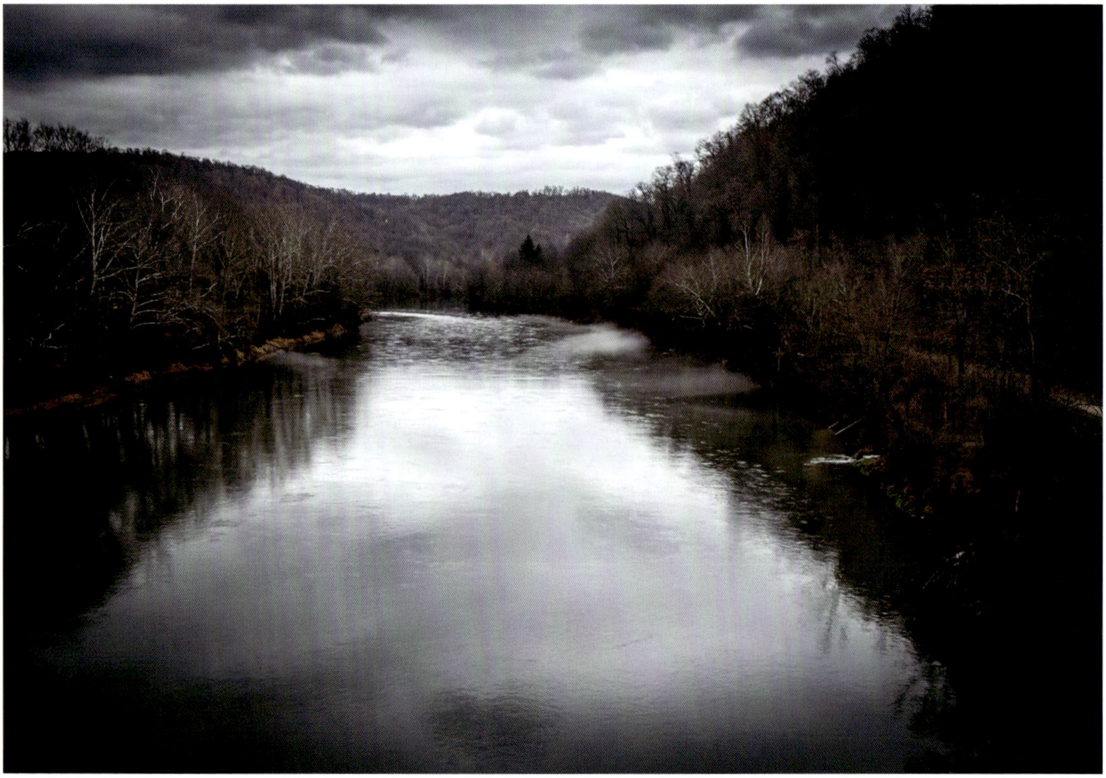

Youghiogheny River

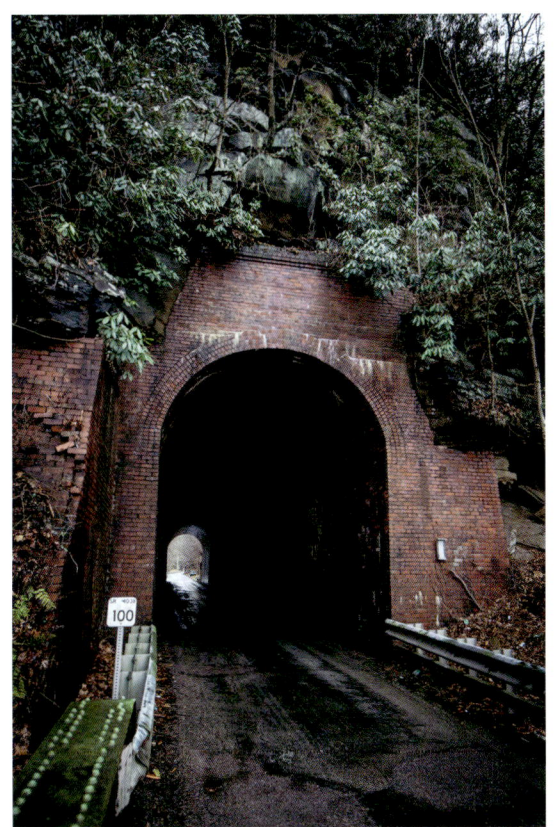

Tunnel 1

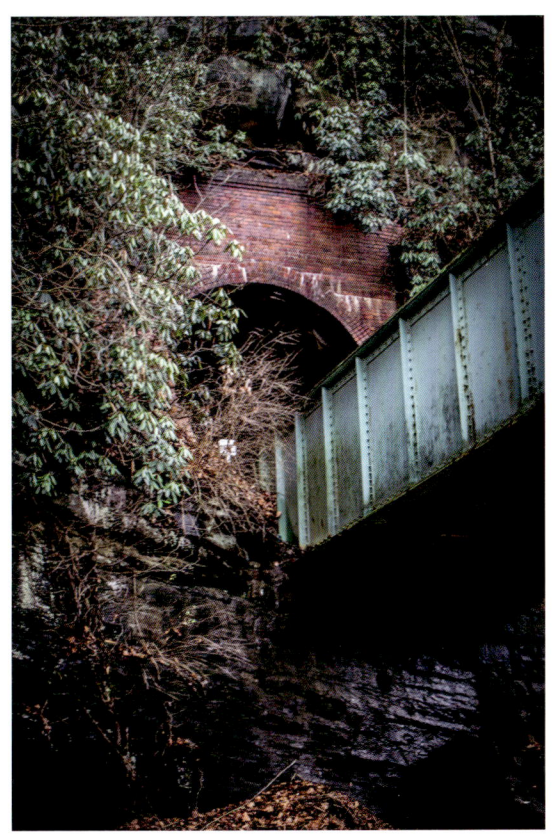

Tunnel 2

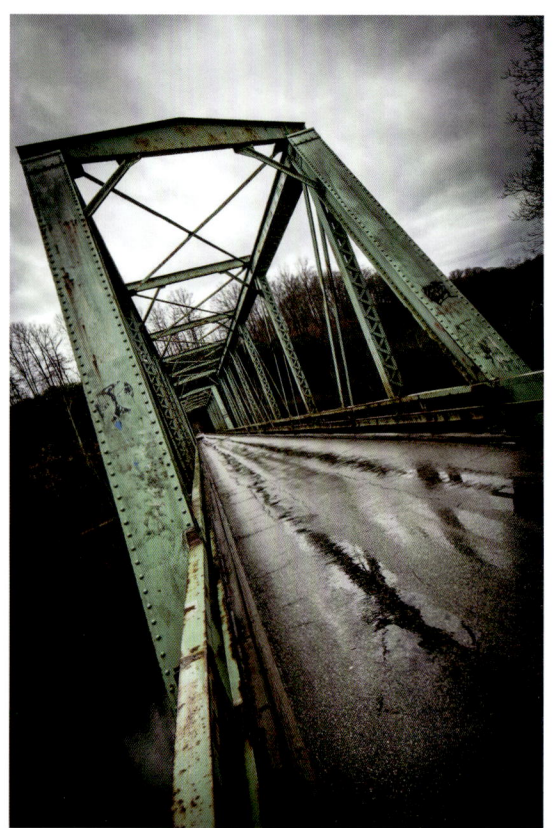

Rain

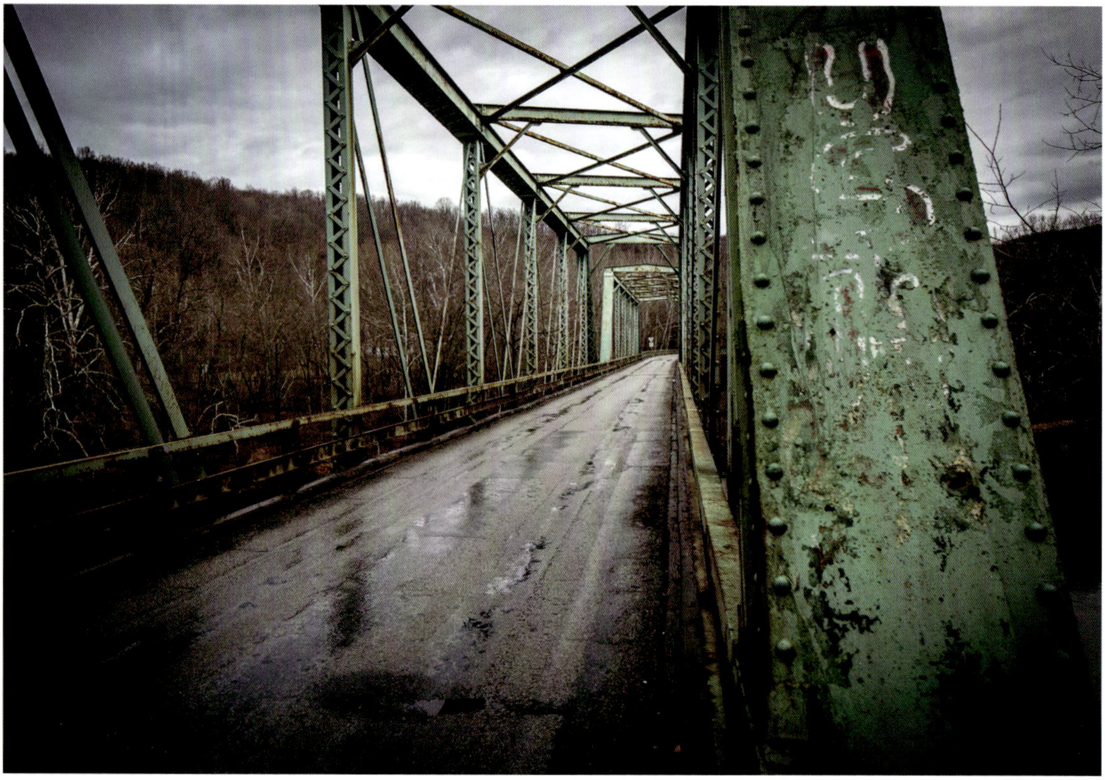

View

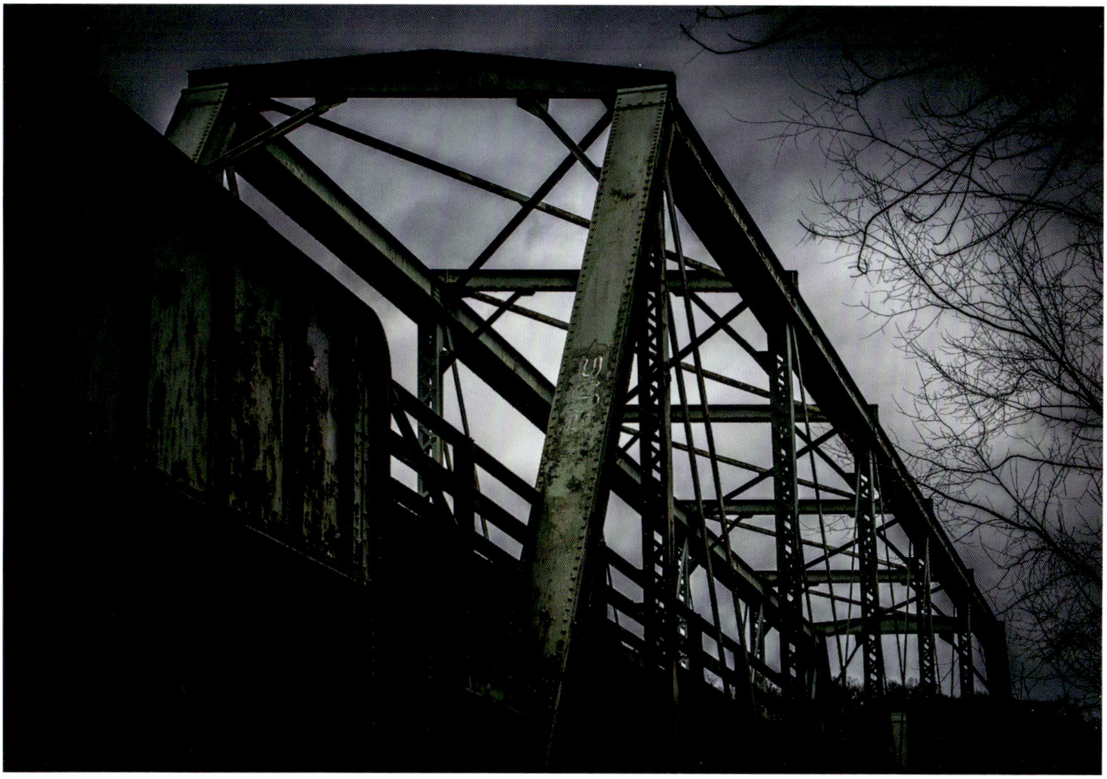

Fog

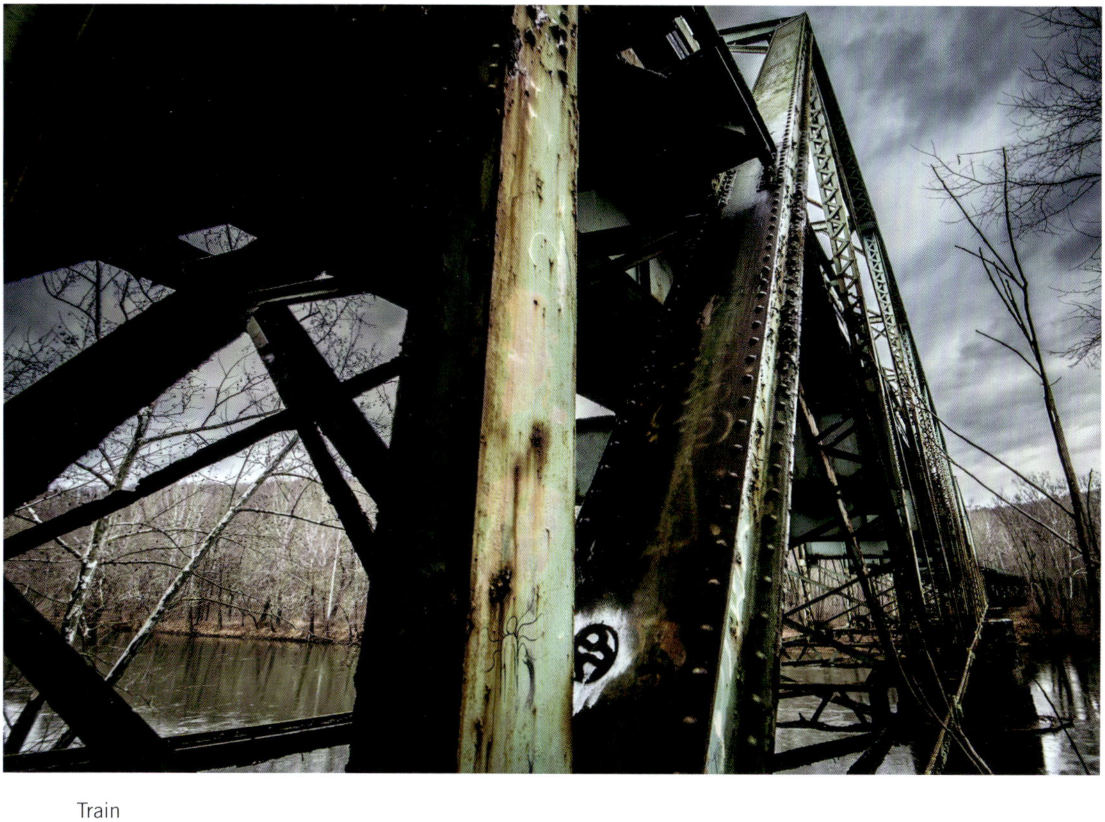

Train

MATHIES COAL CO.

The Mathies Coal Co., near New Eagle, PA (forty-five minutes south of Pittsburgh), opened in 1944. It was said to be the last bituminous coal mine in Pennsylvania to use rail haulage to transport the coal from the mine. The company closed abruptly in 2002, resulting in the unemployment of more than 150 employees.

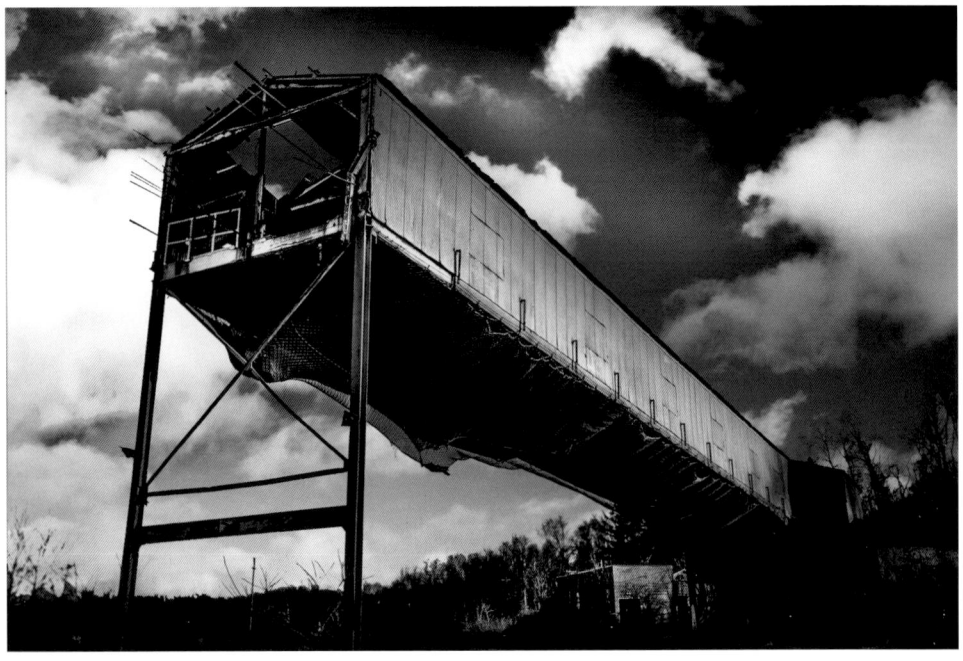

Sky

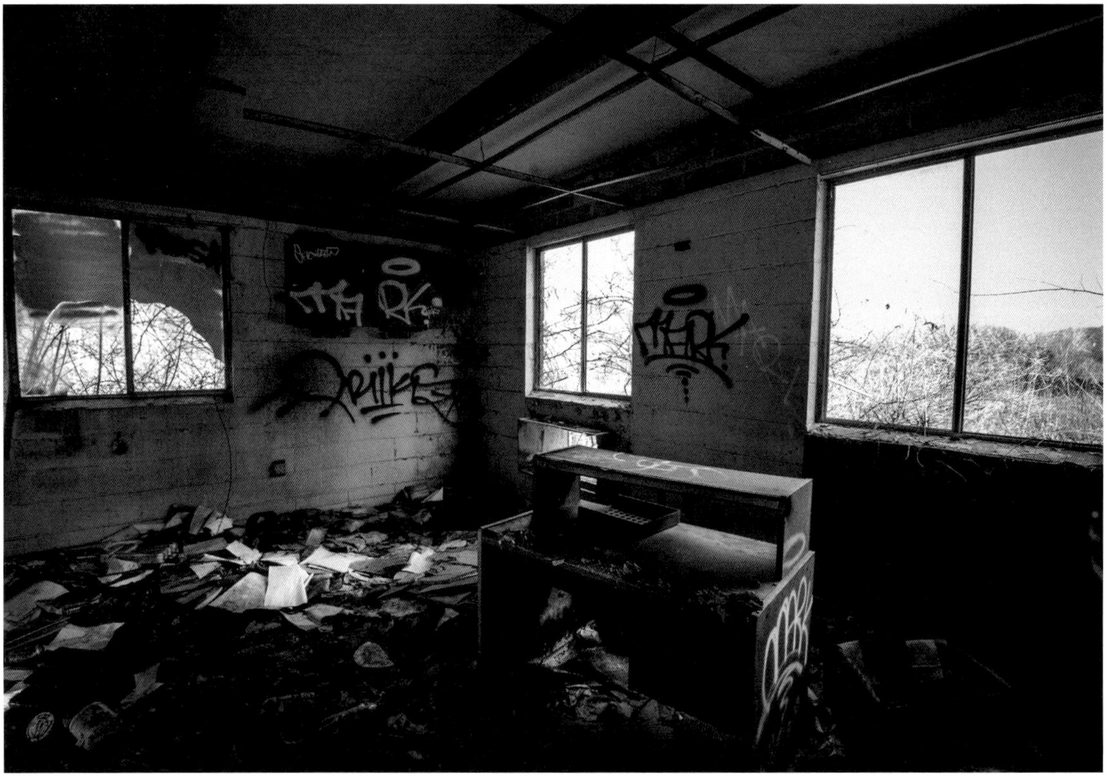

Desk

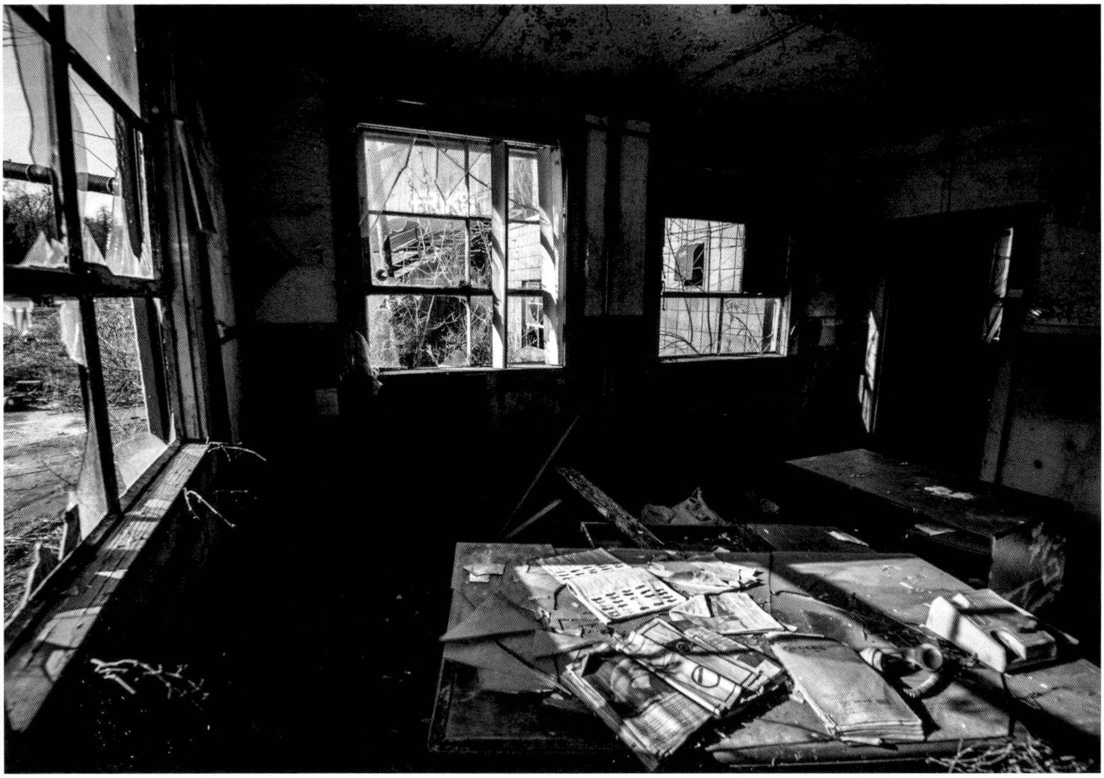

Windows

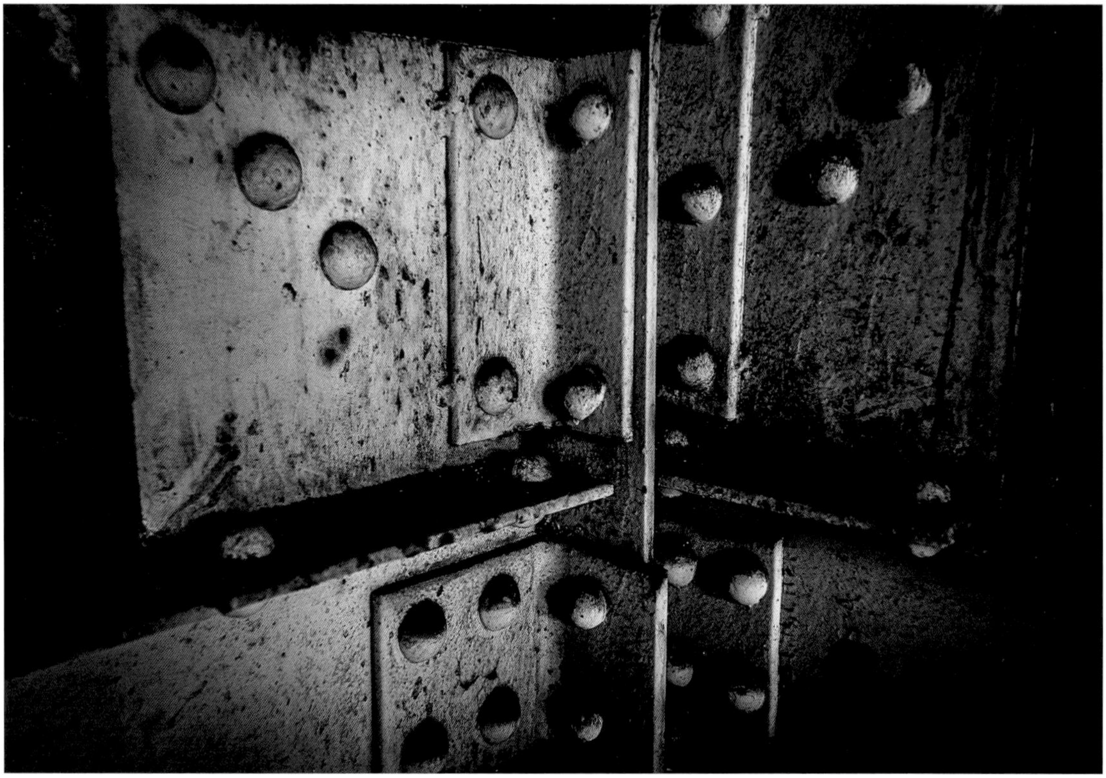

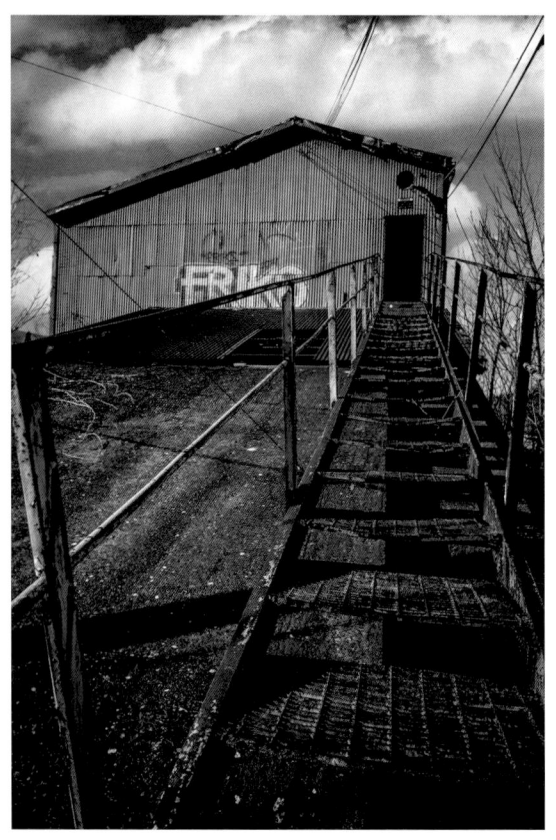

Bolts

Stairs

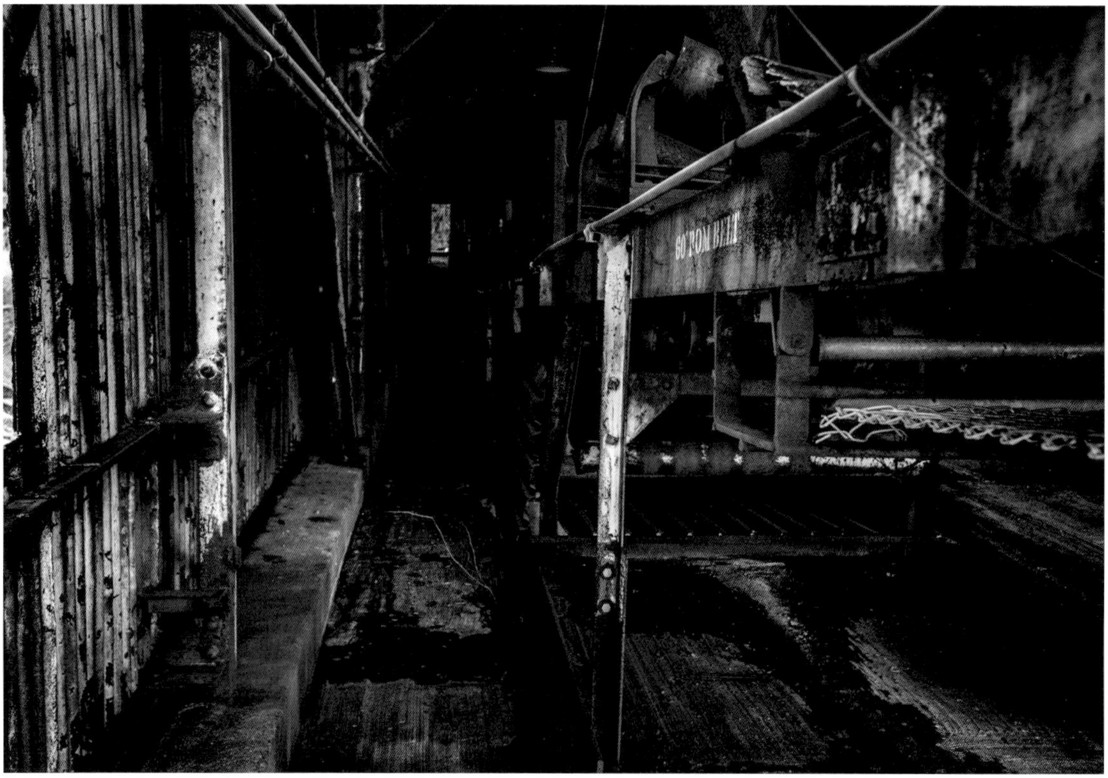

60" Pom Belt

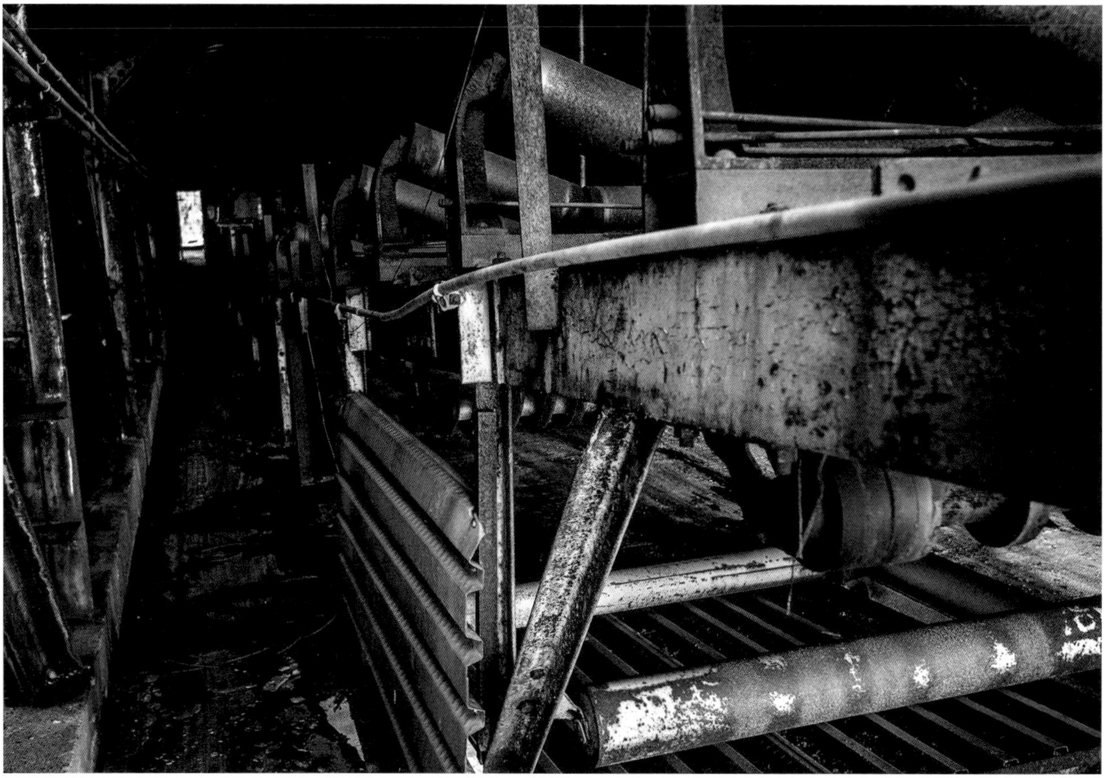

Conveyor

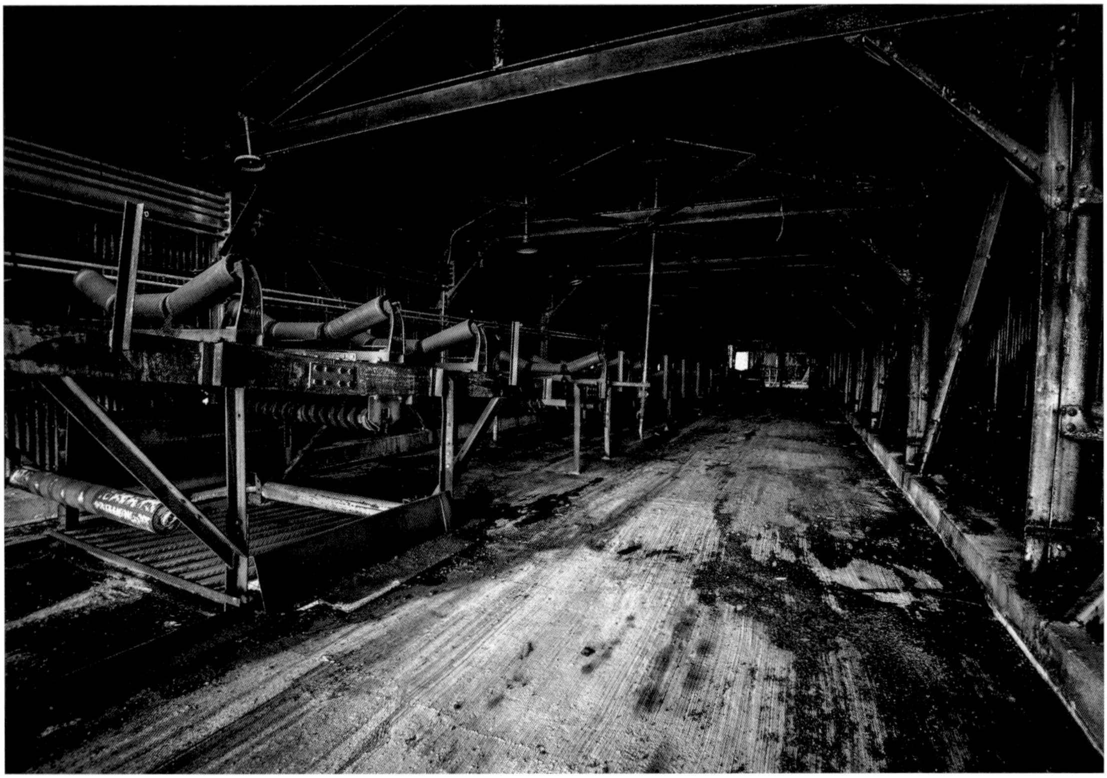

Tunnel

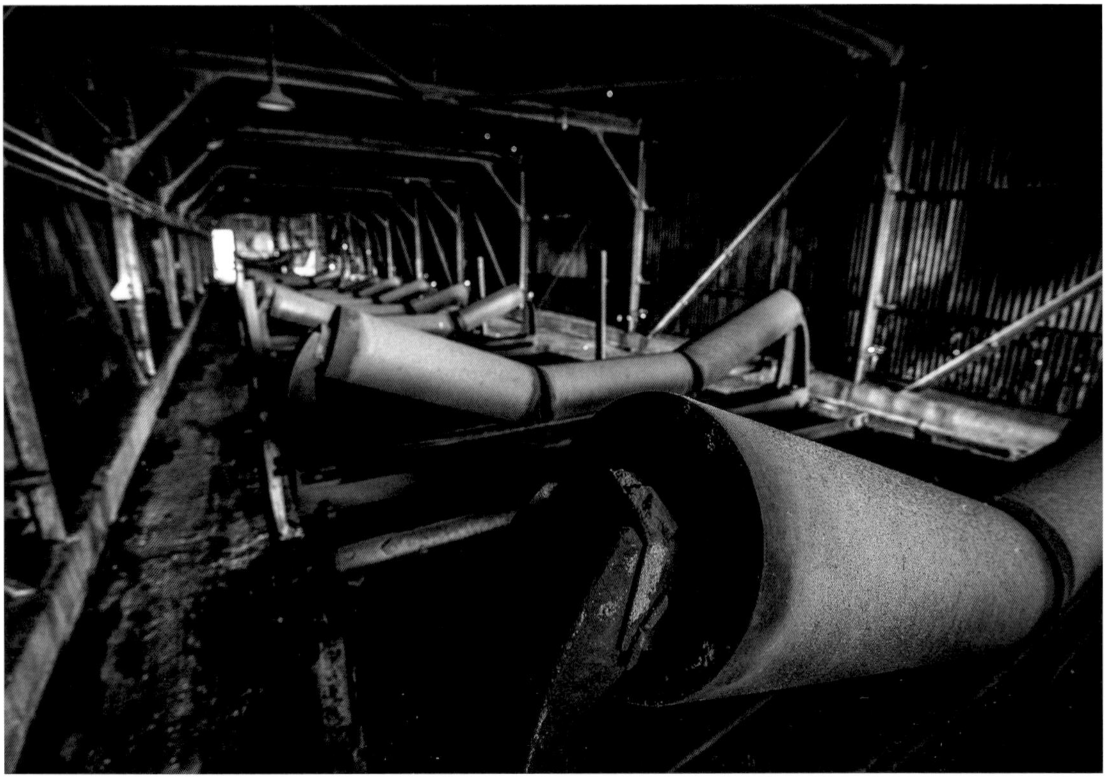

Pipes

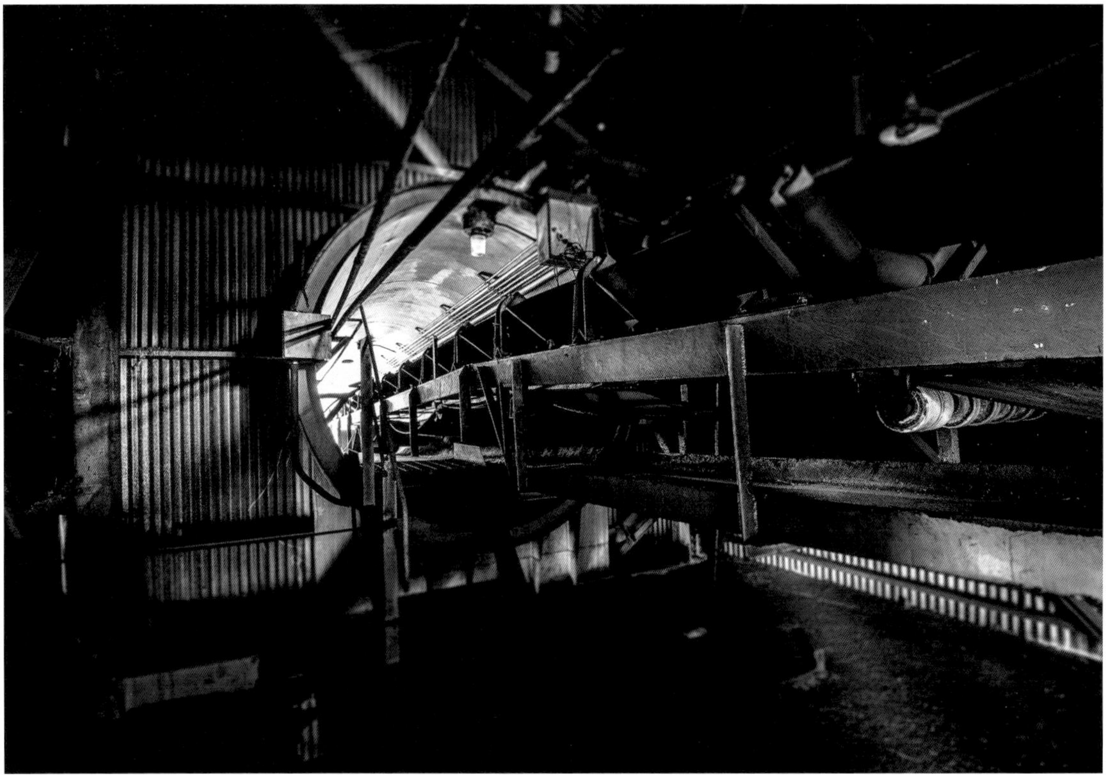

Wormhole

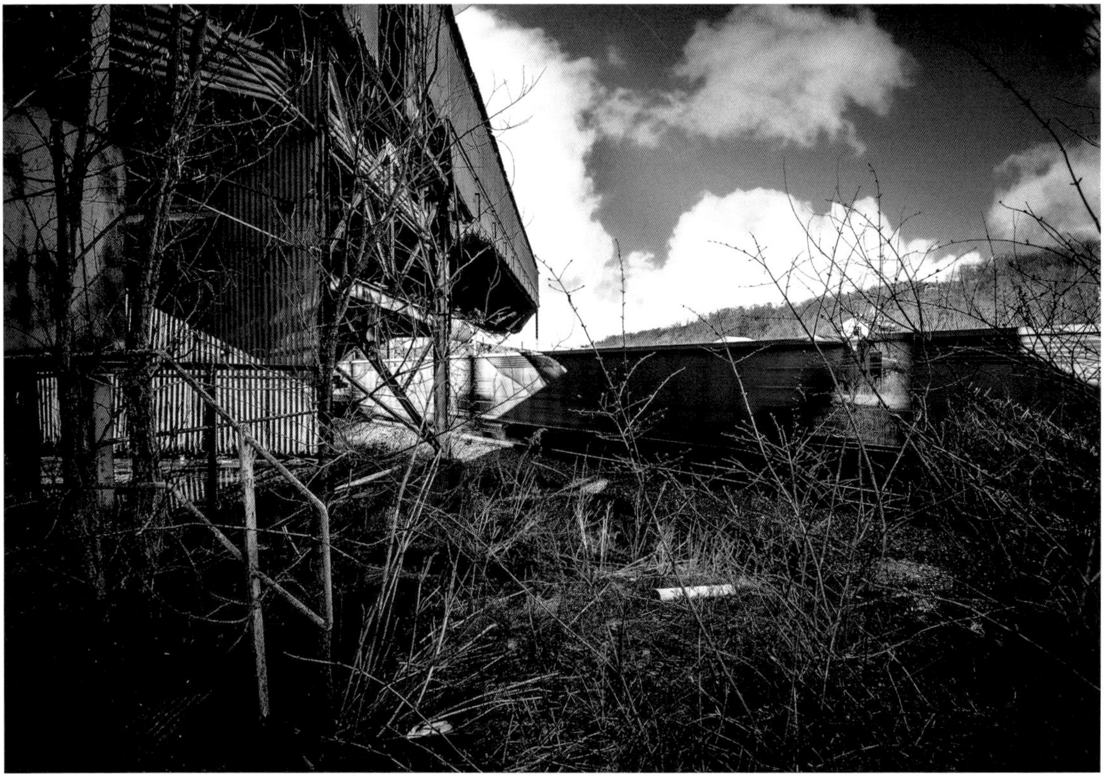

Train

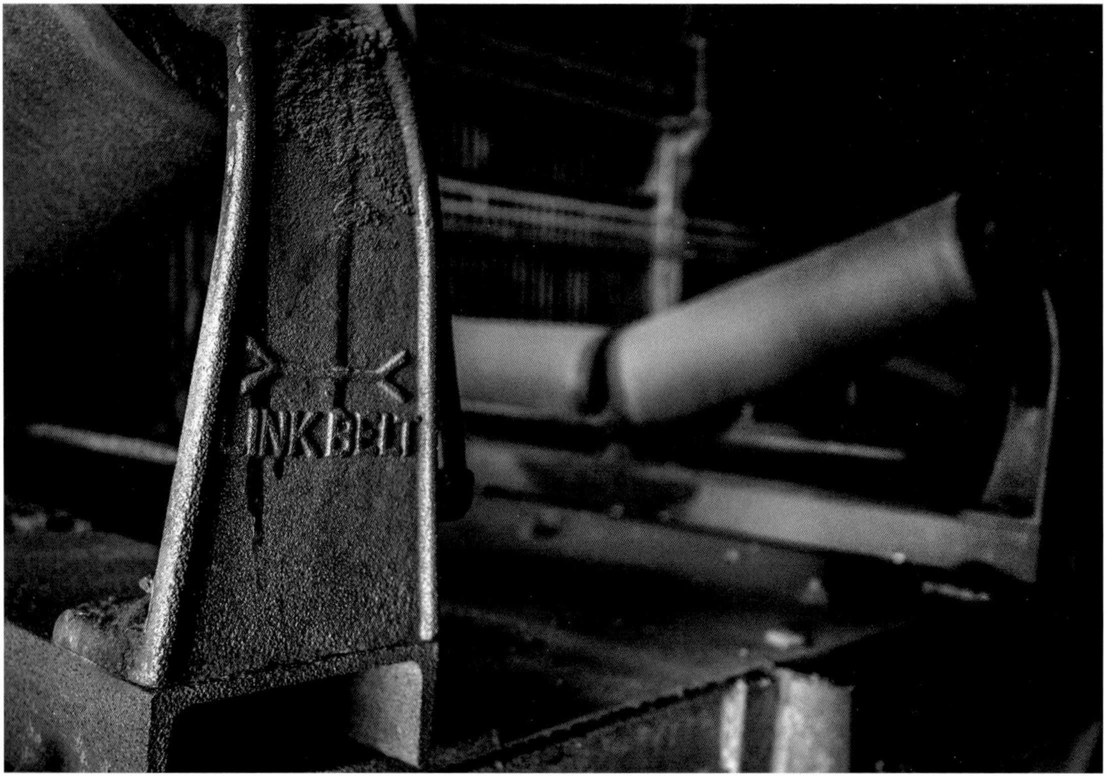

Link Belt

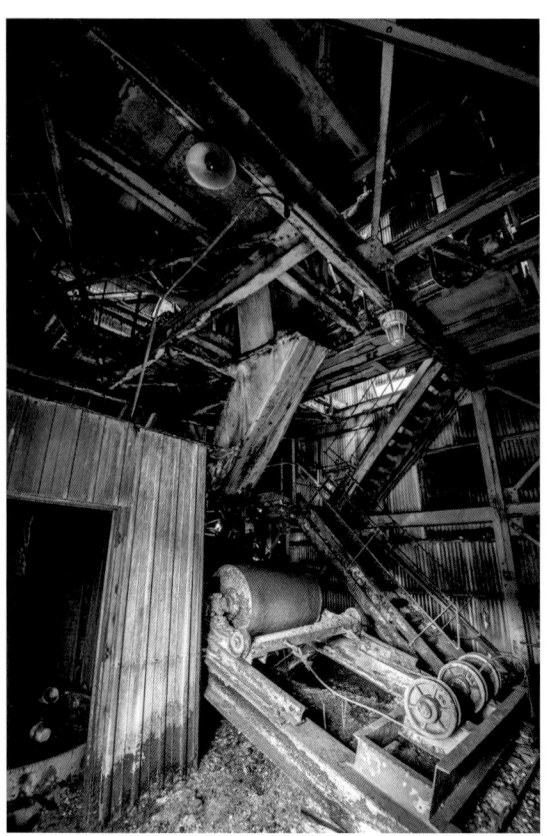

Ladder

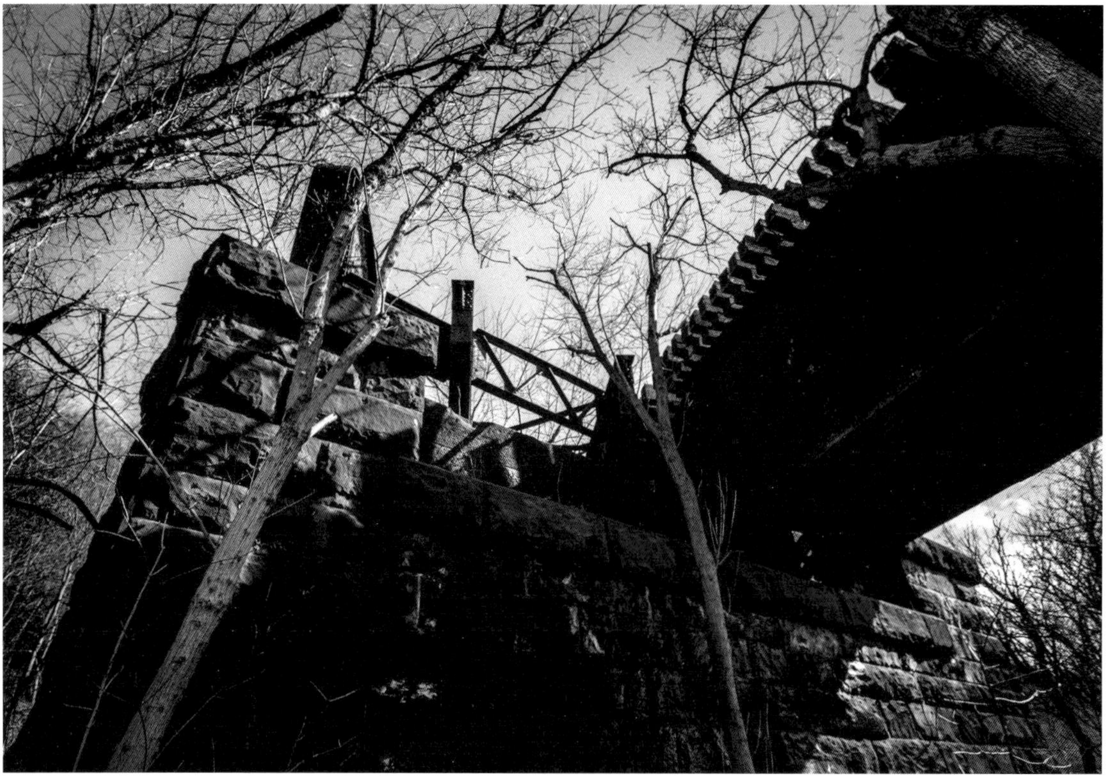

Trestles

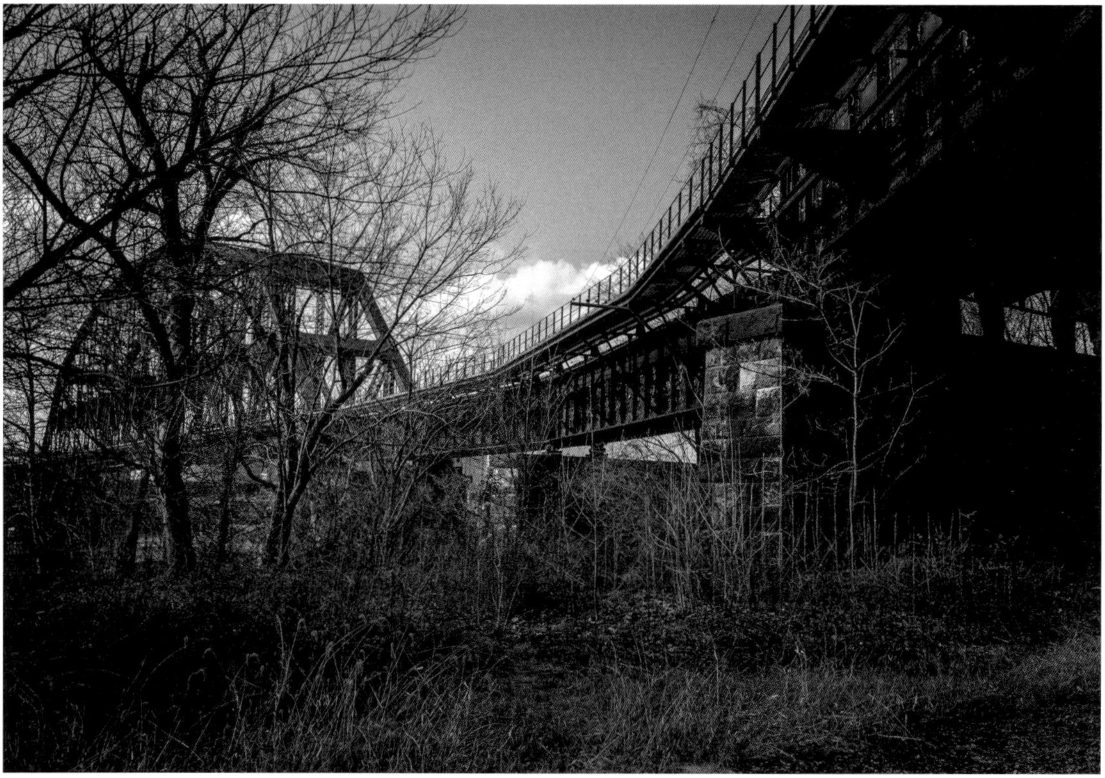

Bridge

HOMESTEAD MUNICIPAL BUILDING

The Homestead Municipal Building was built in 1904 and was the original site of the borough's police and fire stations. The jail's most famous resident was Mother Jones, the labor activist described a century ago as the most dangerous woman in America. She came to the Monongahela Valley to rally support for the Steel Strike of 1919 and was arrested in Homestead for "street speaking without a permit." After the municipality offices moved, the building sat vacant for two decades. It is now the home of a popular craft brewery.

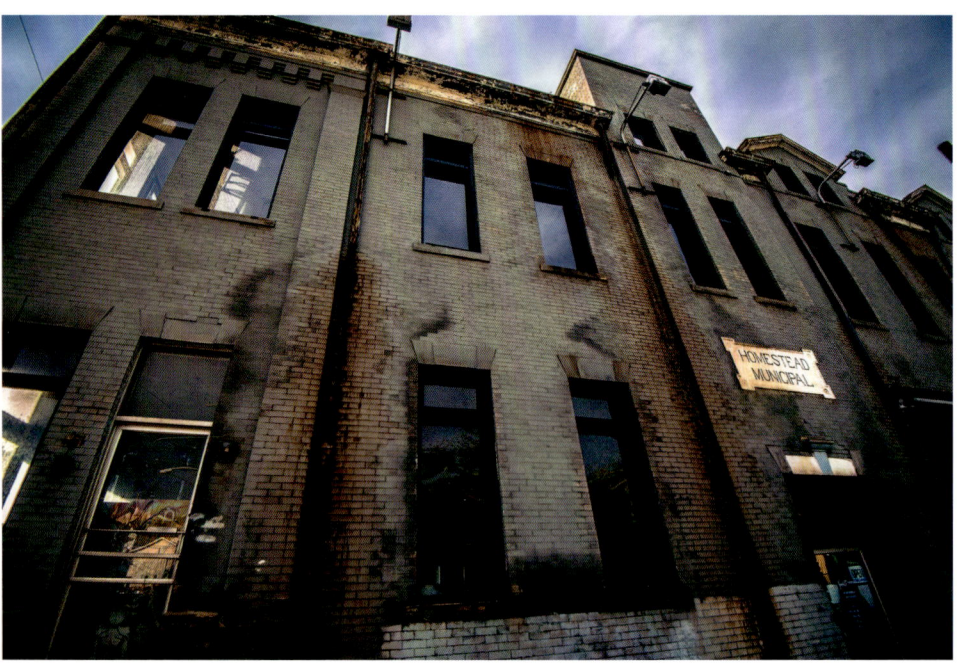

Facade

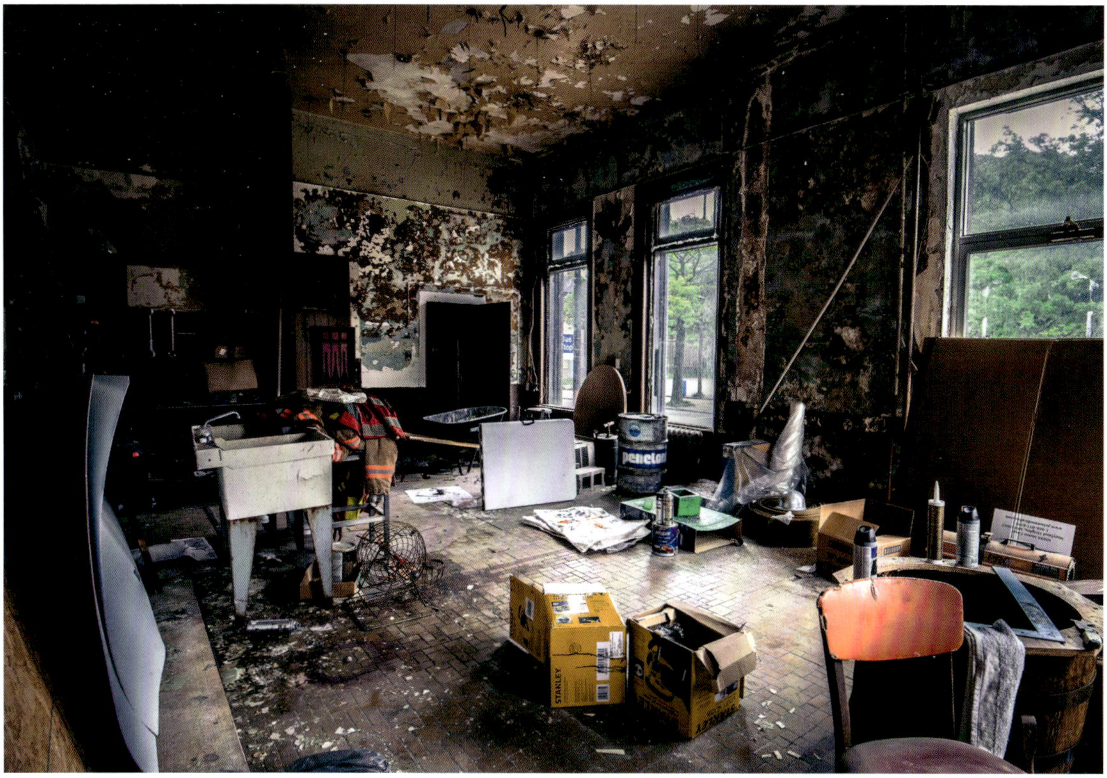

Lobby

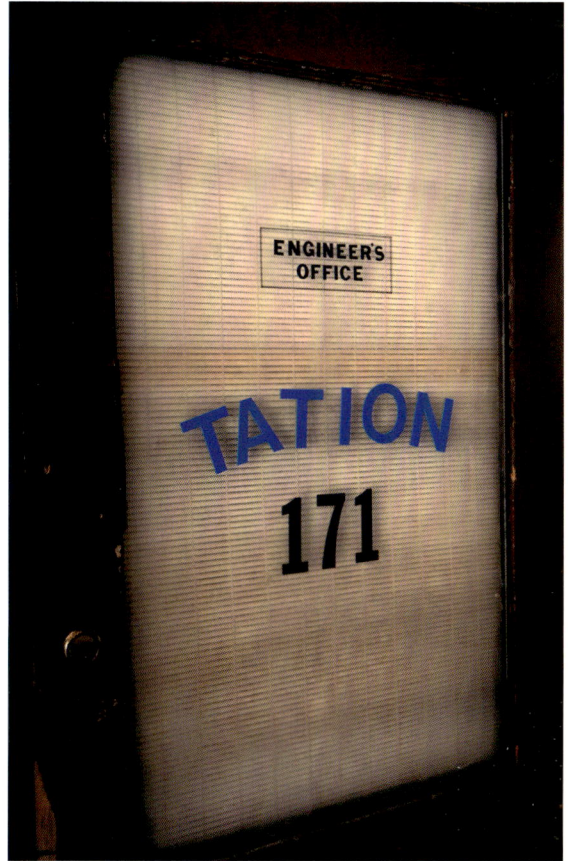

Tation 171

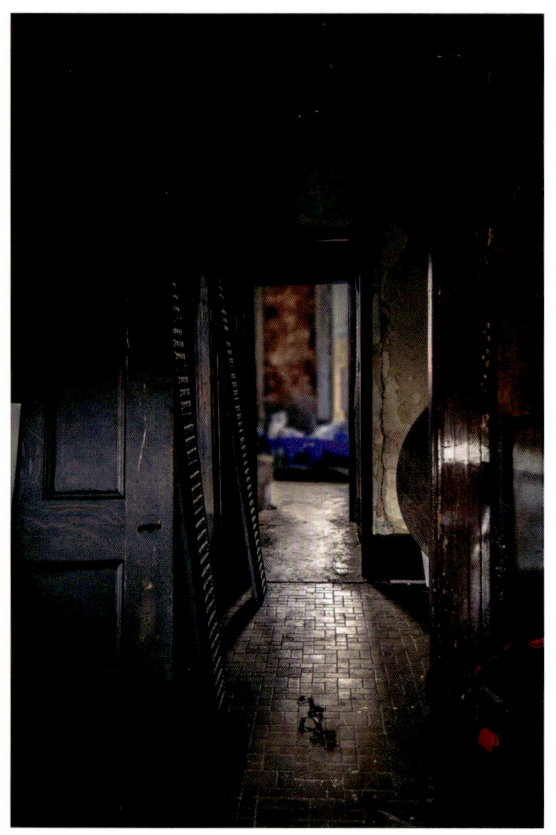

Doorway

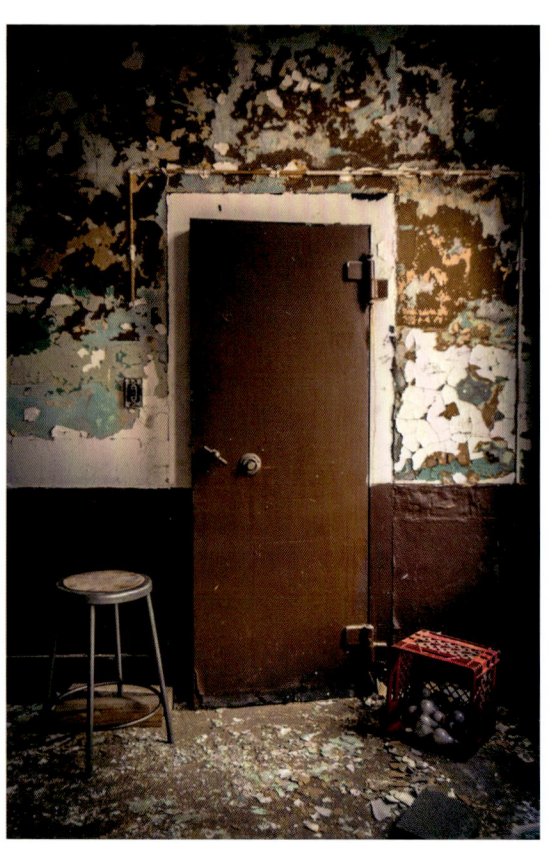

Safe

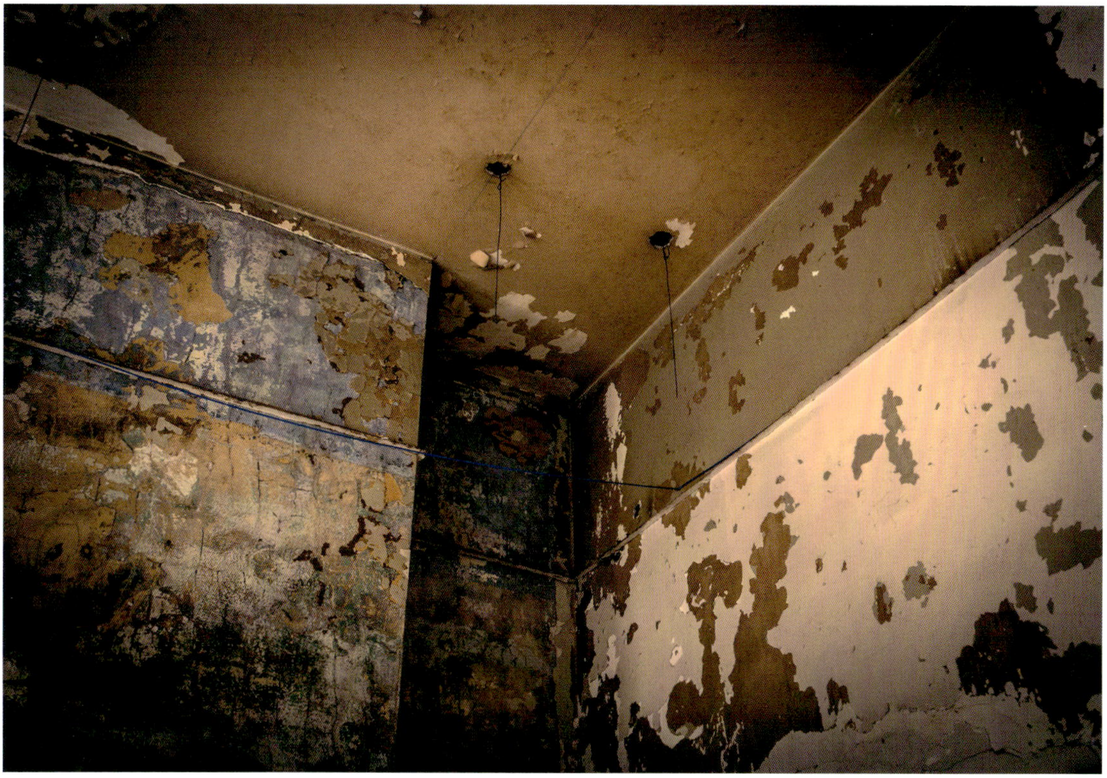

Corner

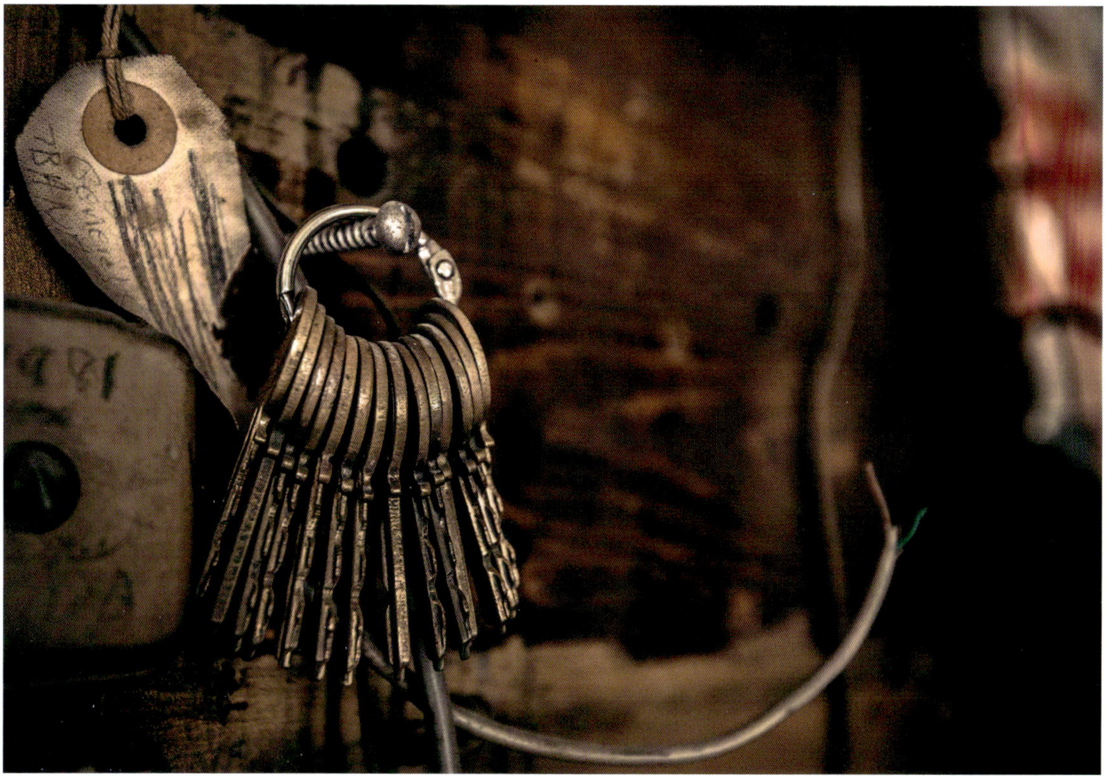

Keys

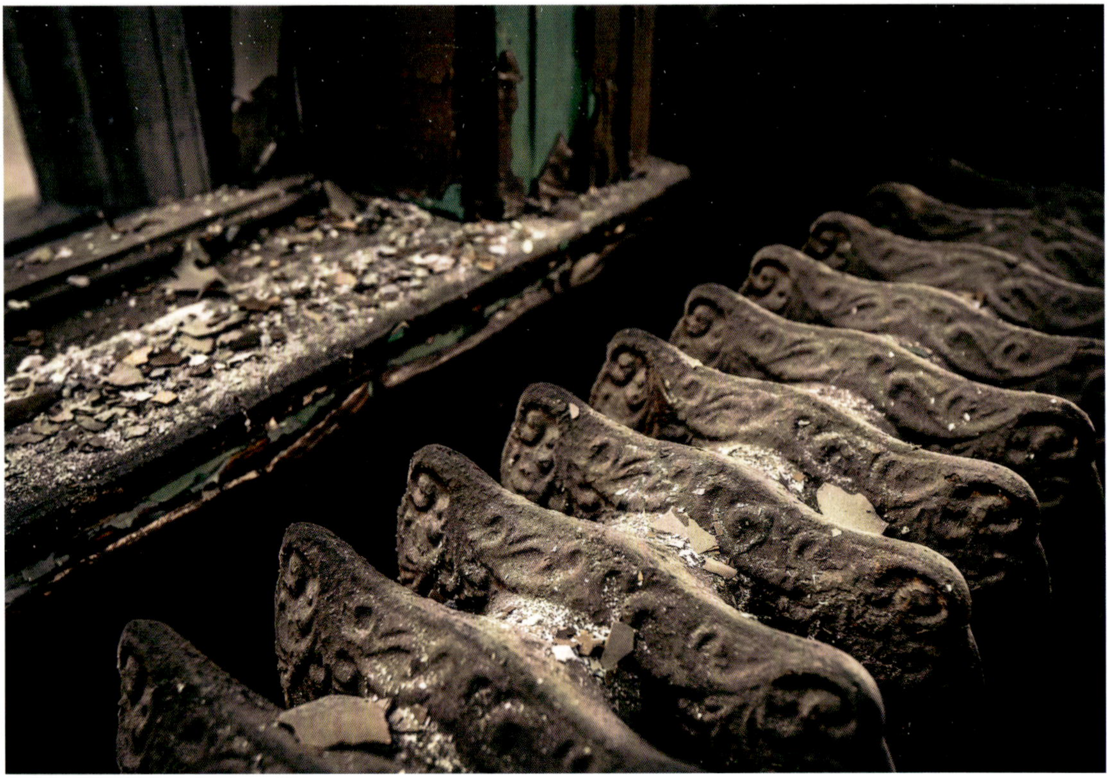

Radiator

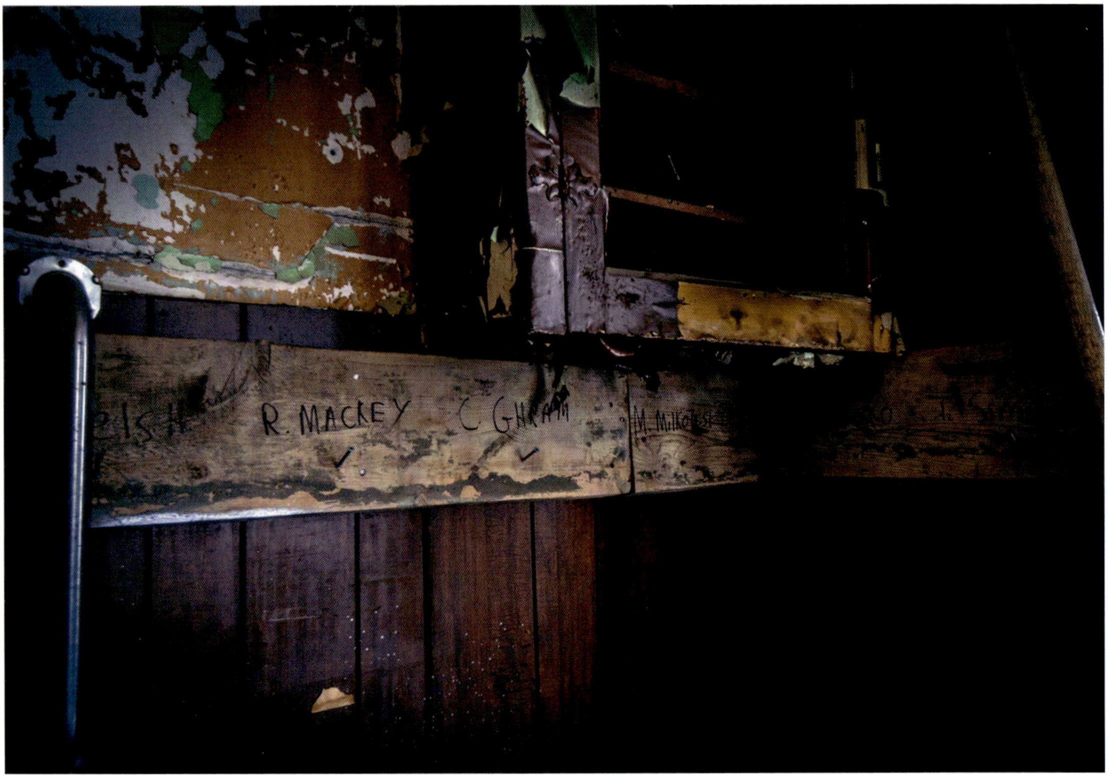

Rack

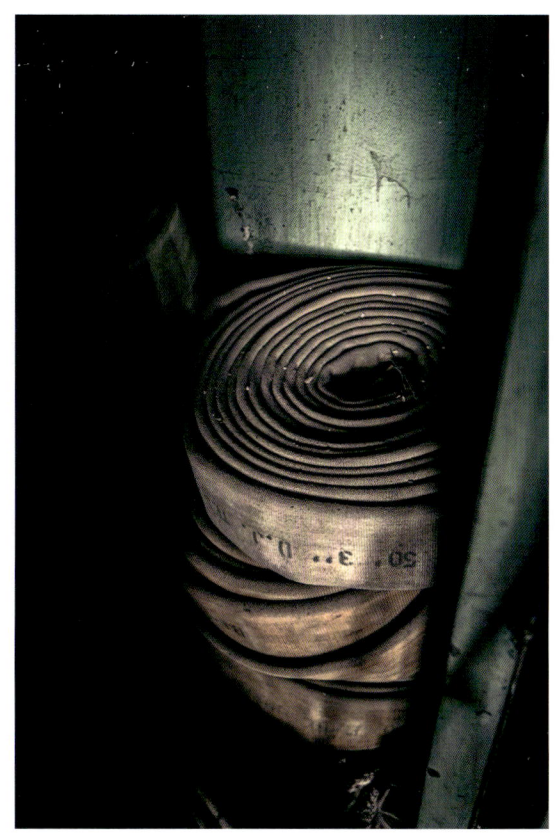
Hoses

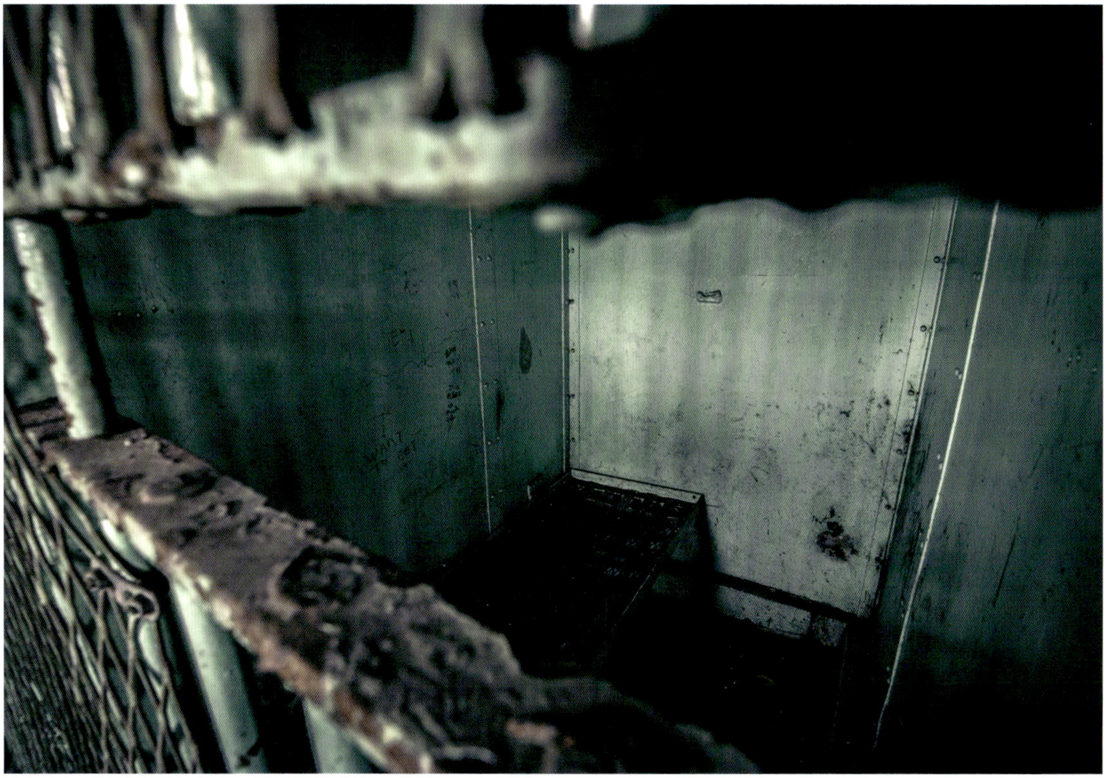

Cell

WILKINSBURG TRAIN STATION

This opulent Beaux Arts-style station was built in 1916, with a vitrified-tile waiting room and massive wooden benches. The station serviced trains on the Pennsylvania Railroad. The Wilkinsburg stop was discontinued in 1975, as only 128 passengers had used the stop in the first six months of that year. The building was listed on the National Register of Historic Places in 1985 but sat vacant and fell into disrepair until a restoration project began in 2016.

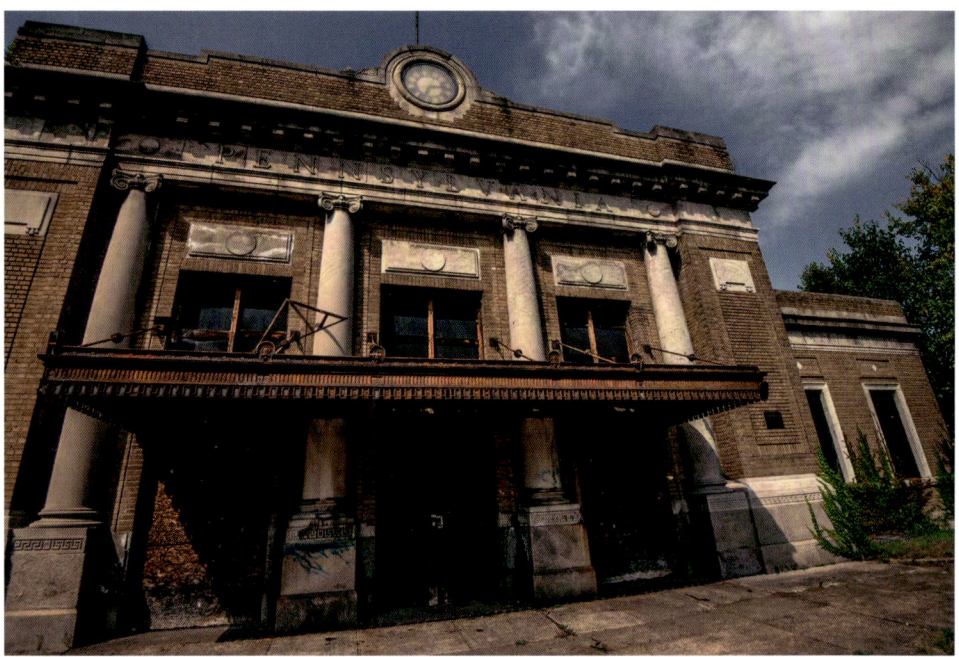

Wilkinsburg Train Station

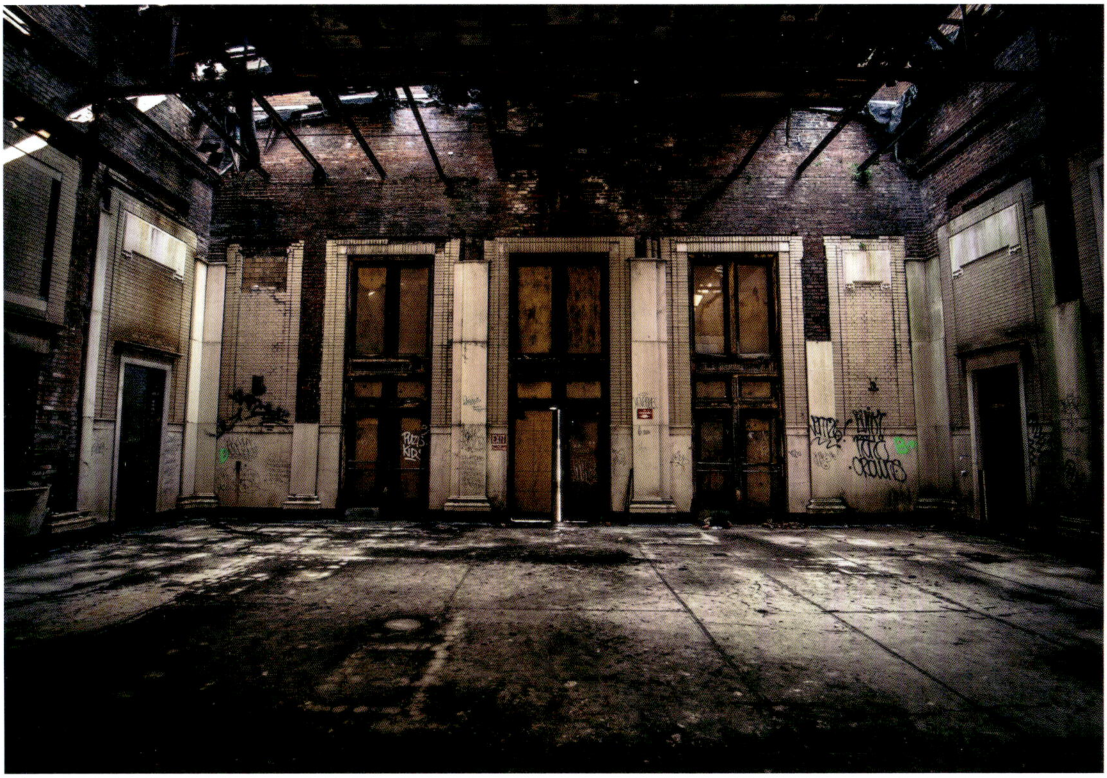

Lobby

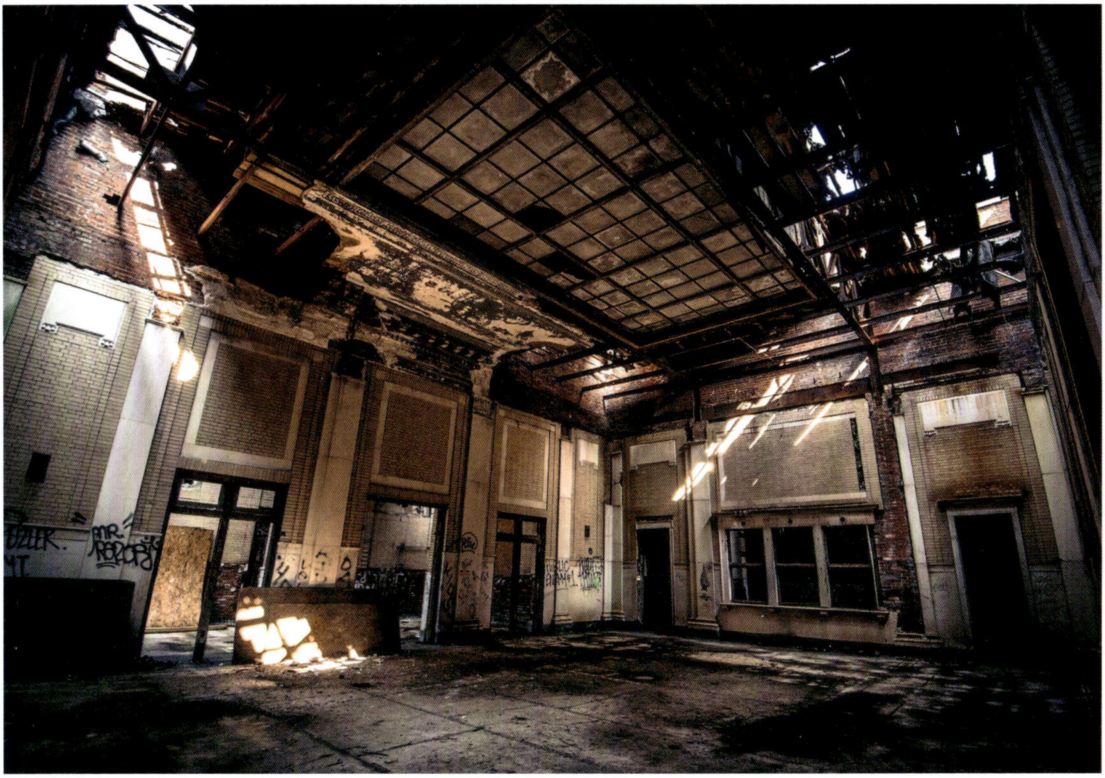

Skylight

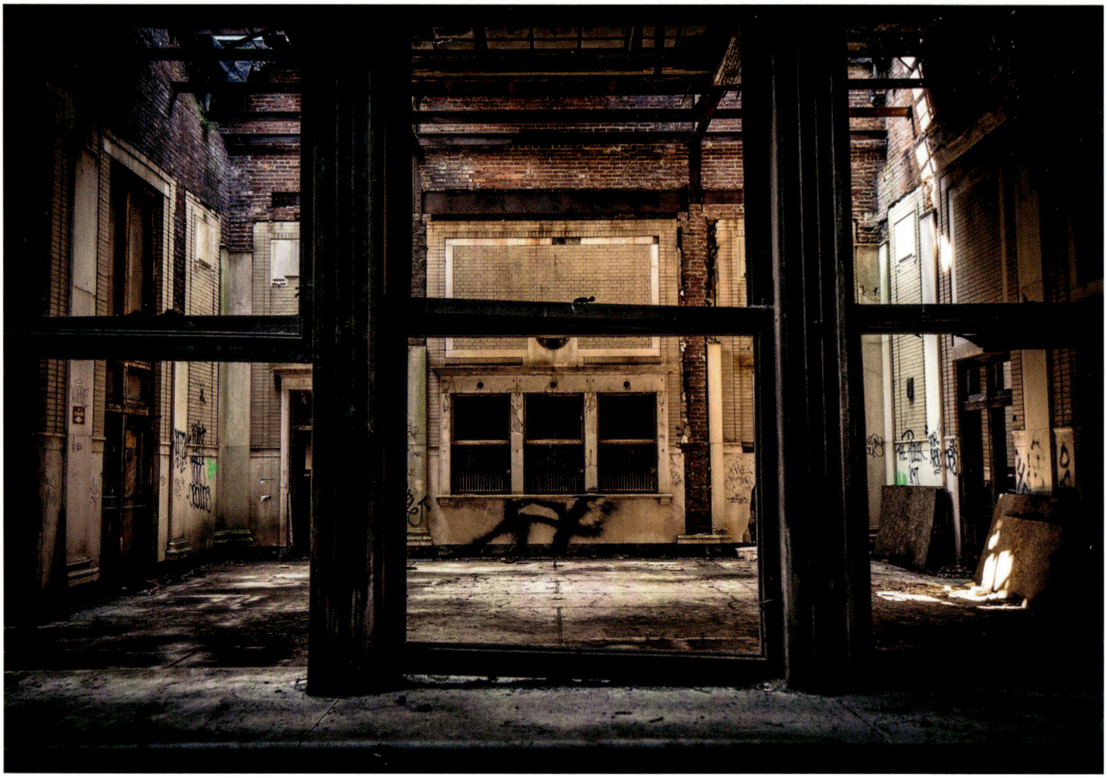

Frame

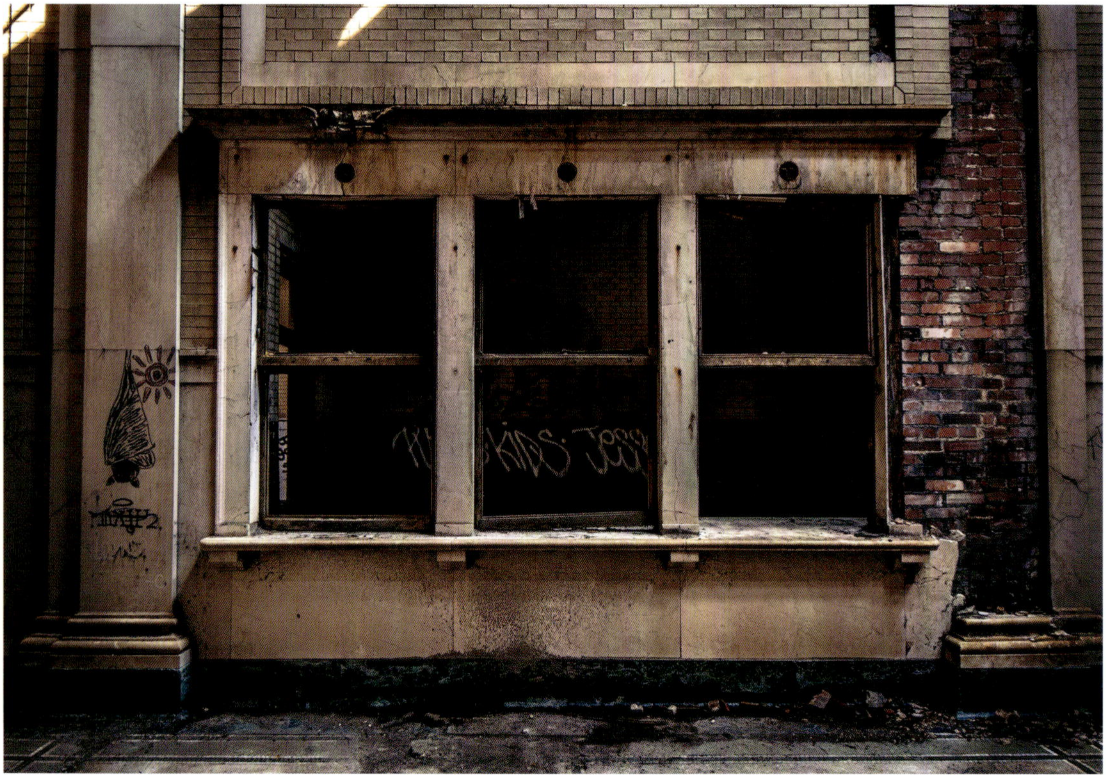

Brown Window

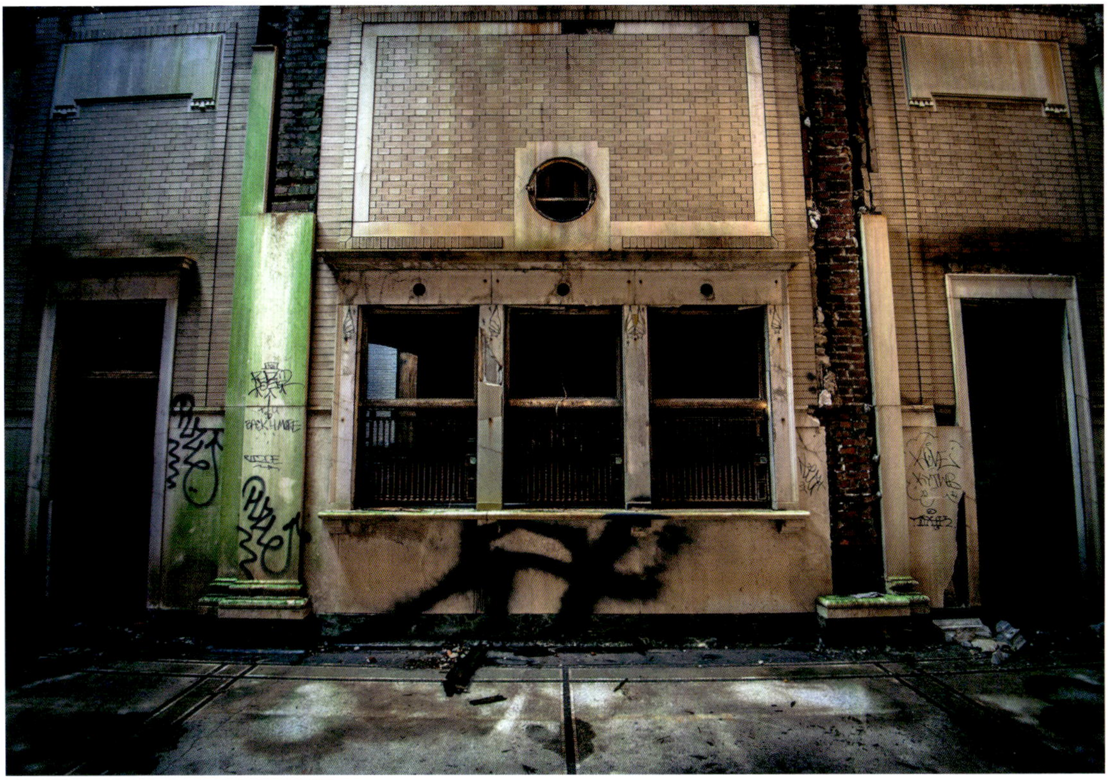

Green Window

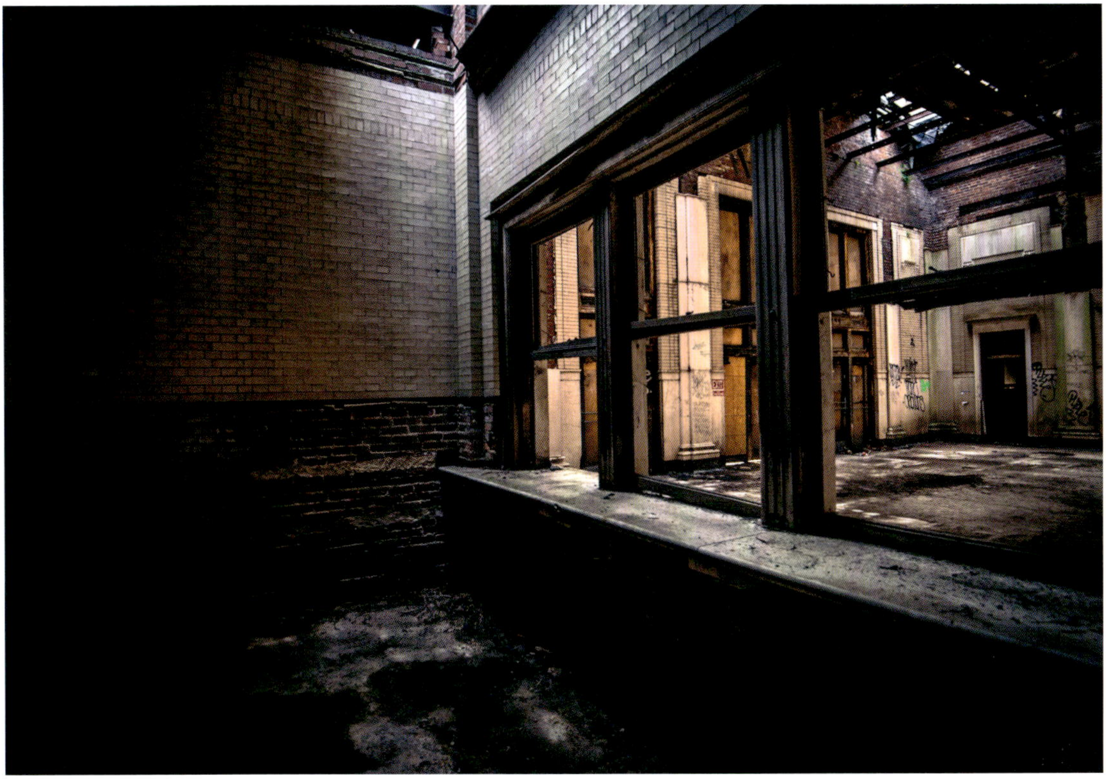

Tickets

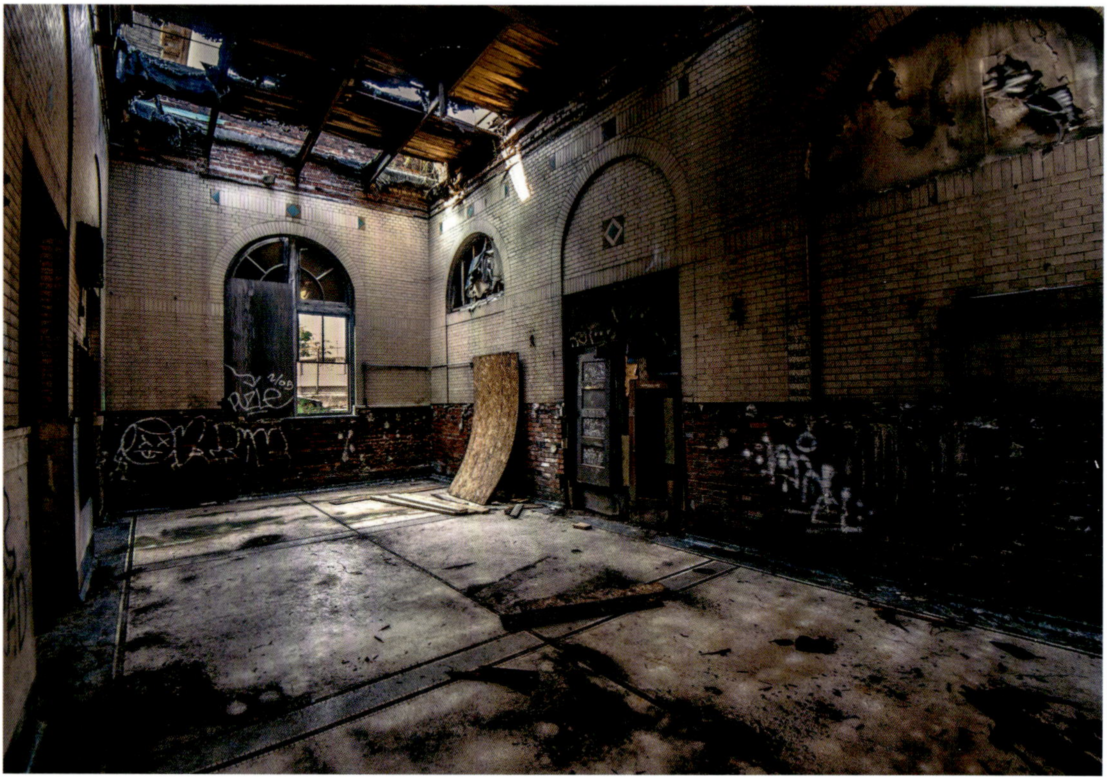

Waiting Room

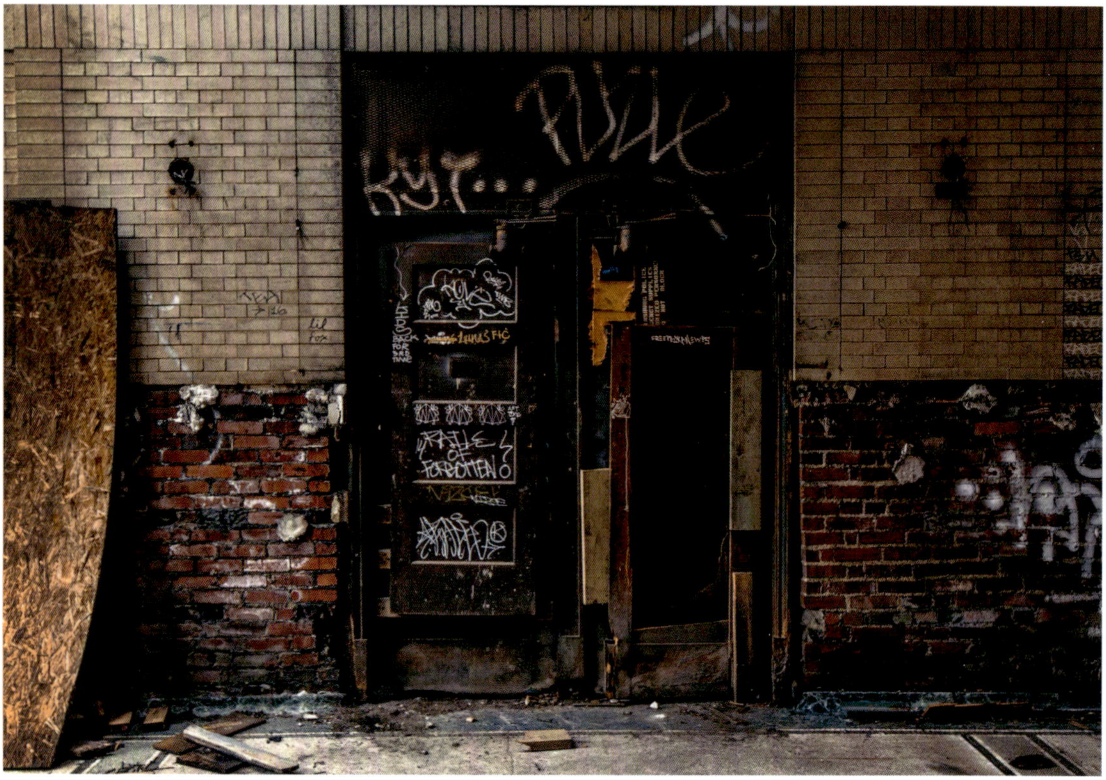

Door Down

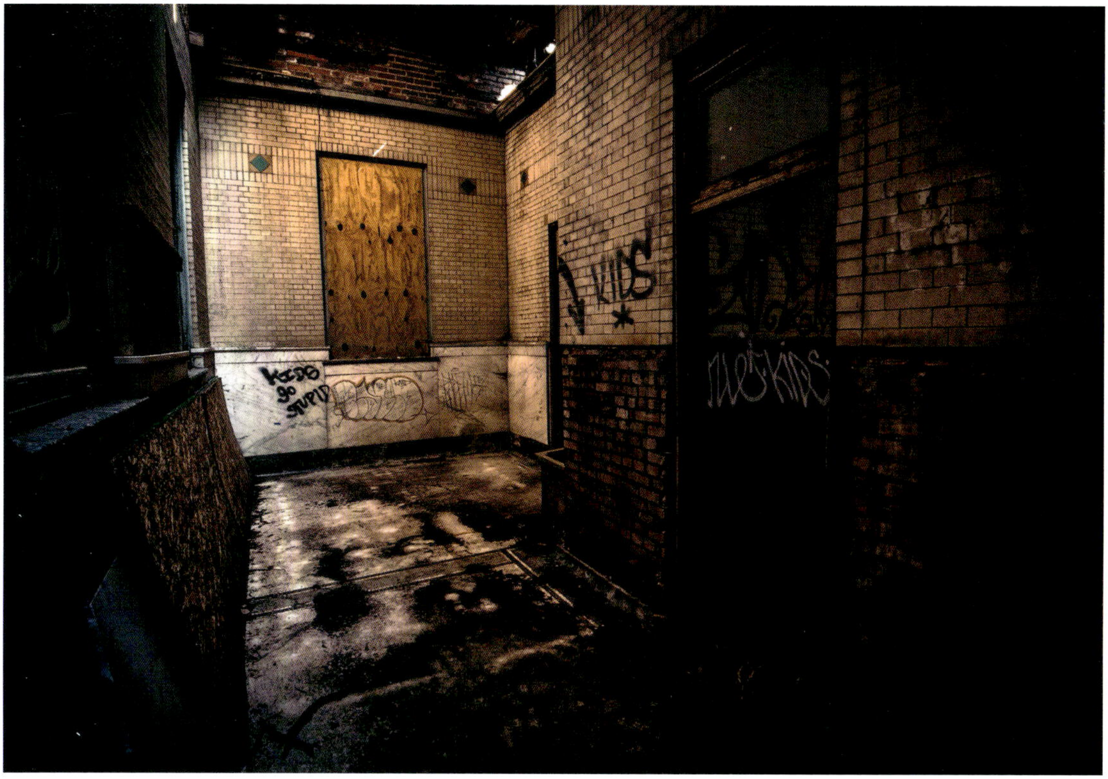

Anteroom

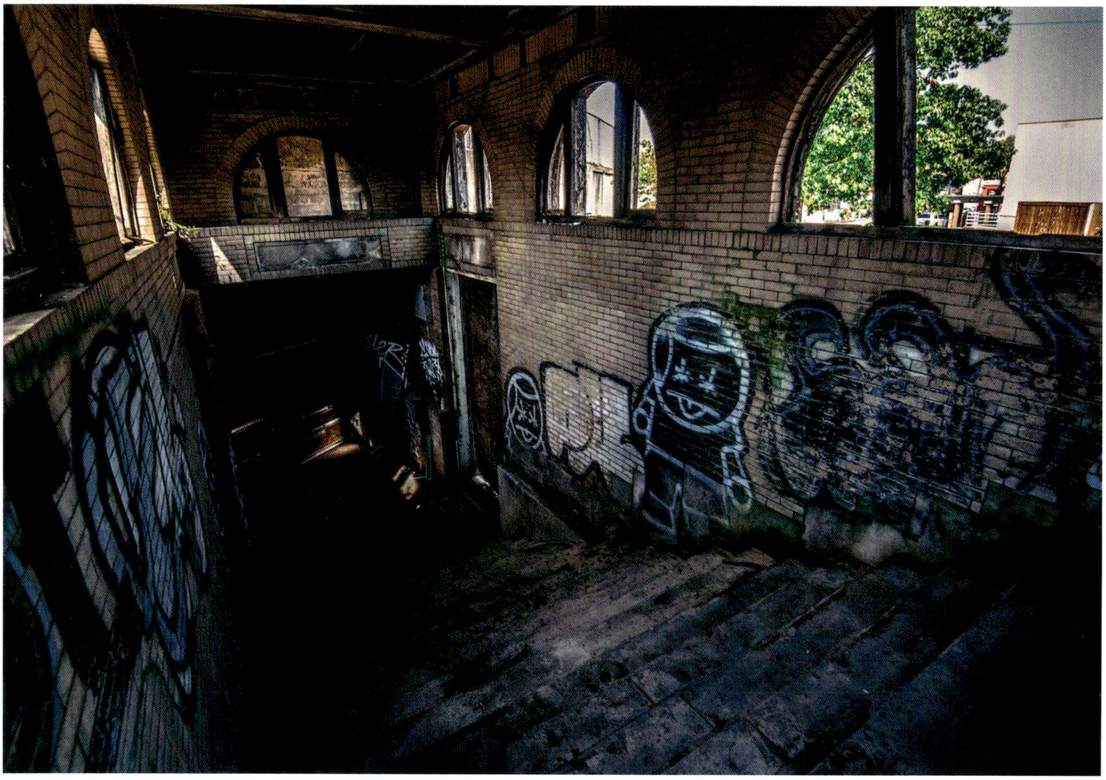

Tunnel Down

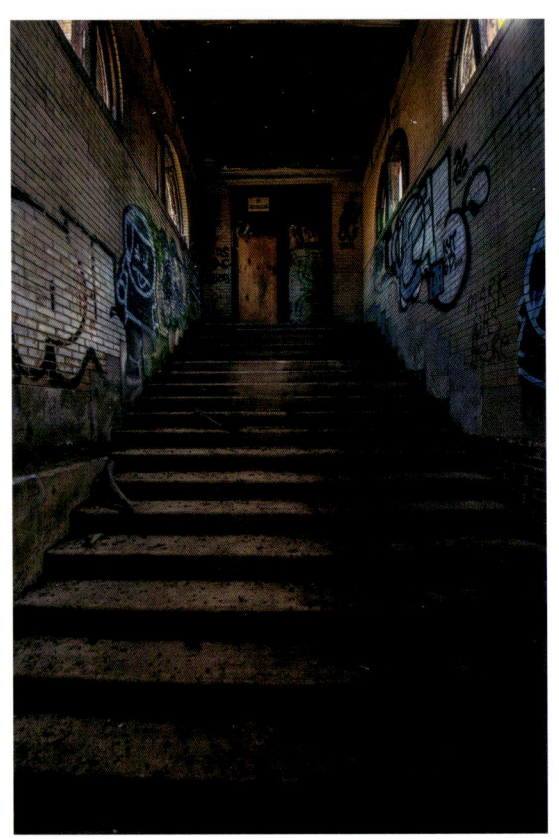
Tunnel Up

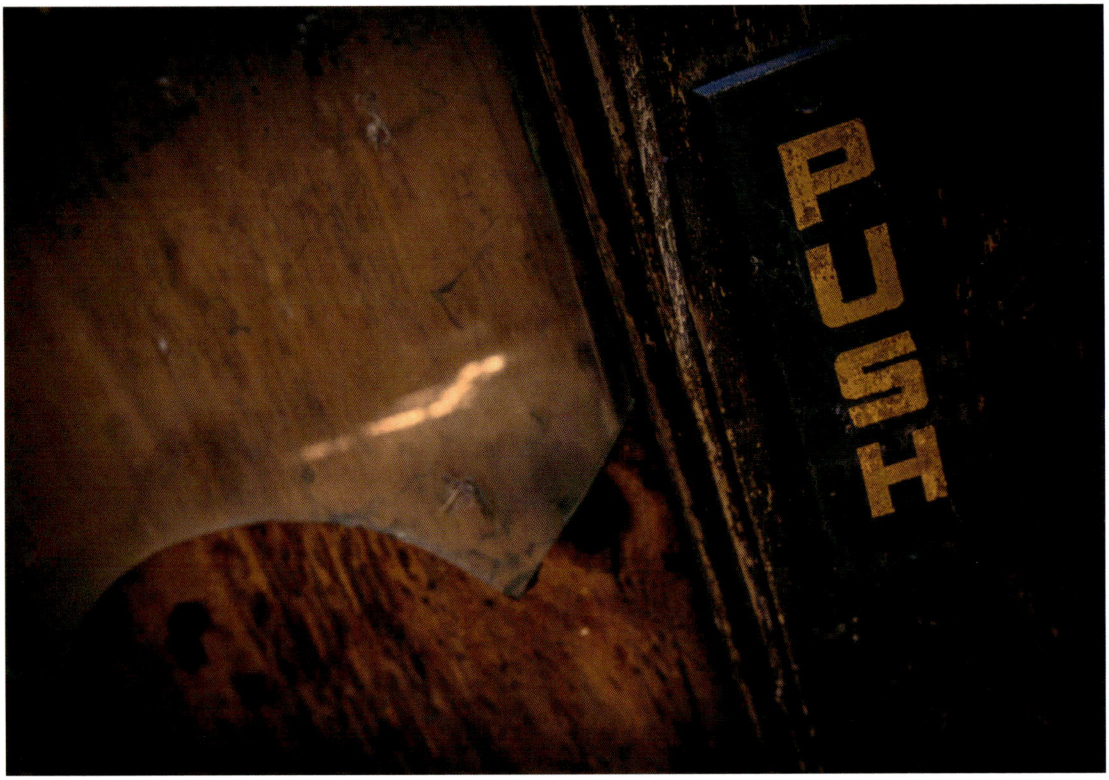

Push

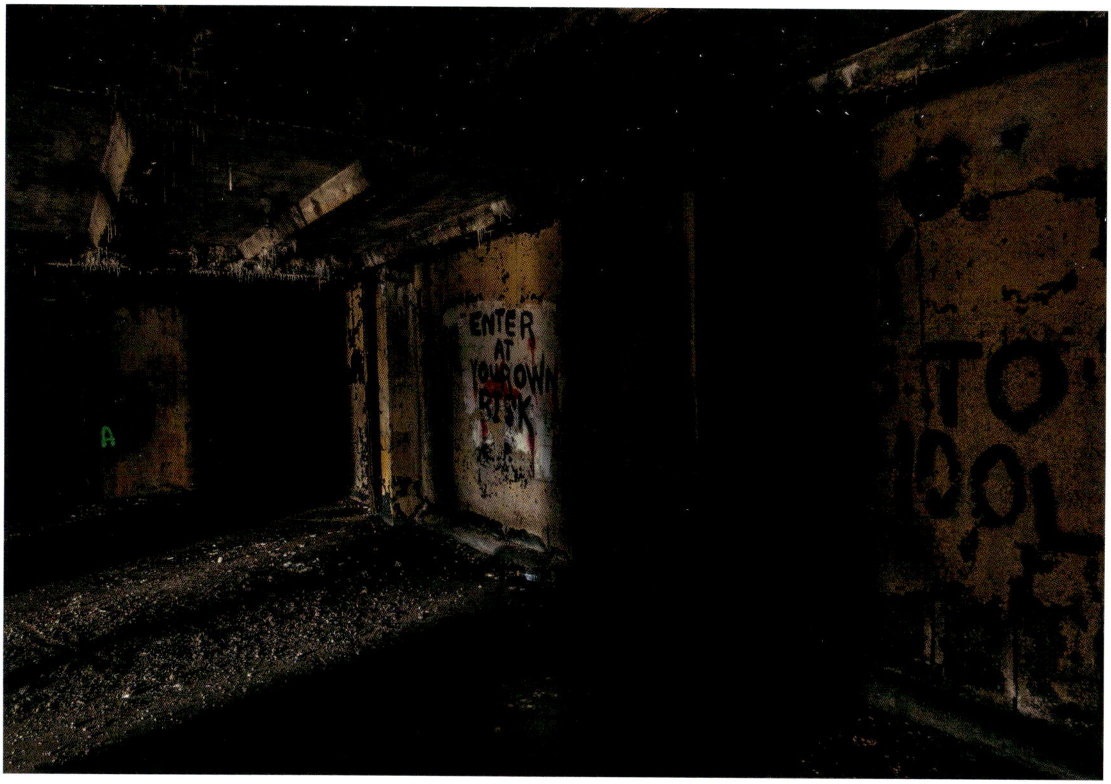

Enter At Your Own Risk

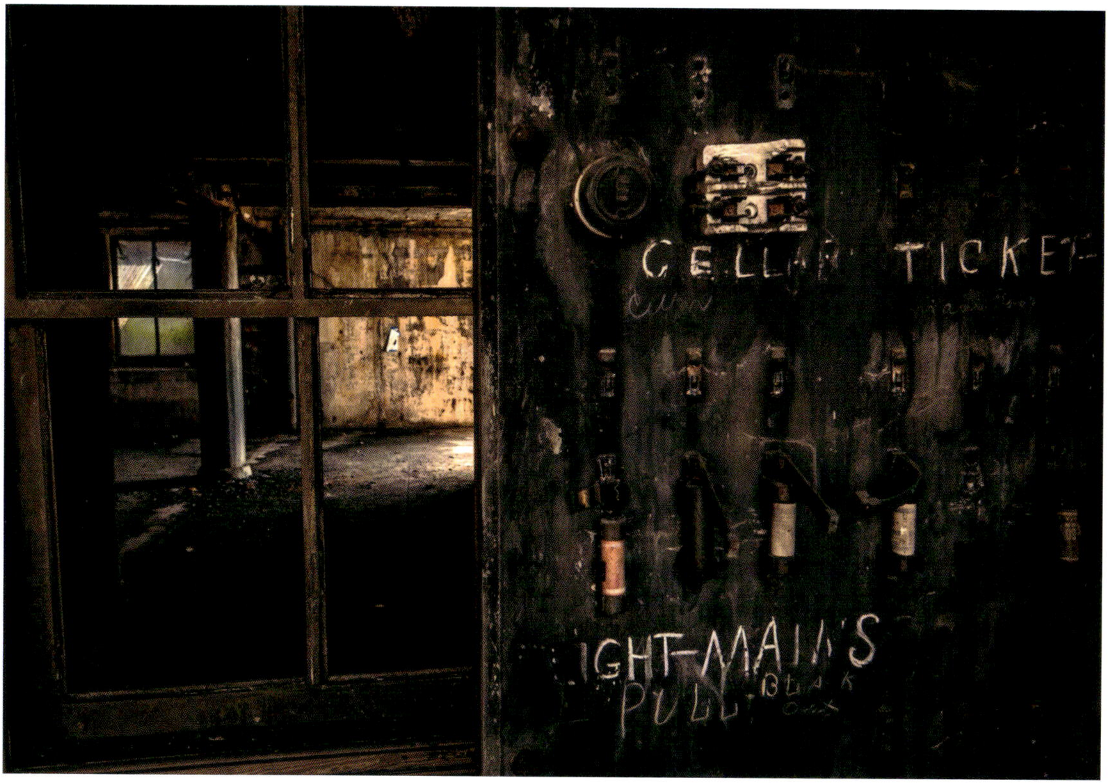

Cellar Ticket

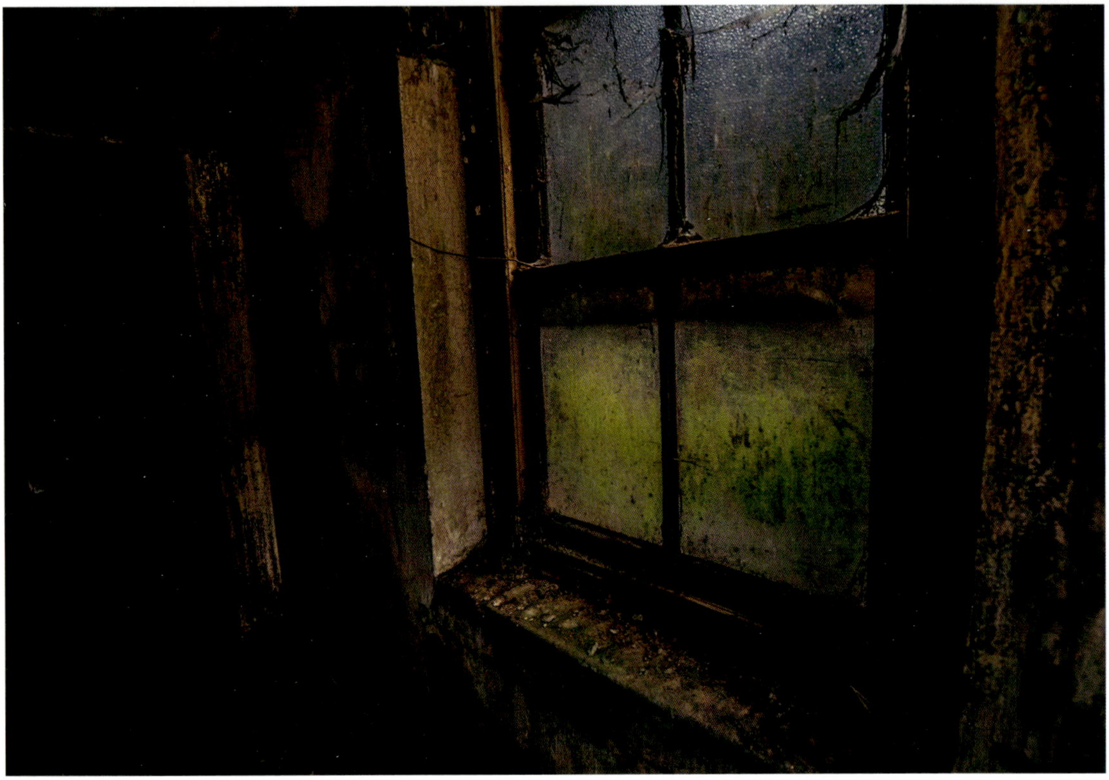

Basement Danger

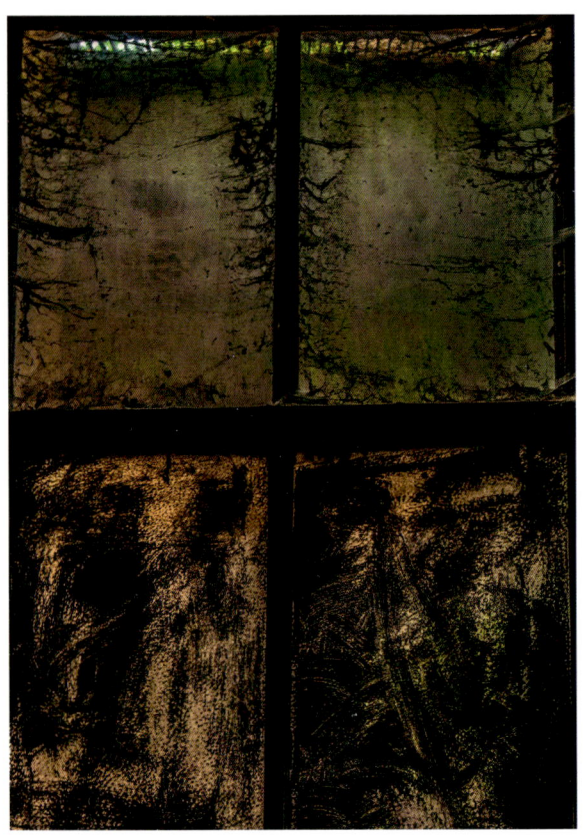

Brown Window

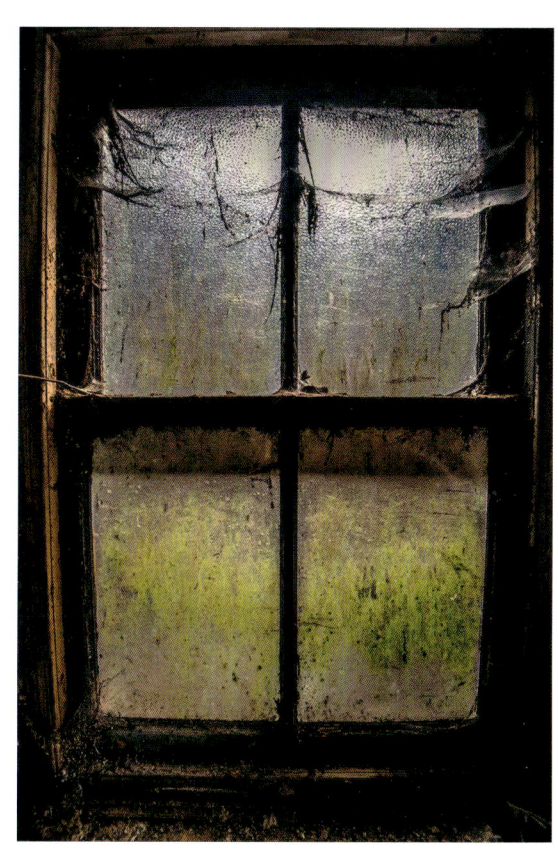

Green Window

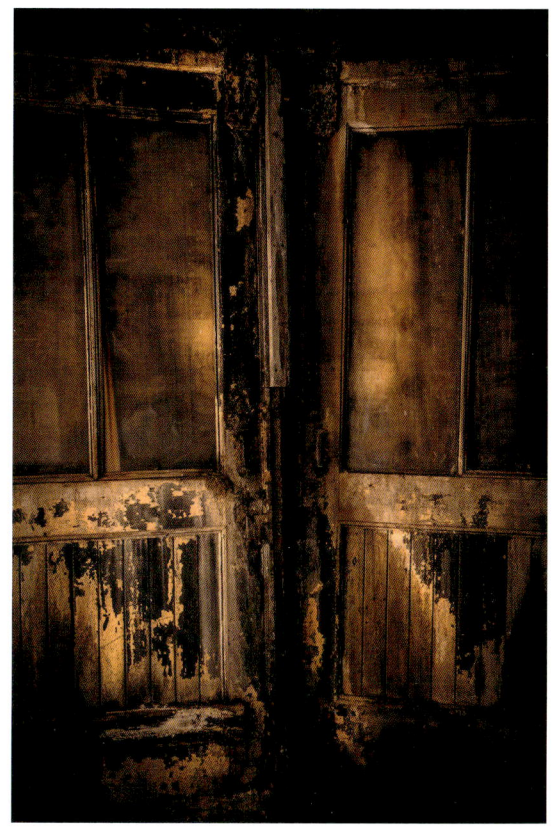

Basement Doors

CARNEGIE LIBRARY THEATER

The Carnegie Library of Homestead, featuring a music theater, a library, and a gymnasium, was built by William Miller and Sons of Pittsburgh in 1898 at a cost of $250,000. Although the structure boasted a grandeur befitting its benefactor, Andrew Carnegie, it was a gift for the area's working-class residents to provide an escape from the harsh working conditions in Carnegie's steel mills. (In his book, *Gospel of Wealth*, he wrote: "The best means of benefiting a community is to place within its reach the ladders upon which the aspiring can rise.") Architectural details include hand-cut Italian marble, stately murals, and richly carved oak woodwork. A renovation of the opulent theater is slated to begin soon.

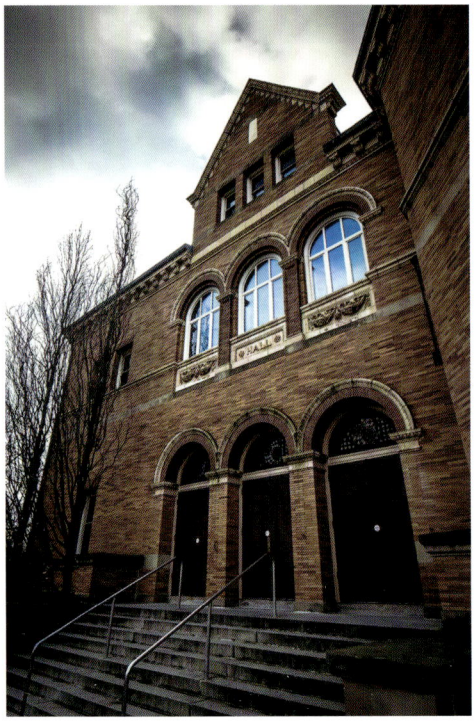

Facade

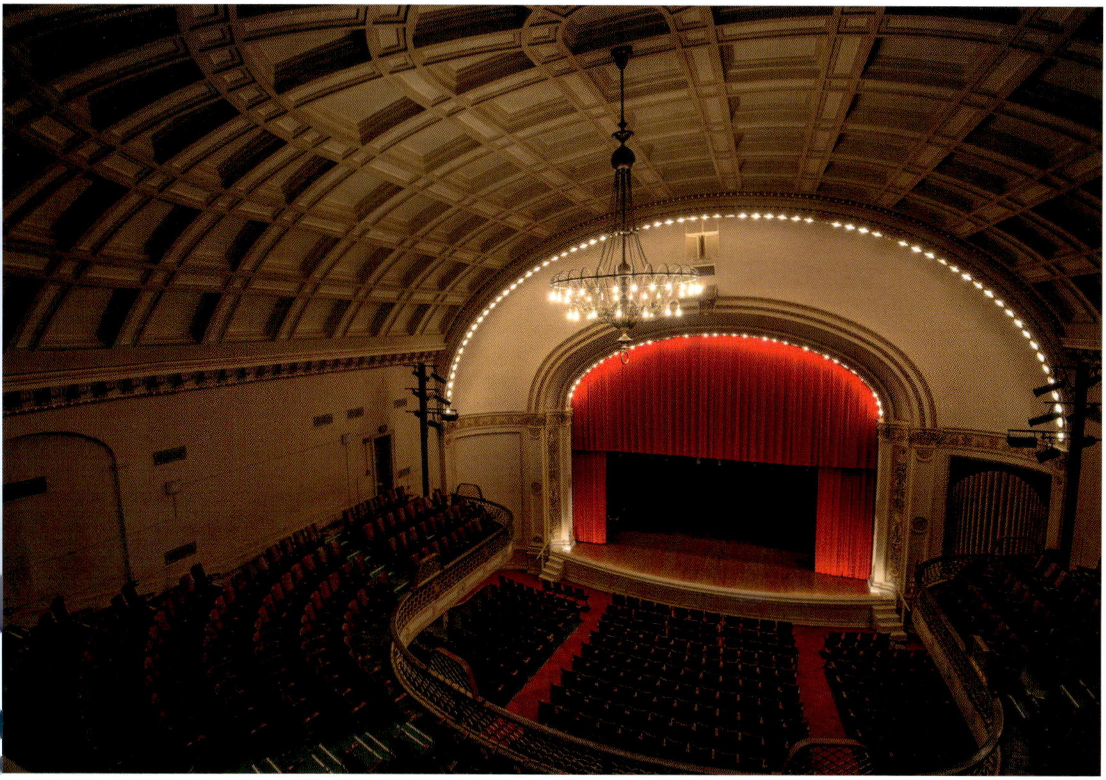

House

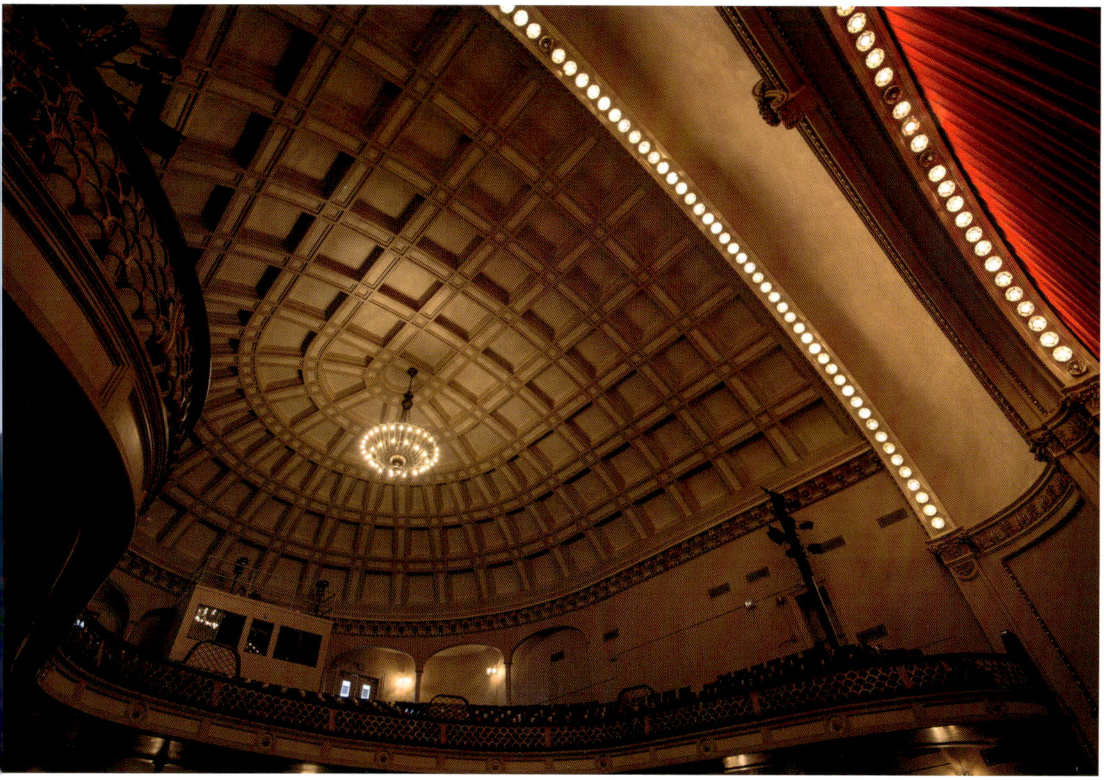

Dome

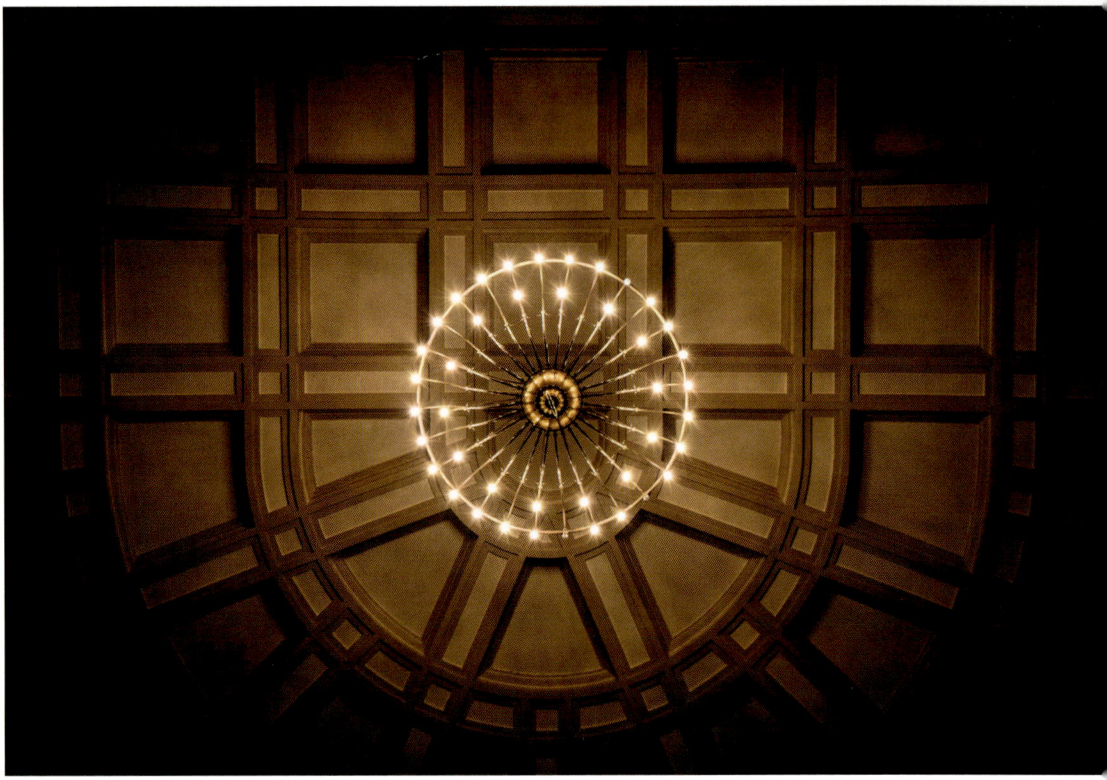

Chandelier

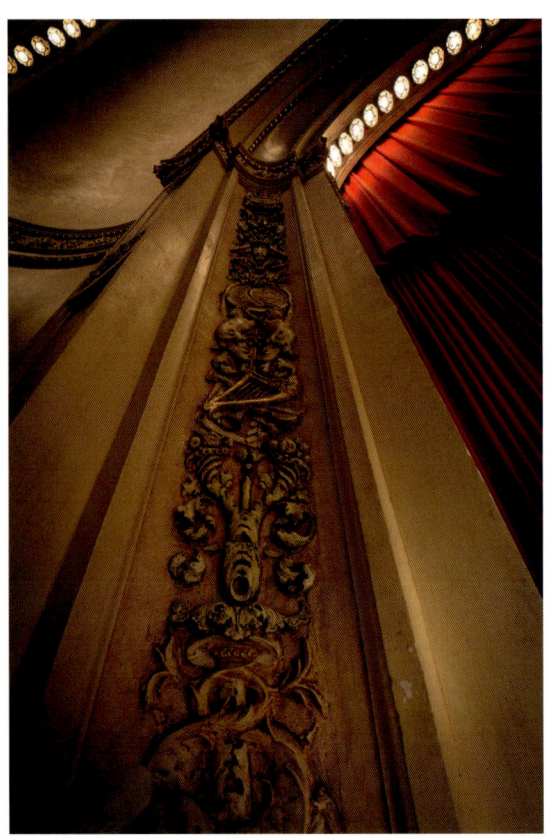

Arch

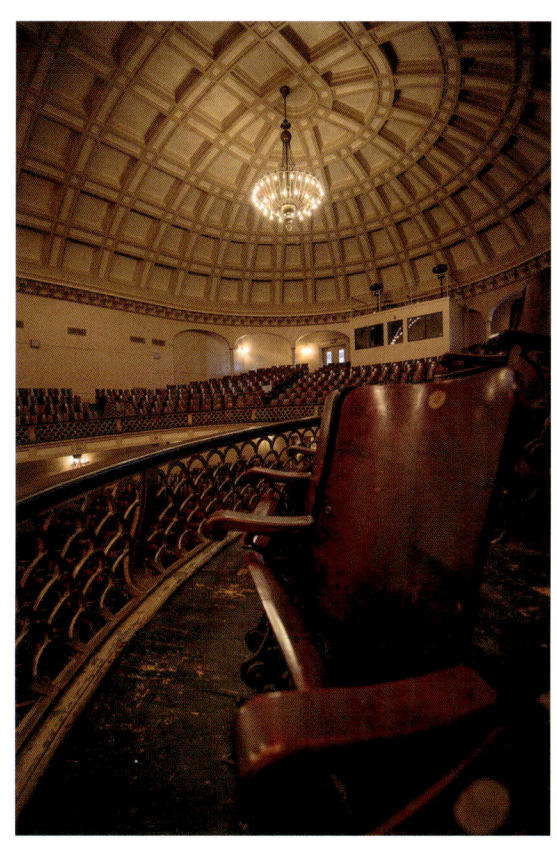

Balcony 12

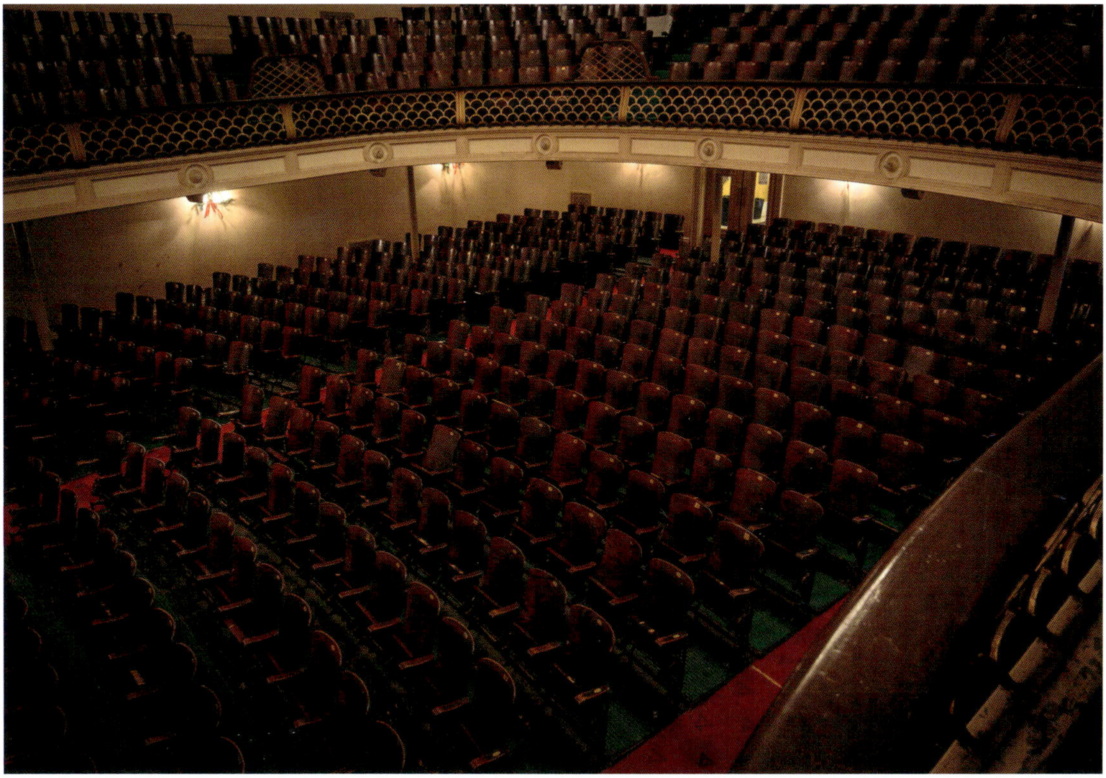

Cheap Seats

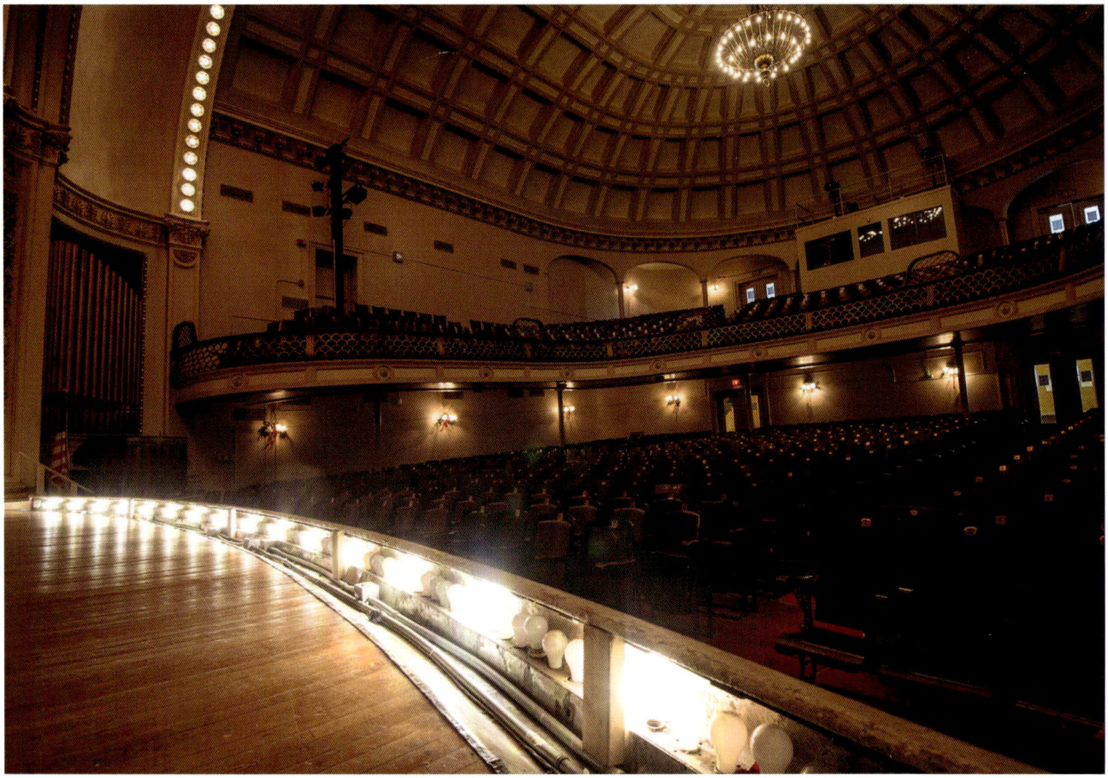

Stage Lights

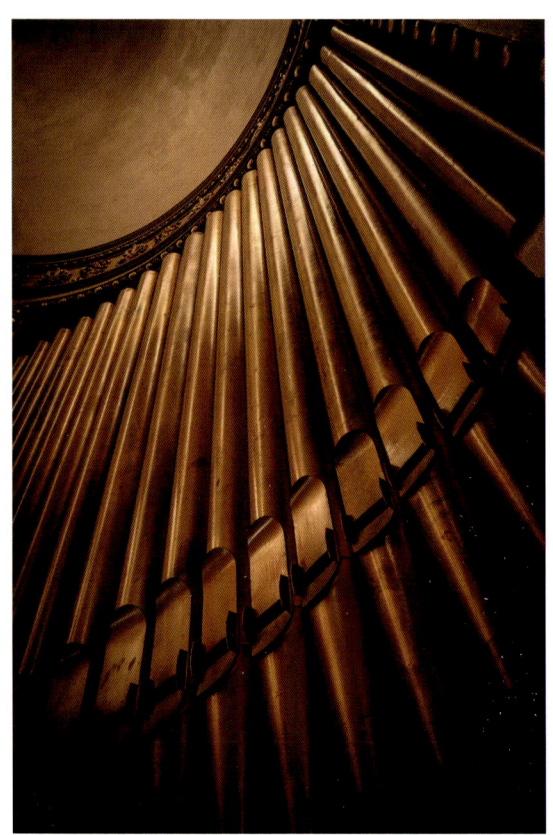

Organ

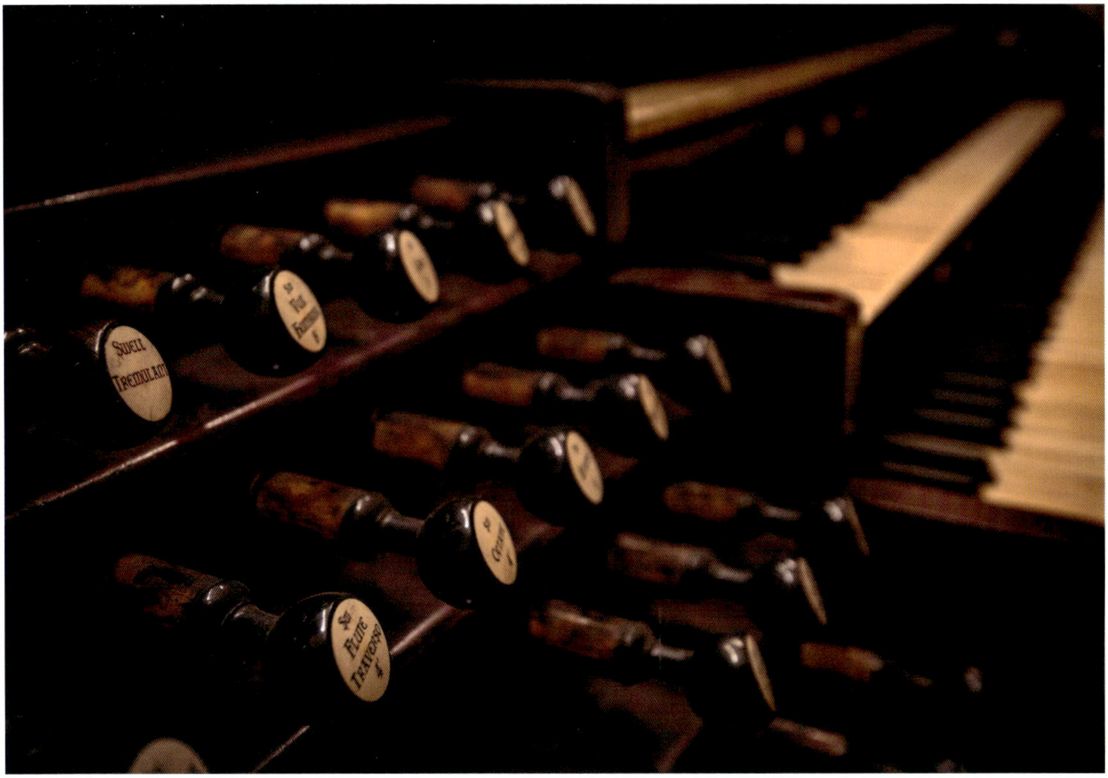

Swell

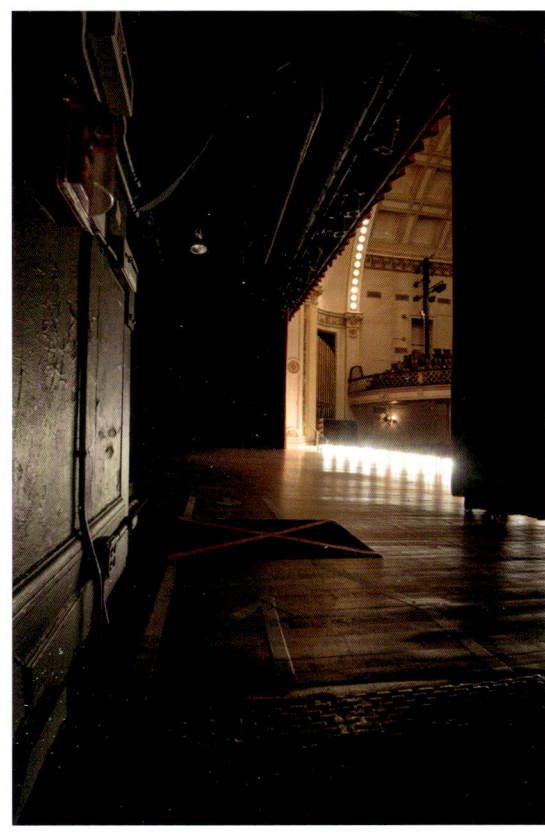

Backstage

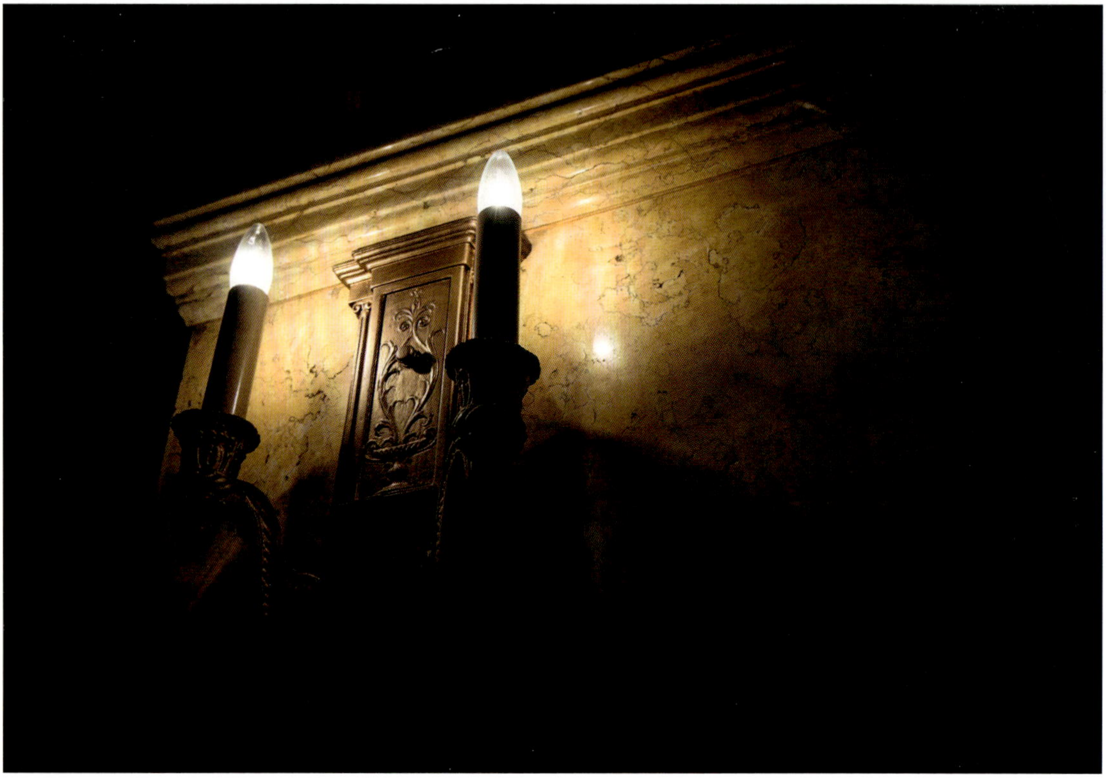

Sconce

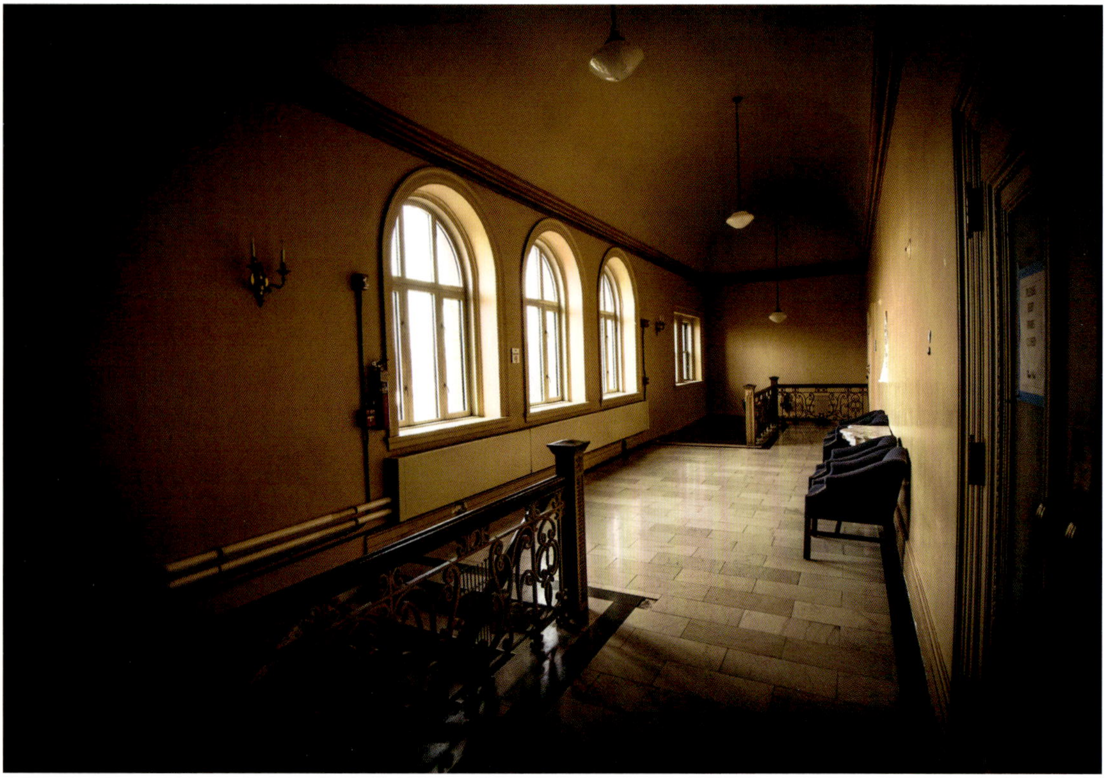

Intermission

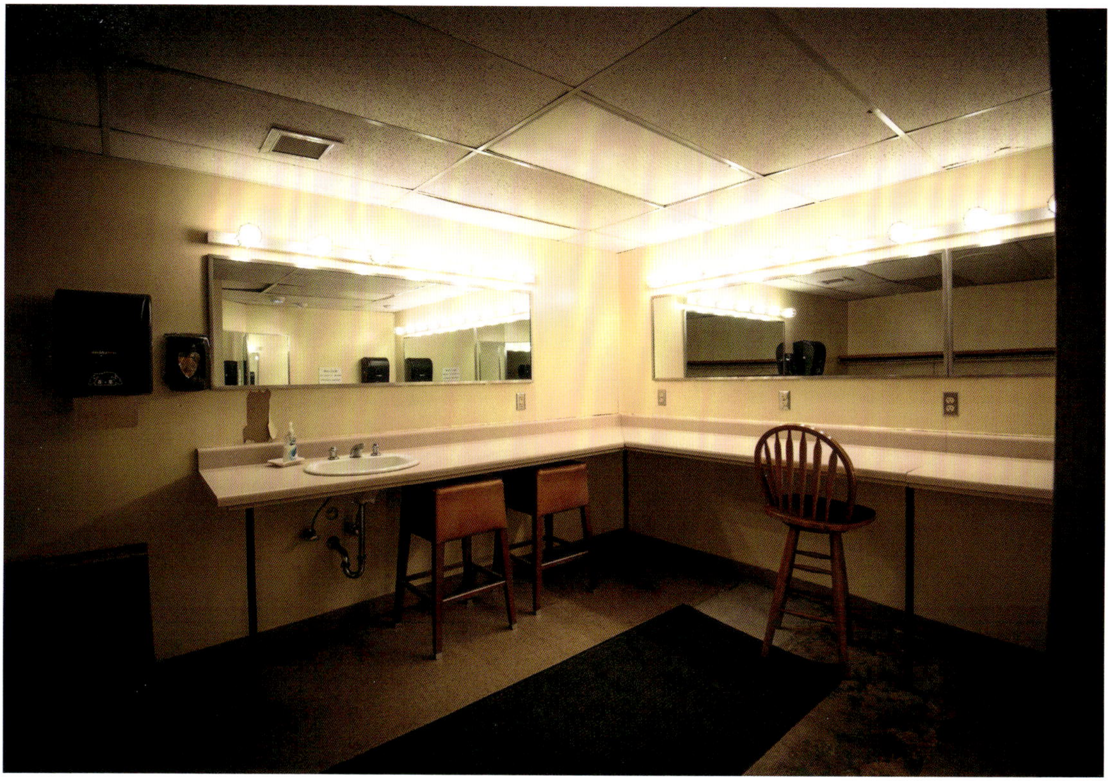

Dressing Room

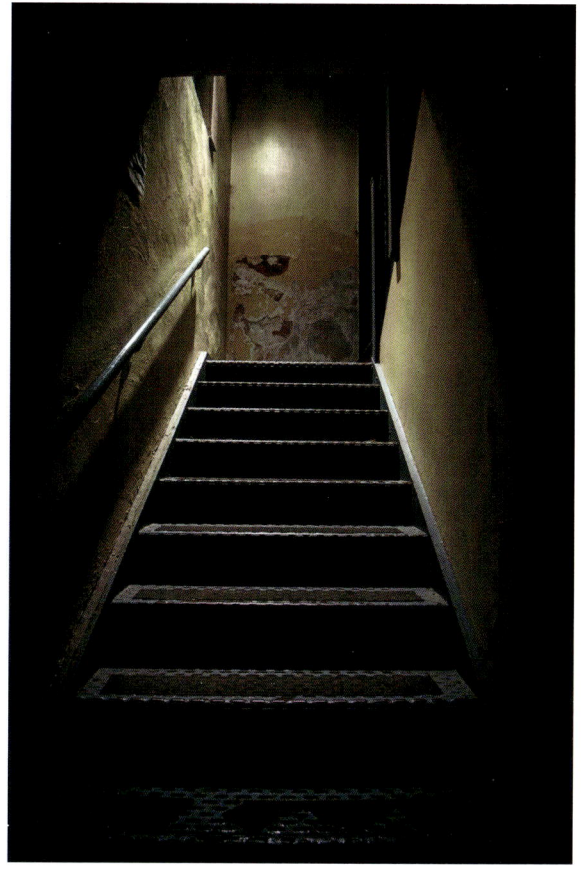

Basement Stairs

WESTERN PENITENTIARY

Pittsburgh's State Correctional Institution — commonly known as Western Penitentiary or Western Pen — was originally built in 1826 a few blocks from the current site. It was relocated in 1882 to its present location on the Ohio River. The English writer Charles Dickens visited the original prison in 1842 and was appalled at the prisoners' conditions. The facility also housed Confederate soldiers during the Civil War. Over its lifetime, the prison held maximum-security inmates in its early years, and later, inmates who required treatment for substance abuse. Western Pen closed in May 2017.

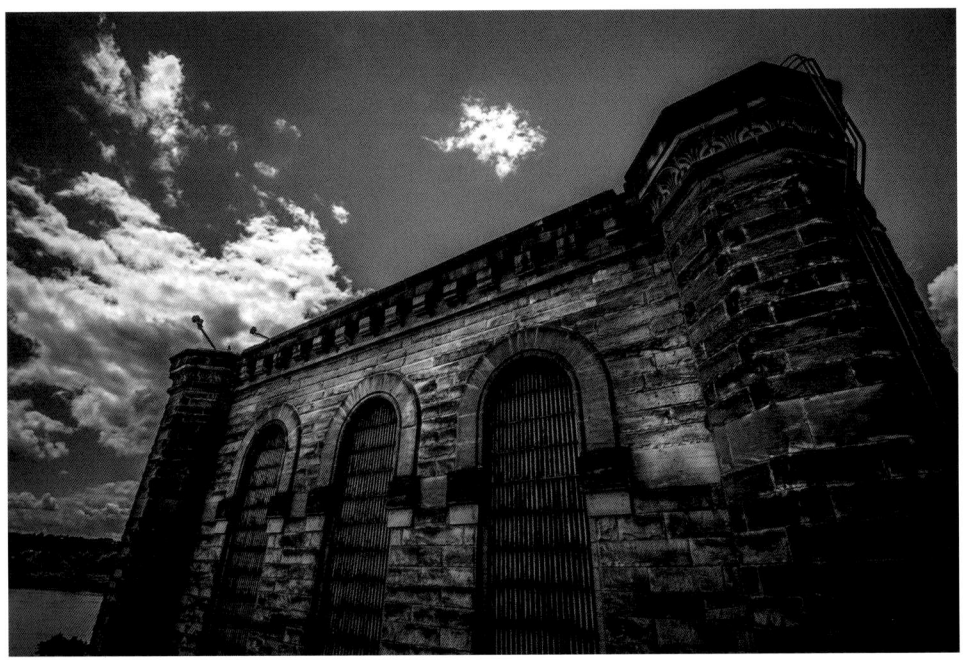

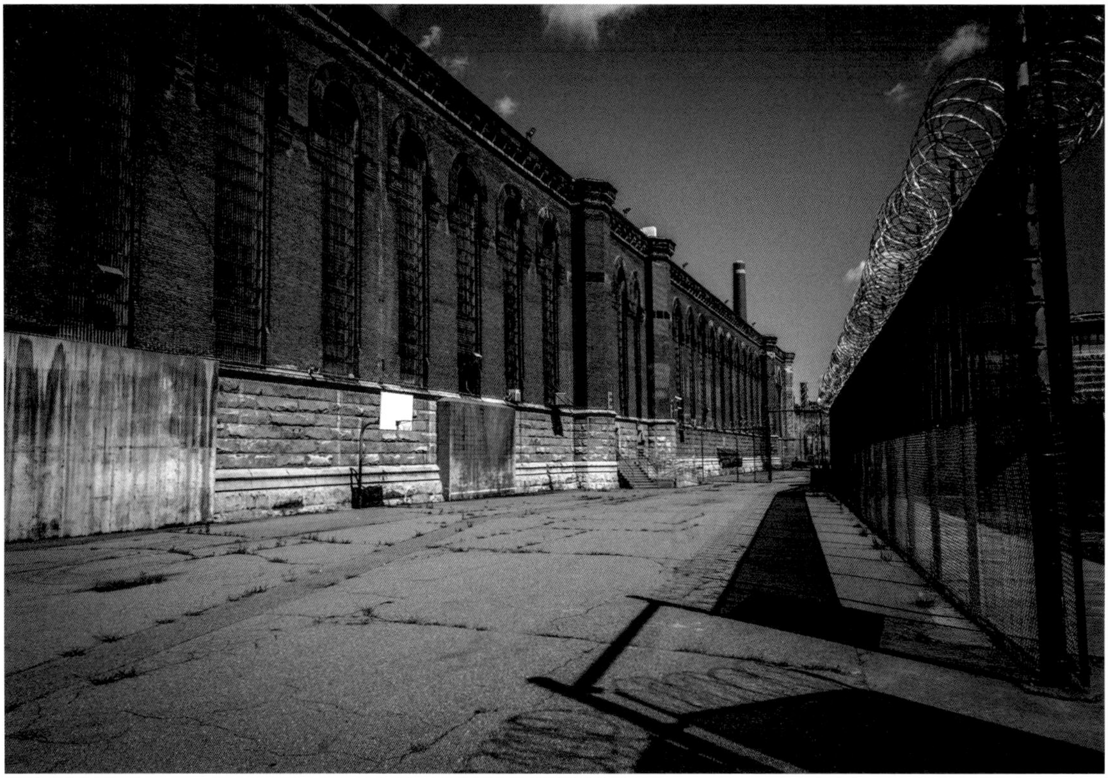

Playground

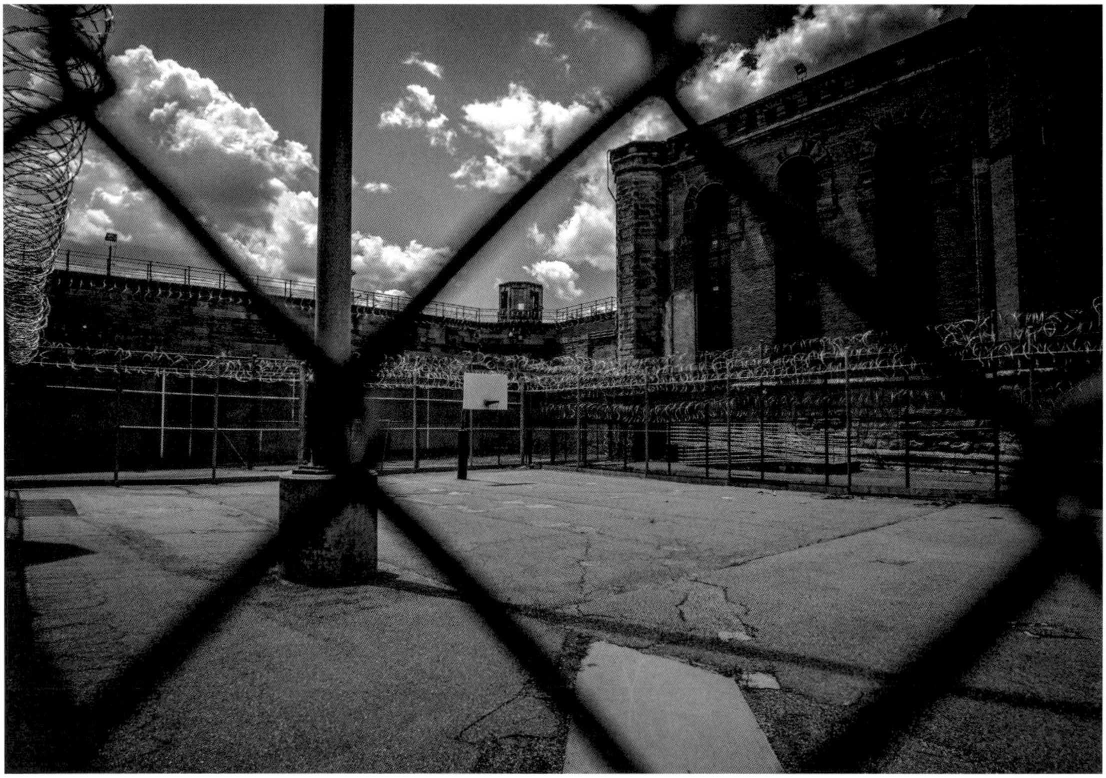

Basketball

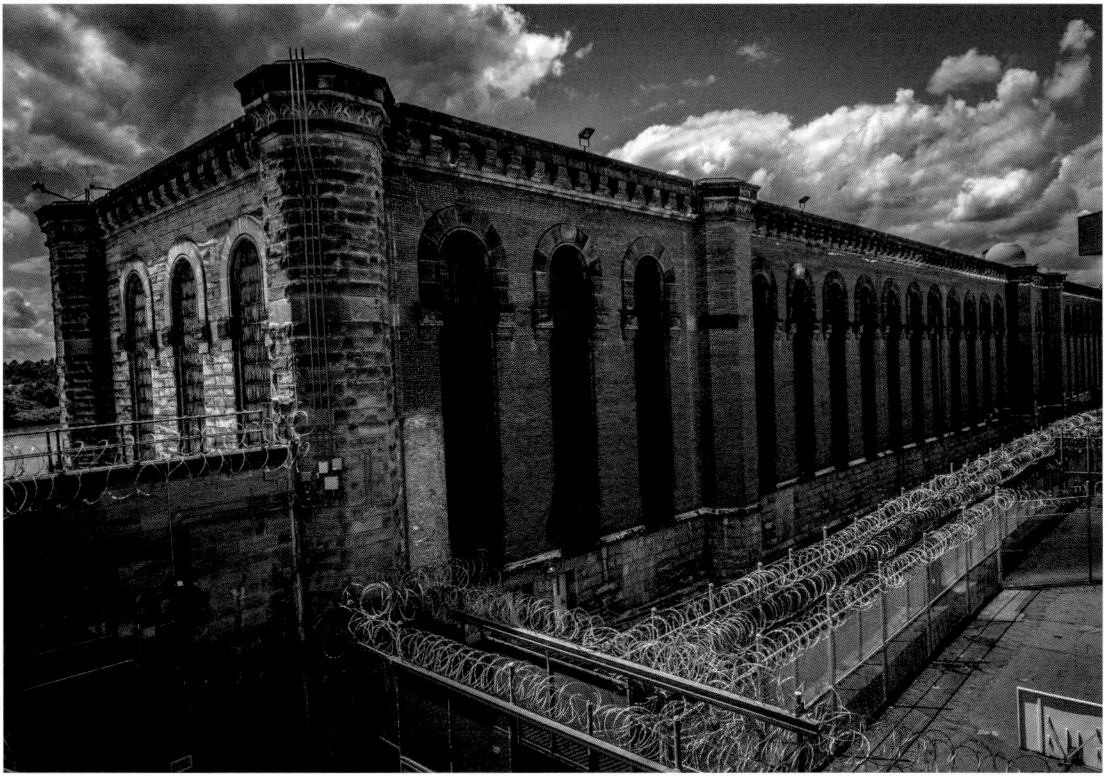

Fortress

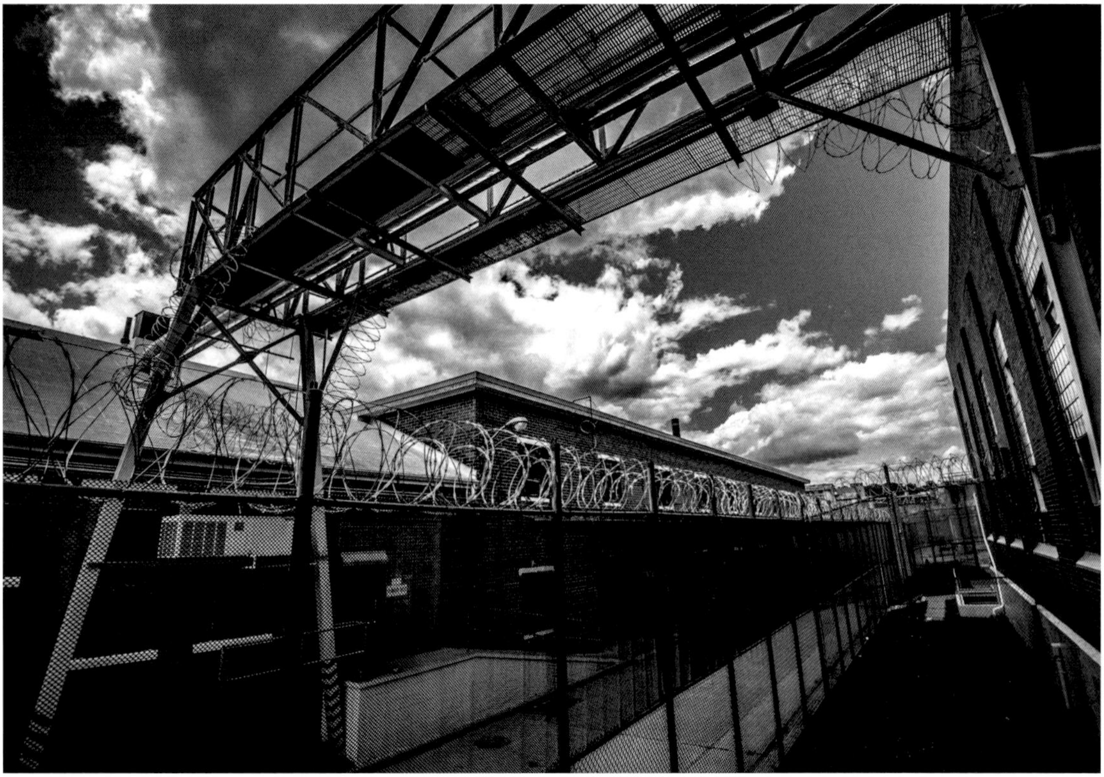

Skyway

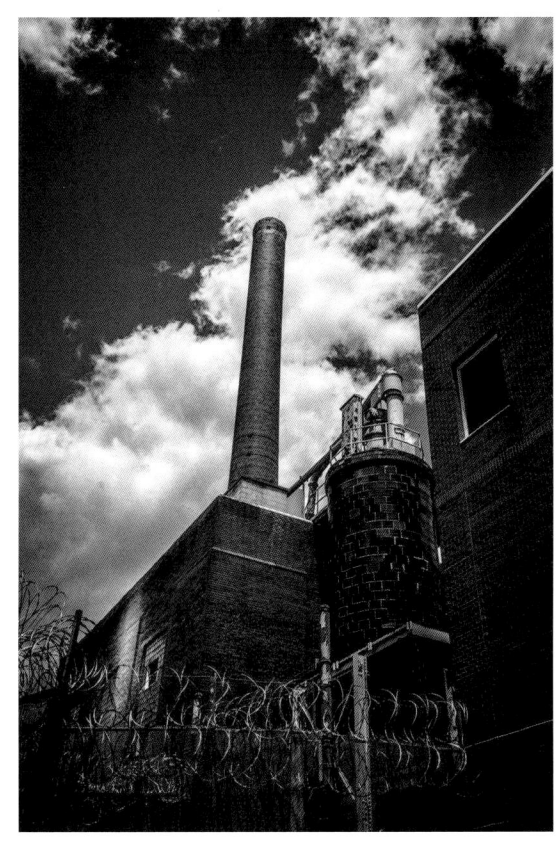

Smokestack

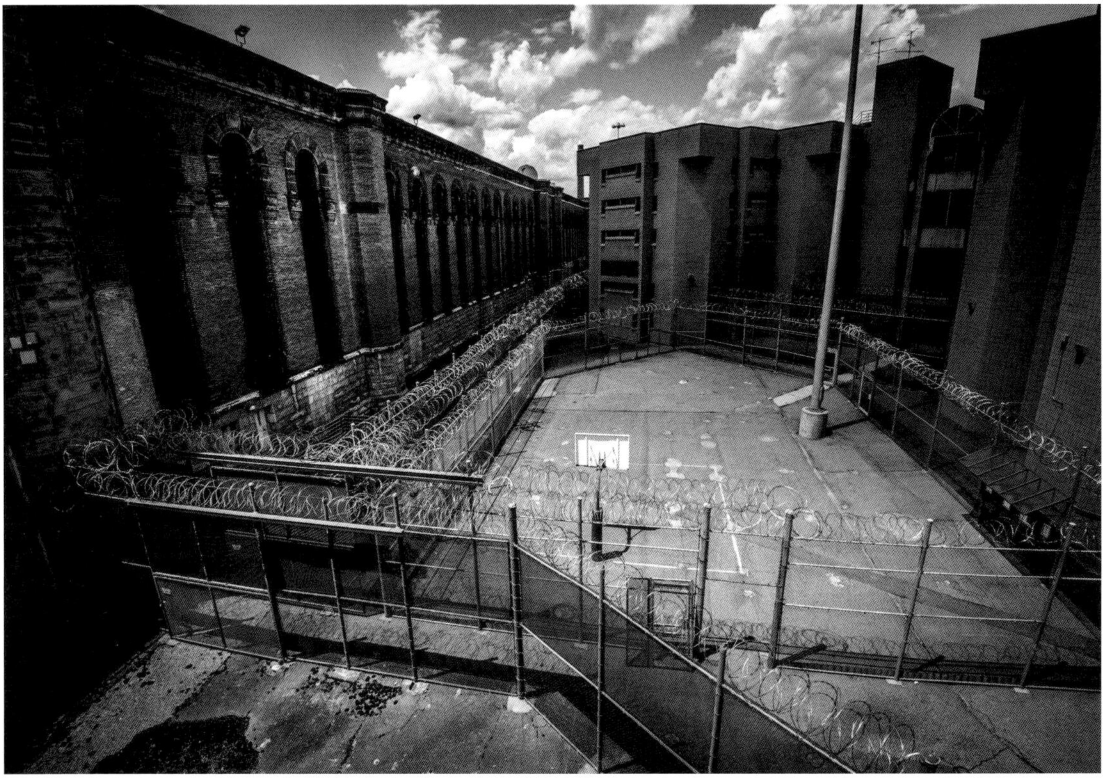

The Yard

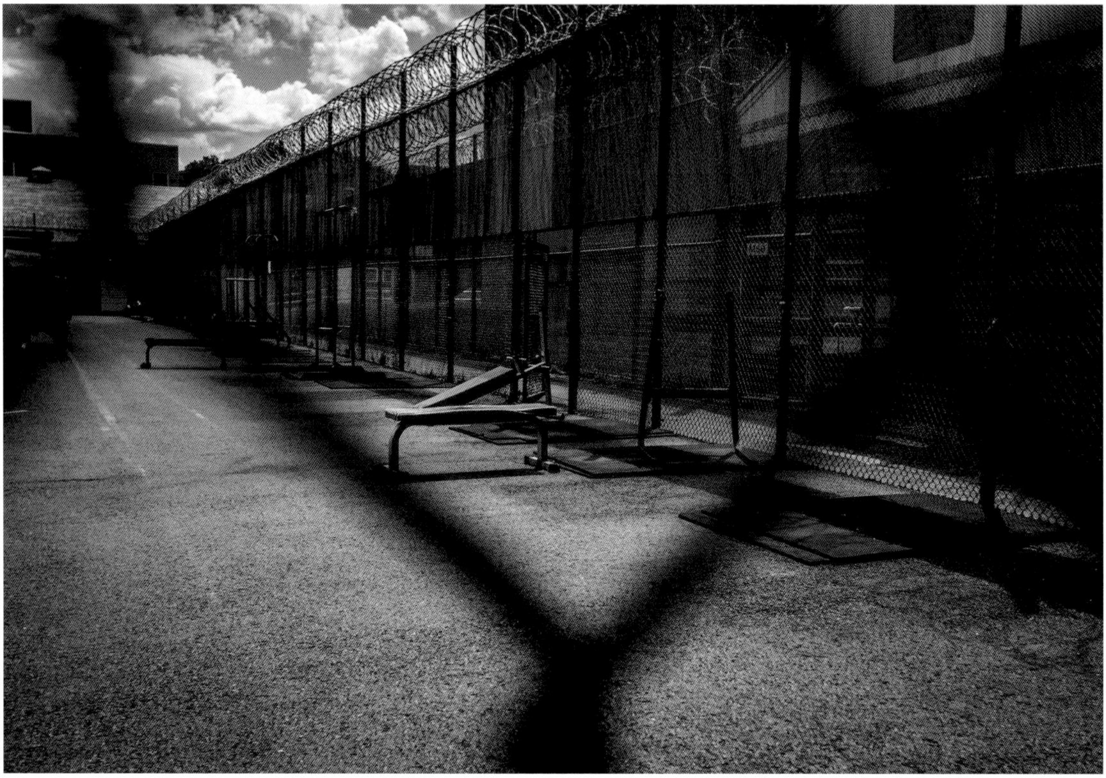

Workout

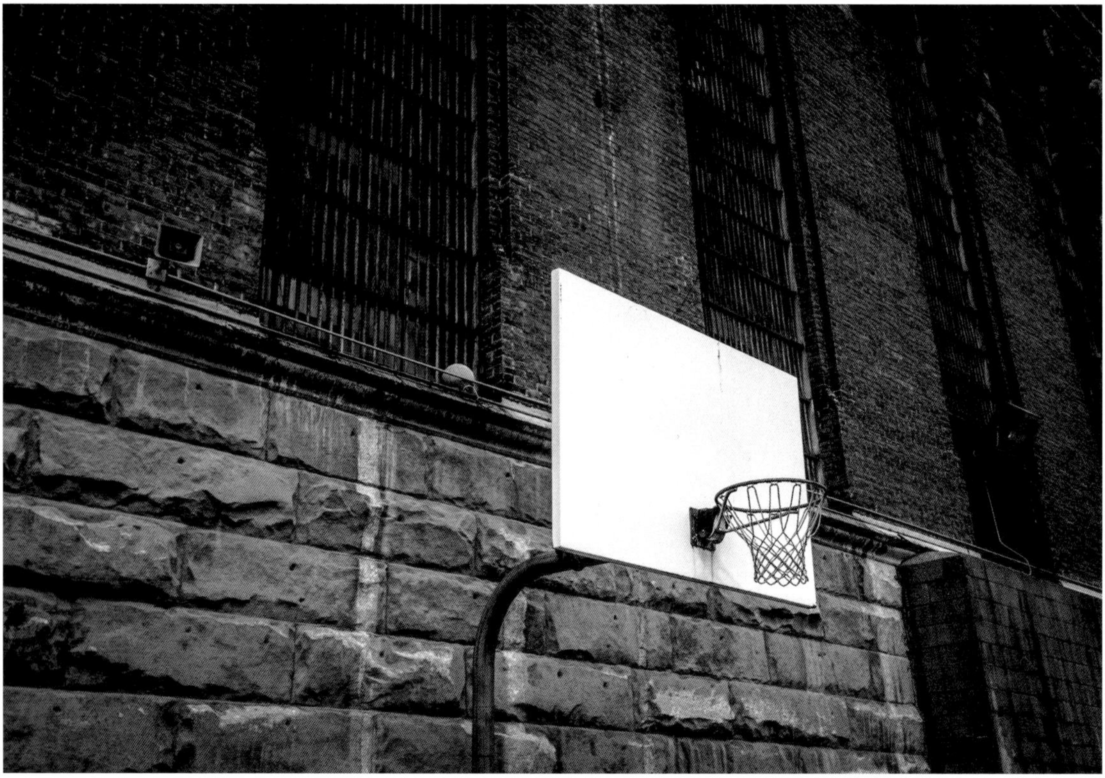

Game Over

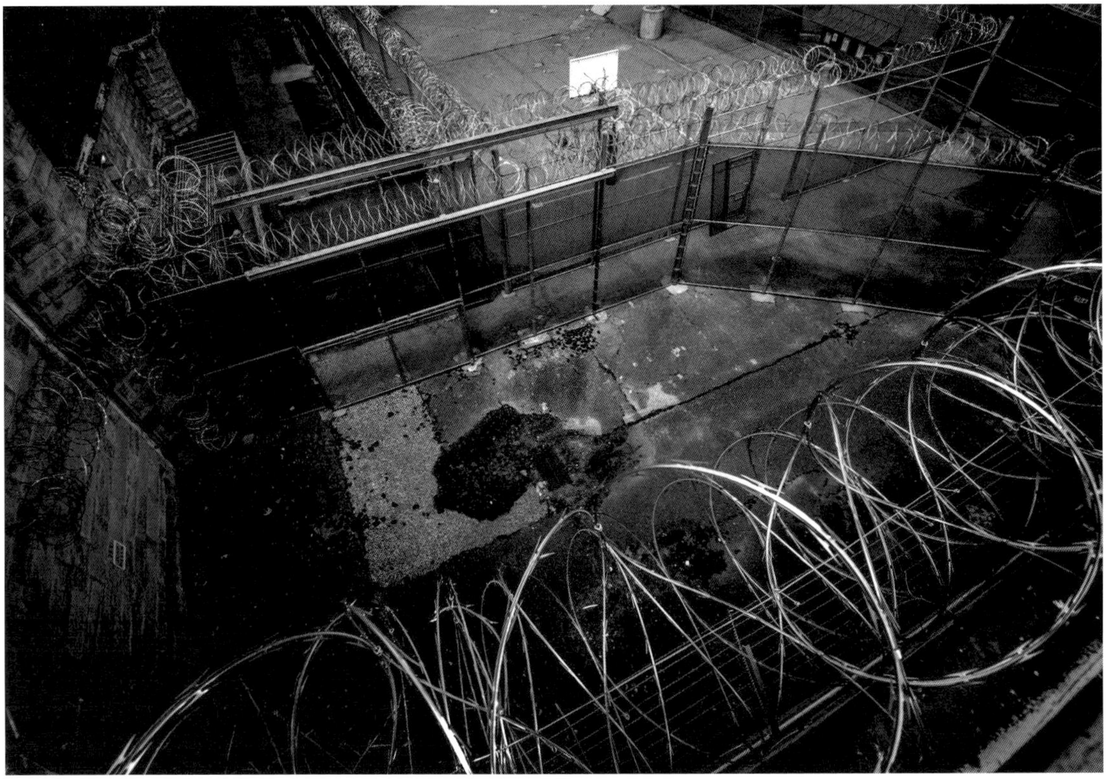

Barbed Wire

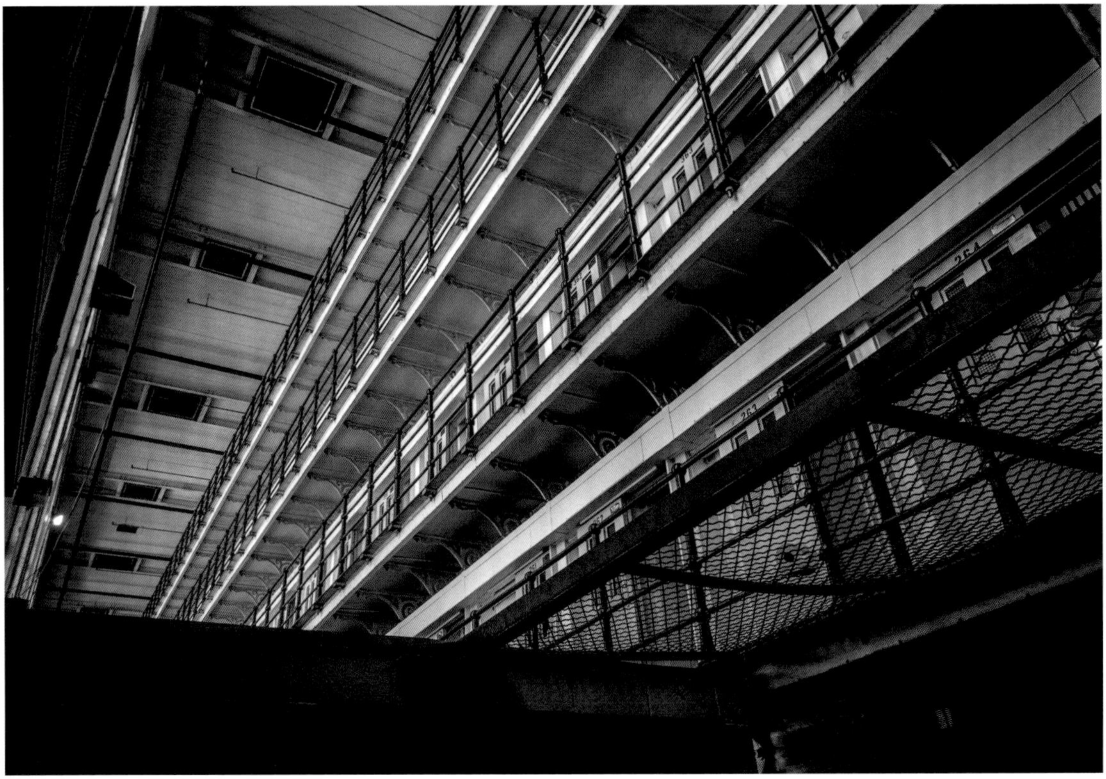

Tiers

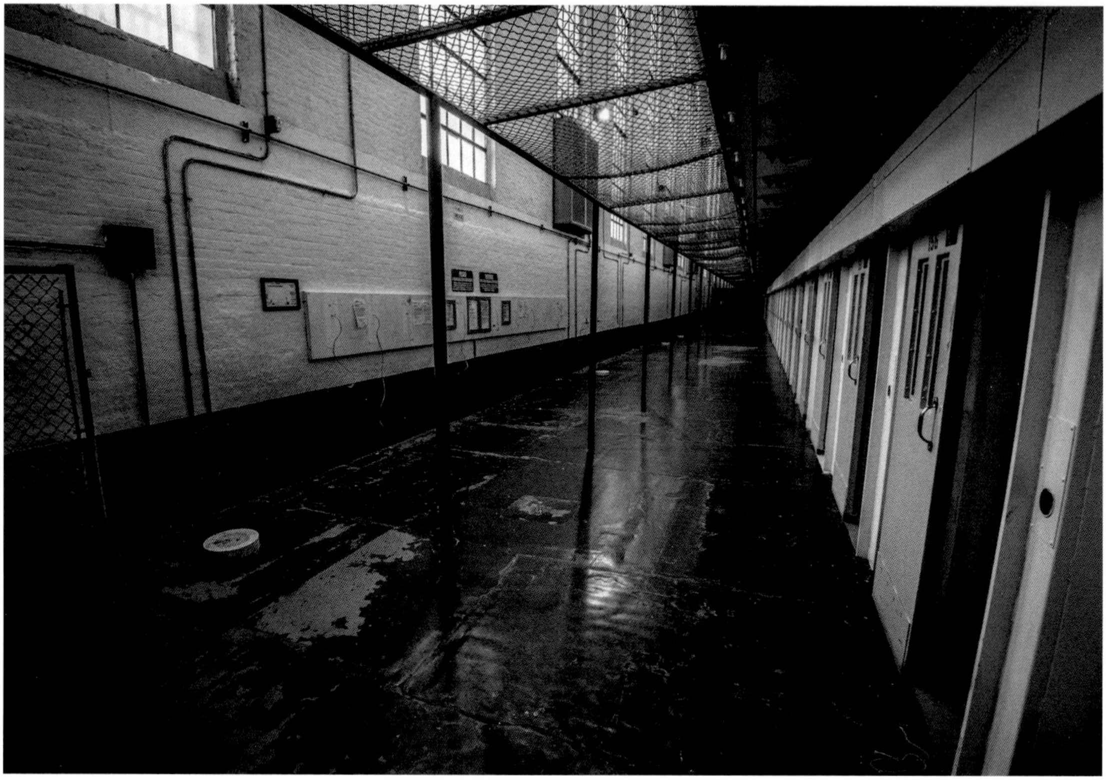

Brick Wall View

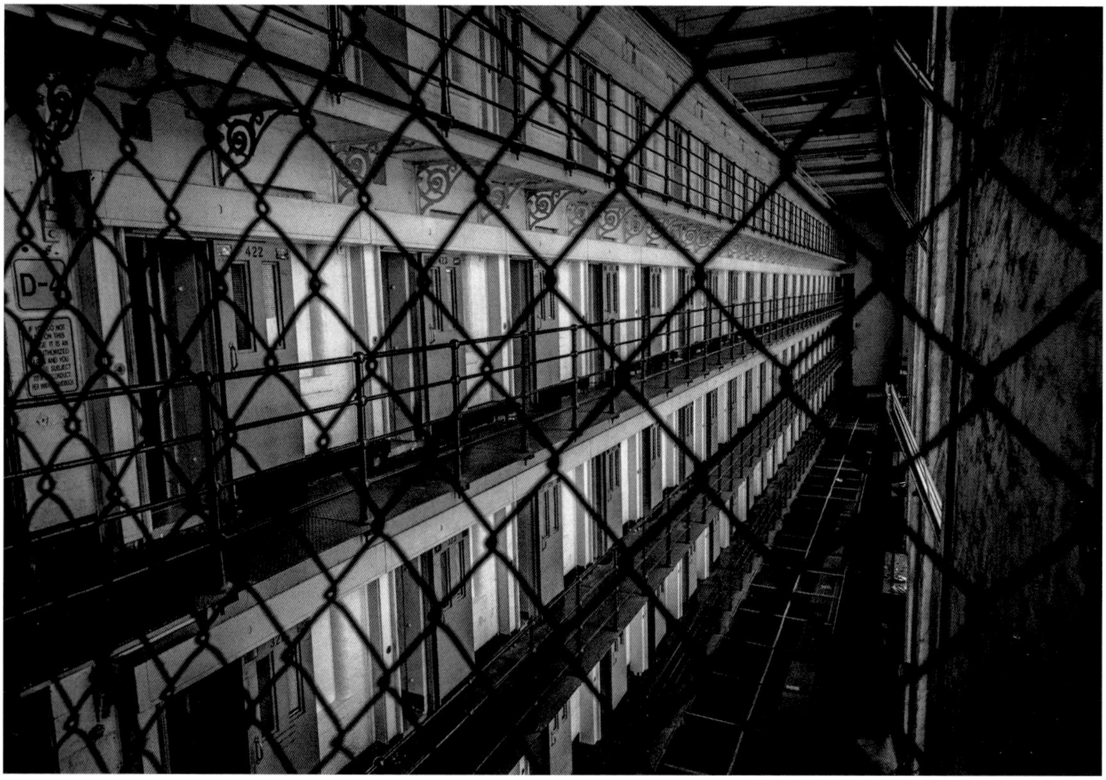

D-4 Block

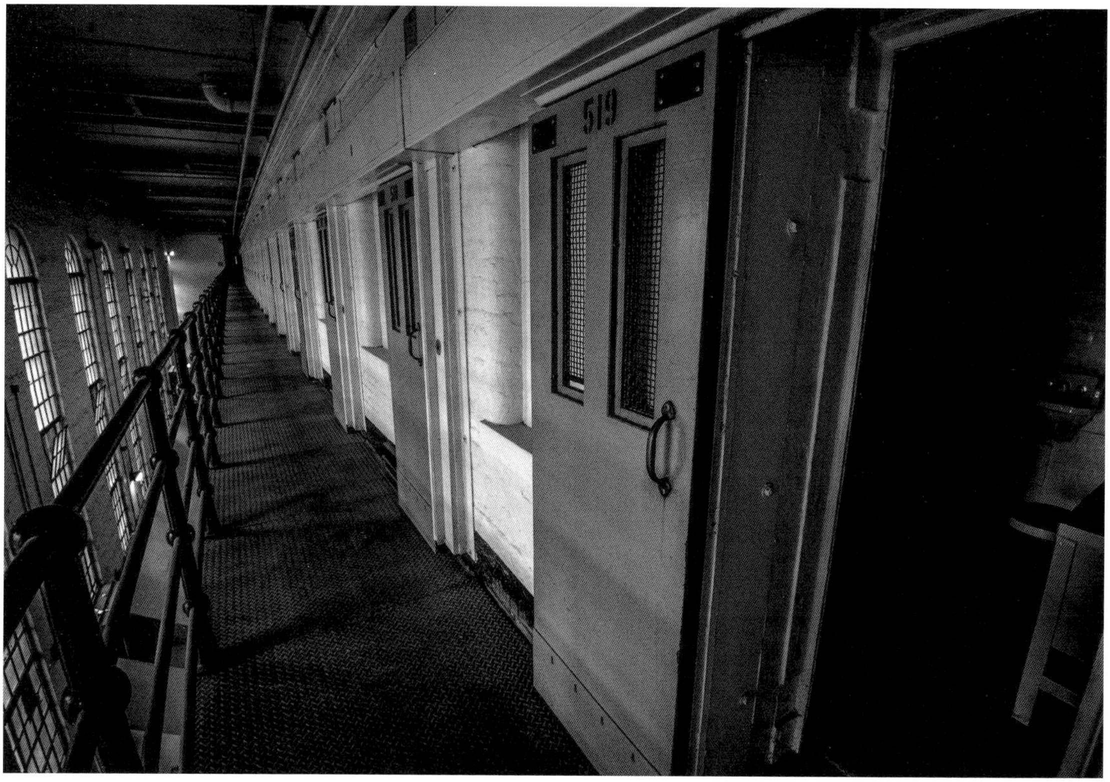

519

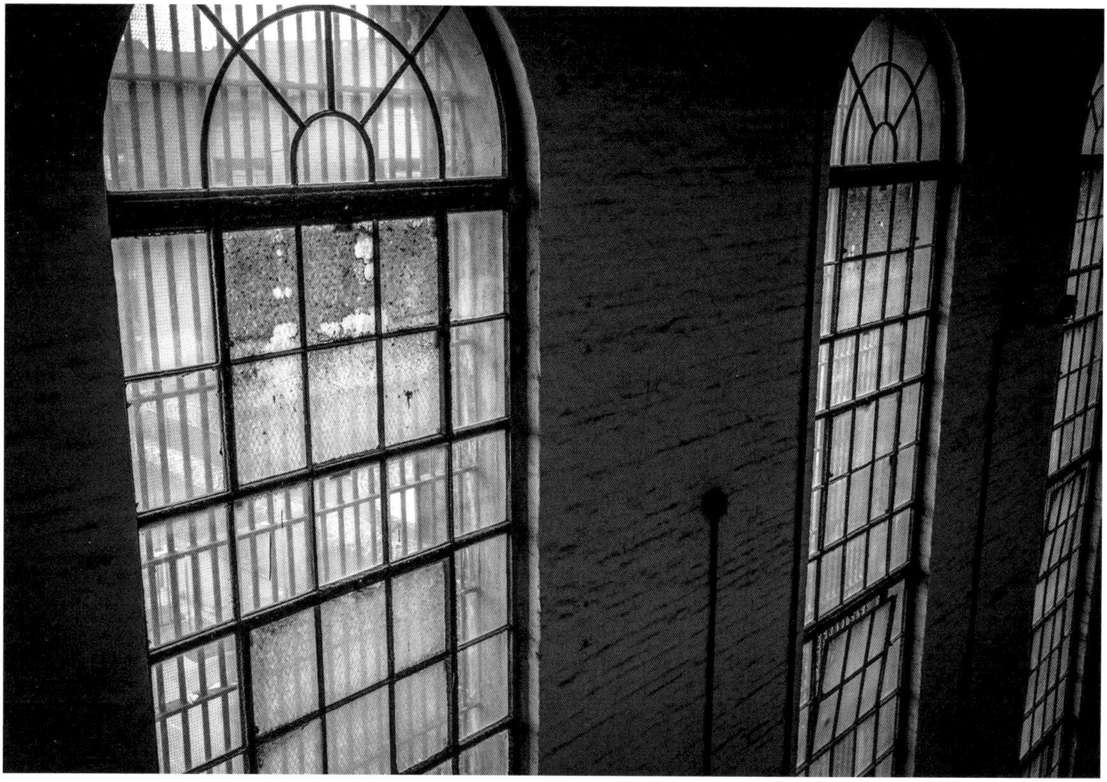

Behind Bars

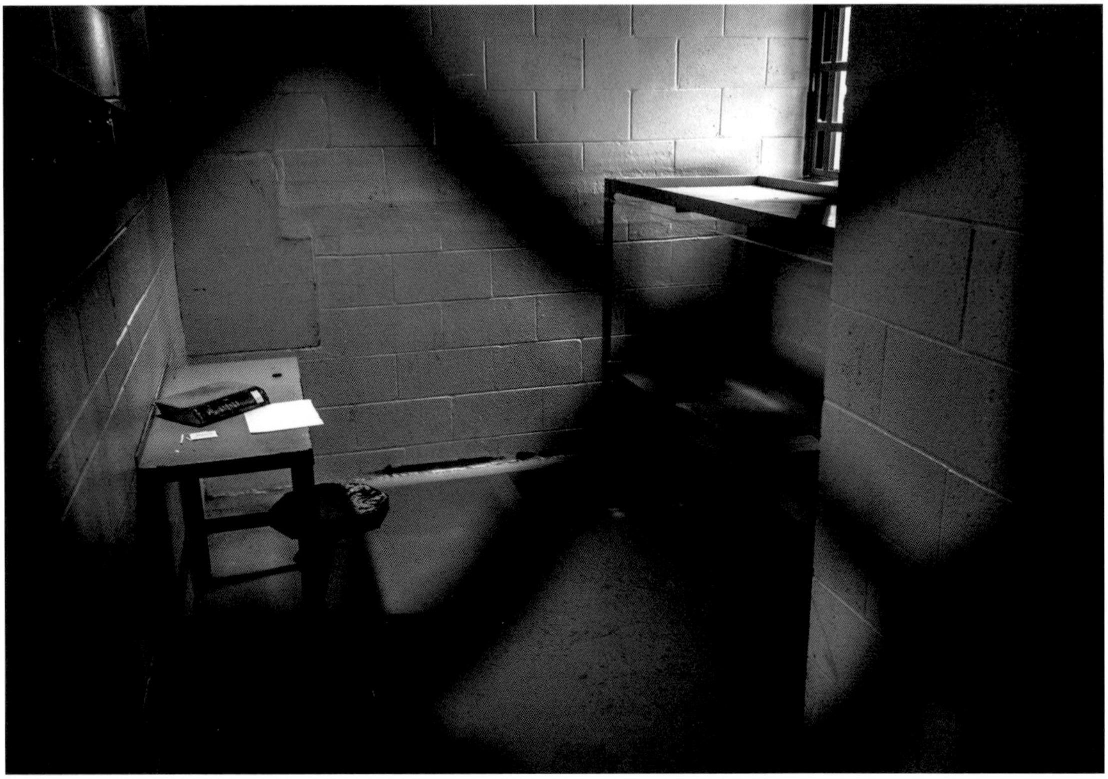

Fenced In

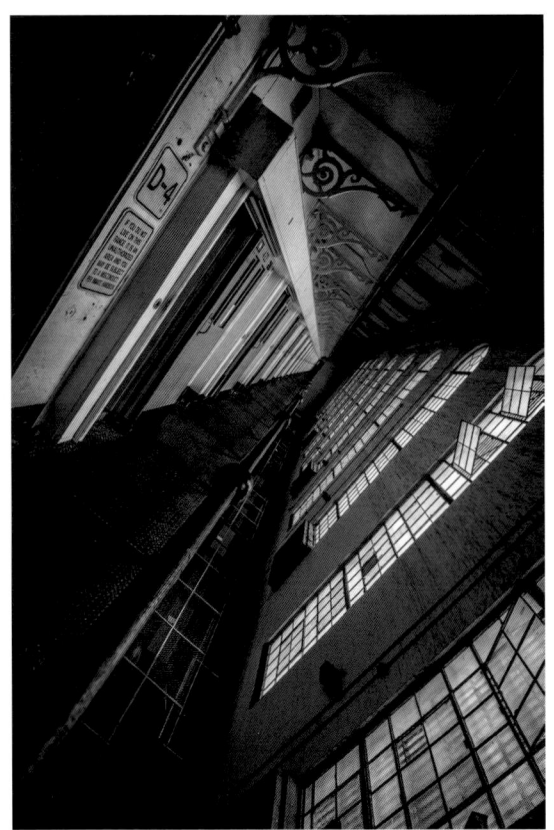

Funhouse

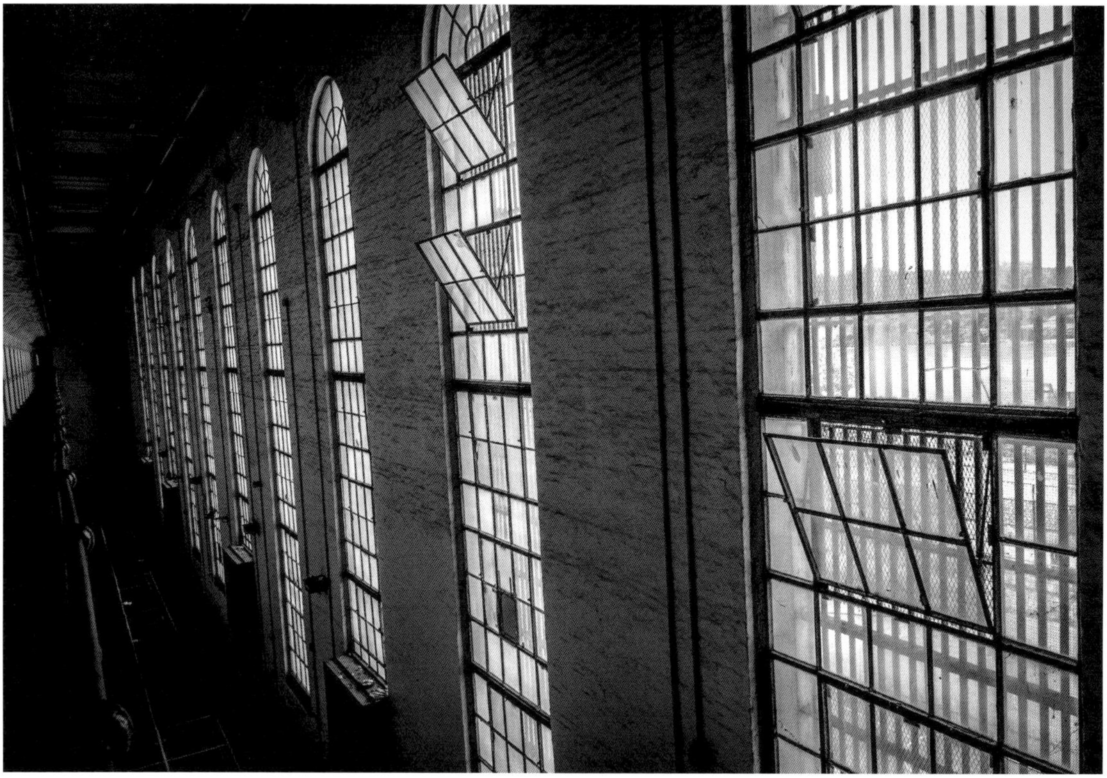

Fresh Air

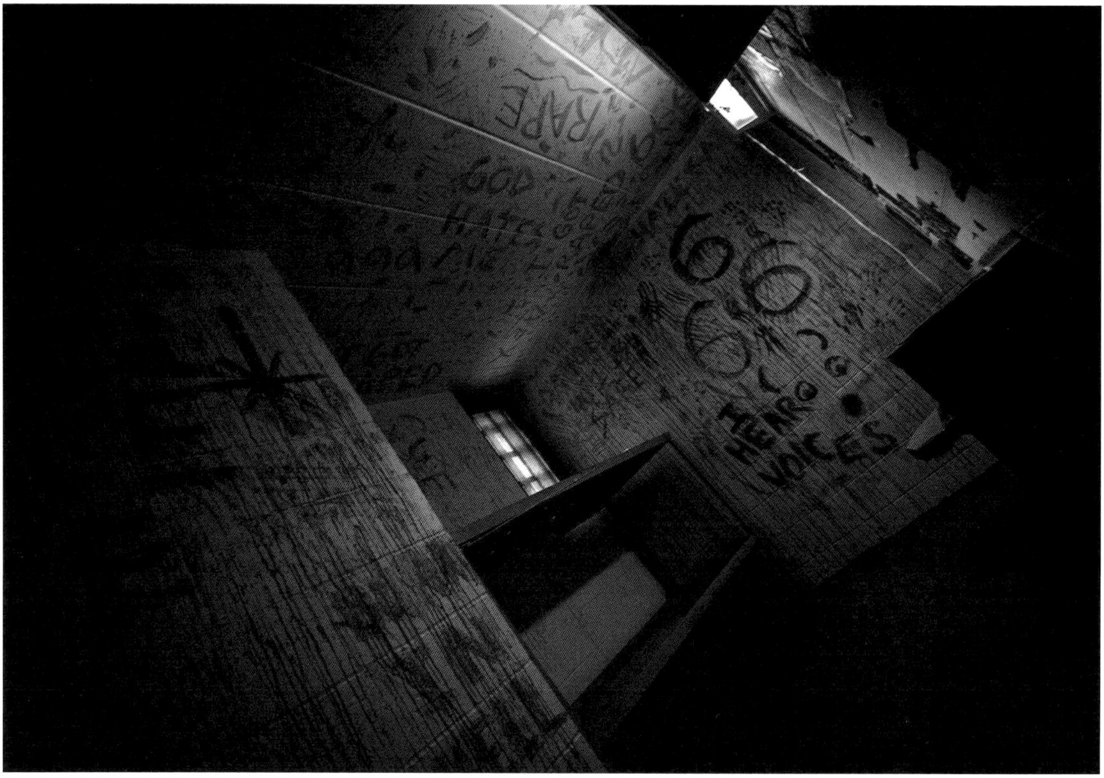

I Hear Voices

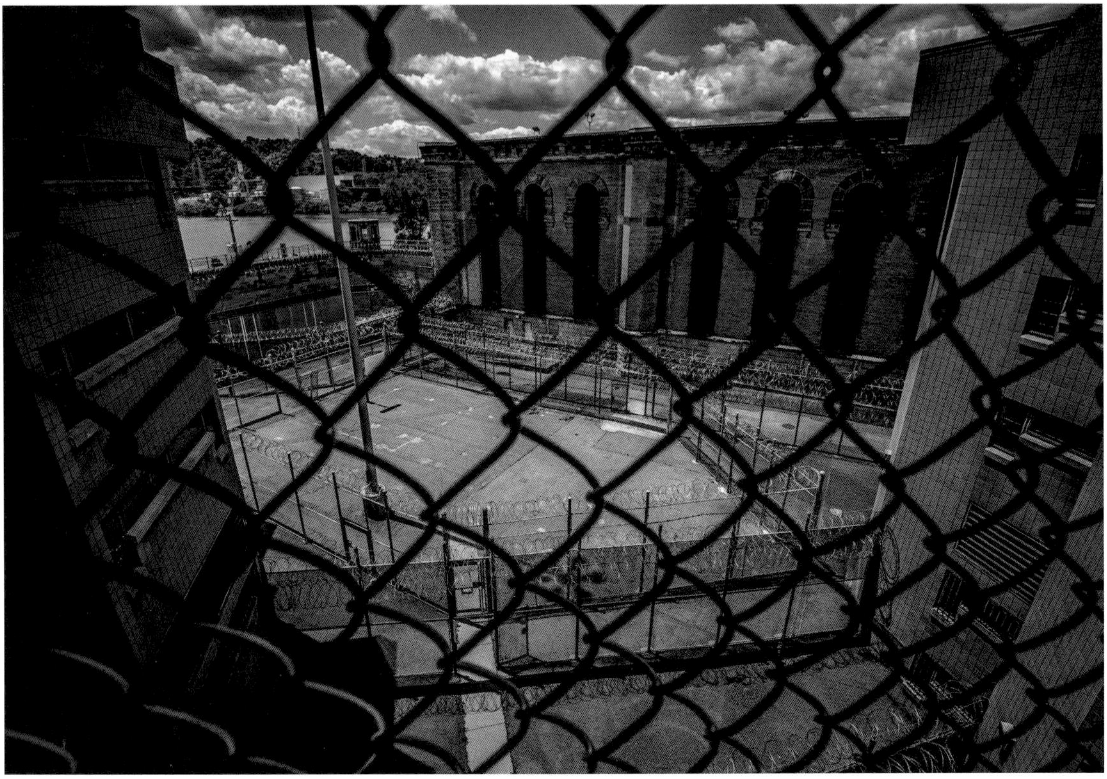

View of the River

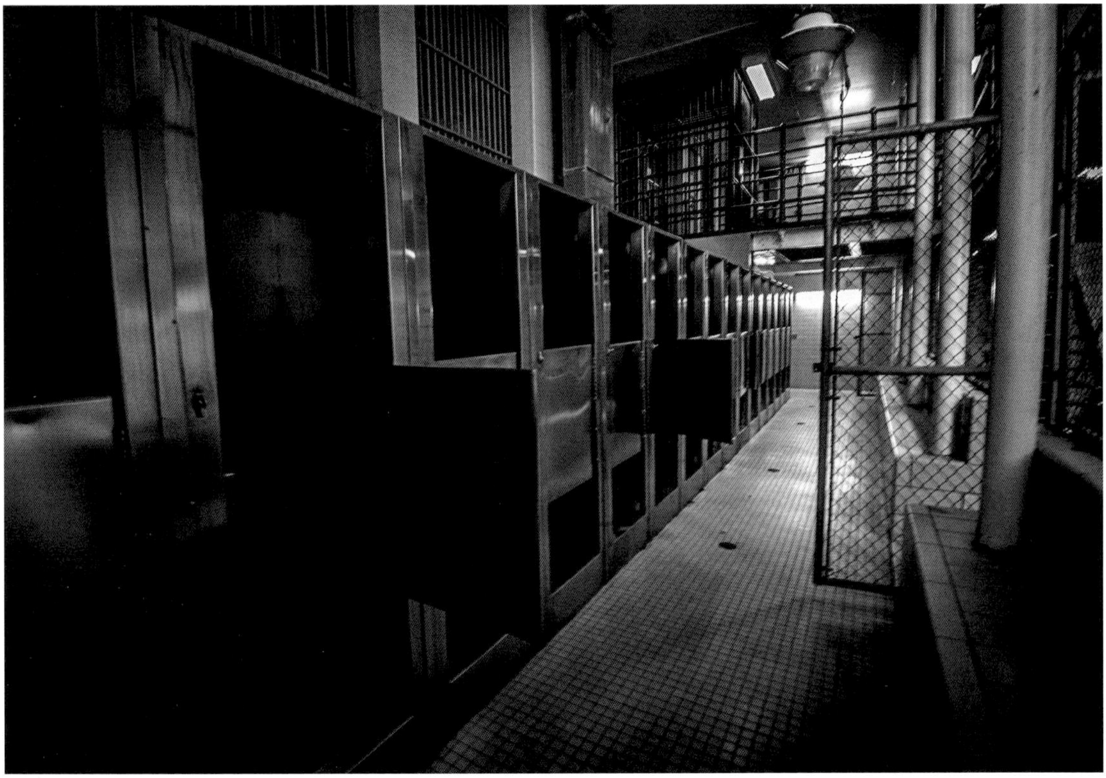

Showers

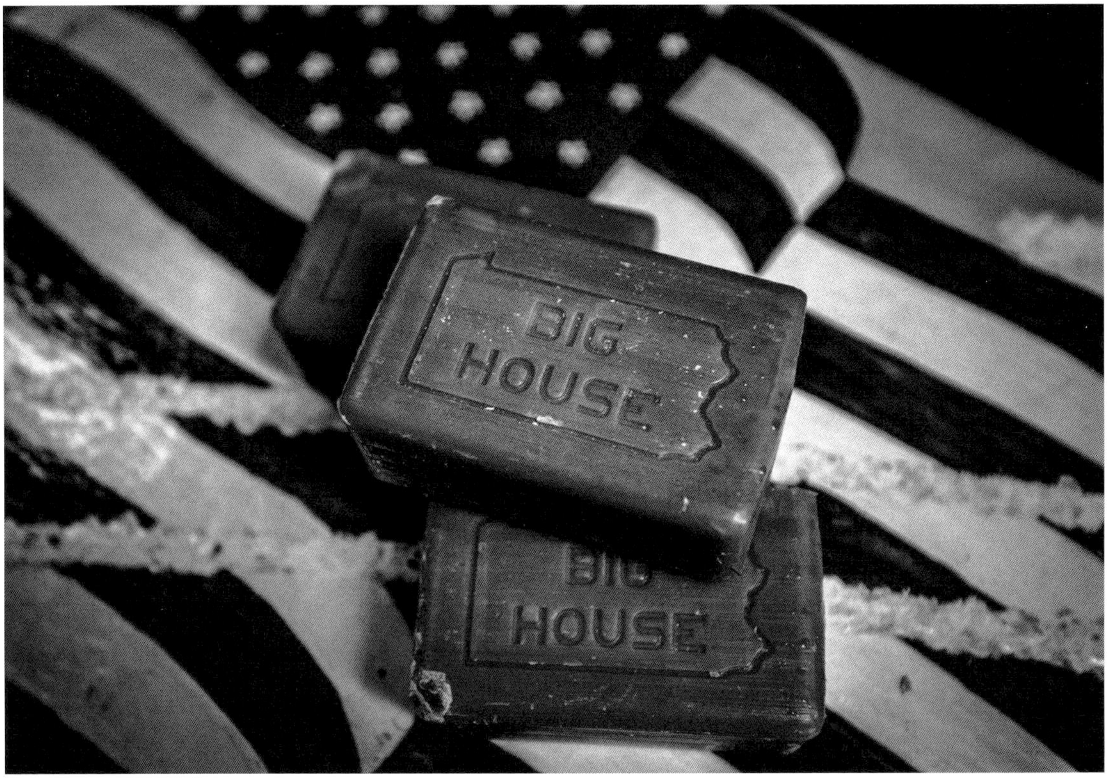

Big House

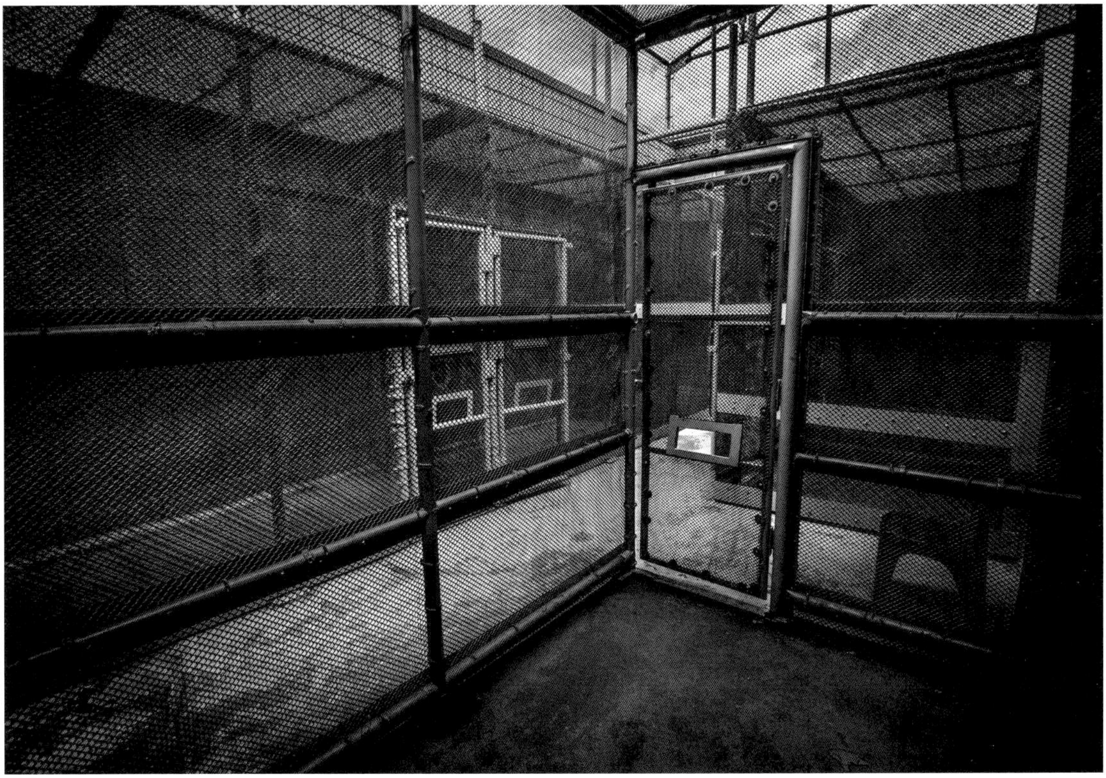

Cages (horizontal)

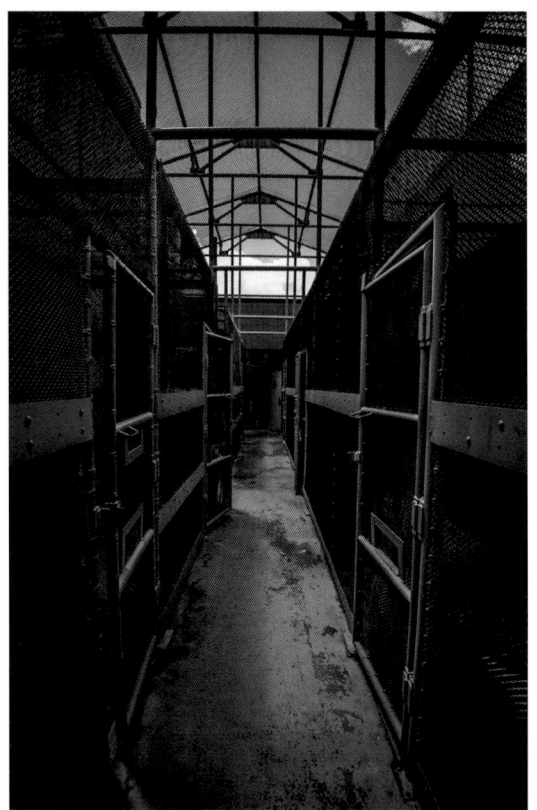
Cages (vertical)

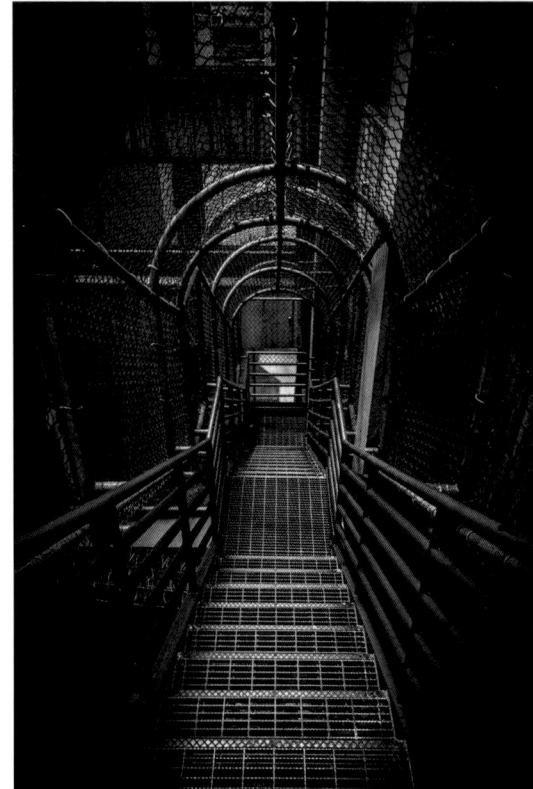
Lockdown

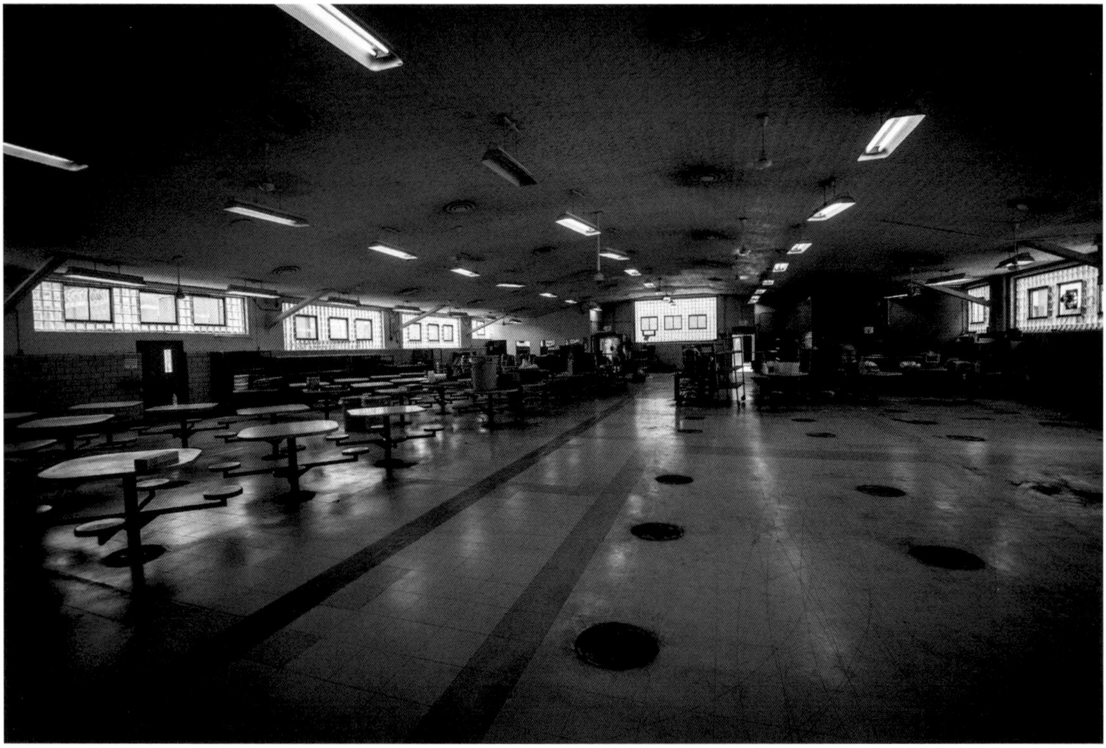

Cafeteria

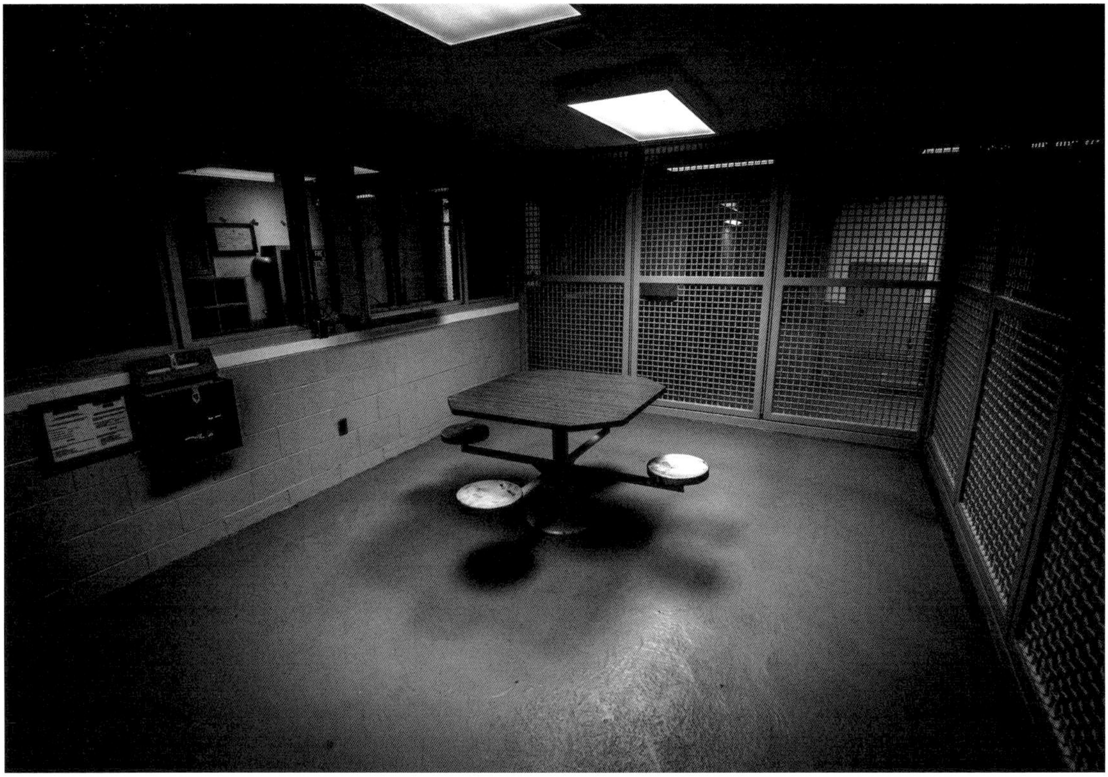

Conference

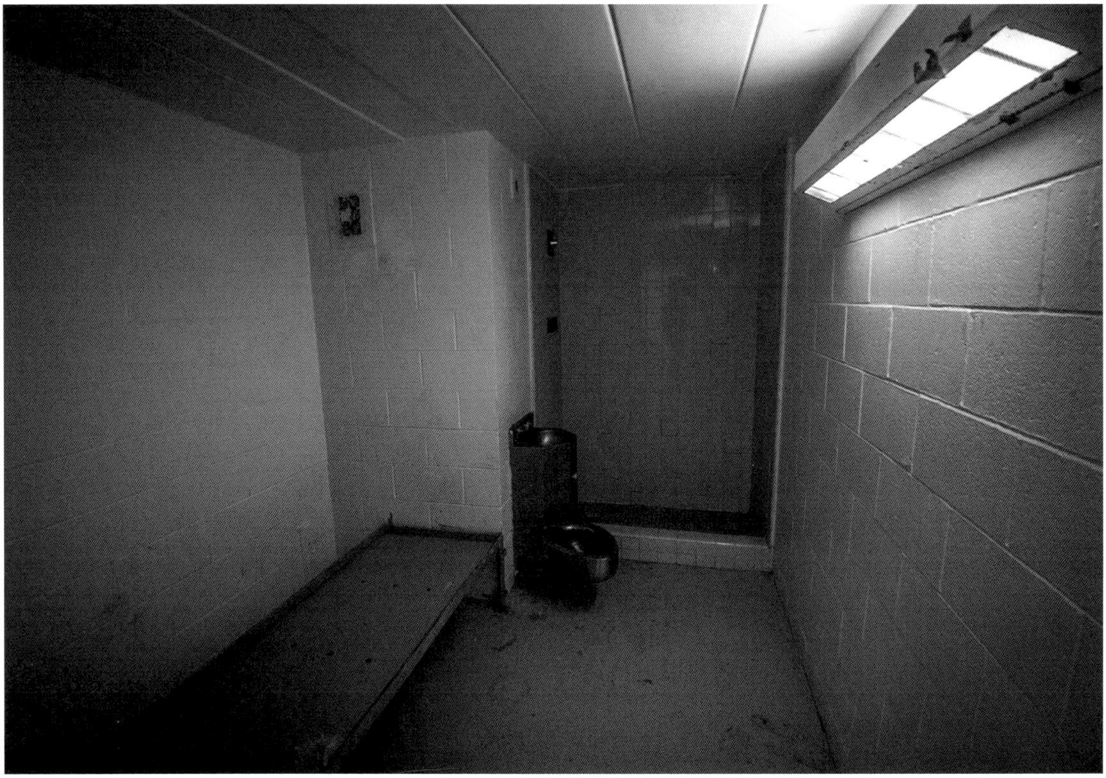

Death Row

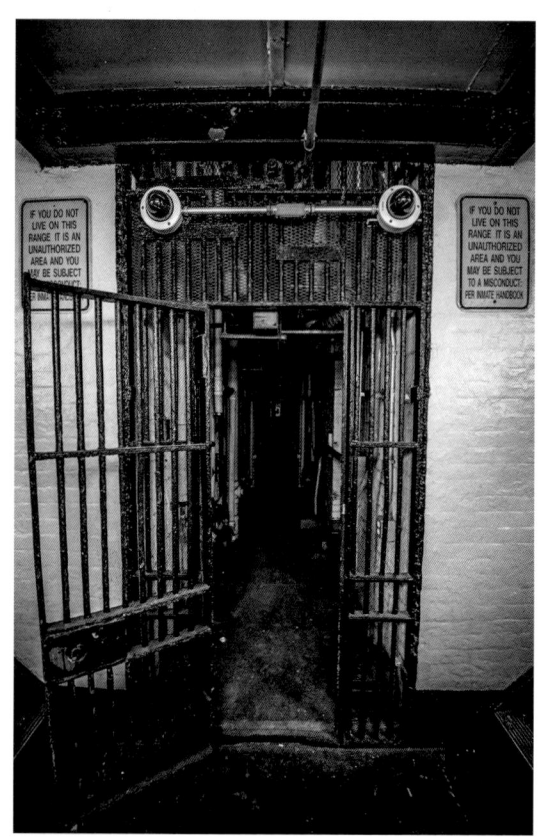

Unauthorized Area

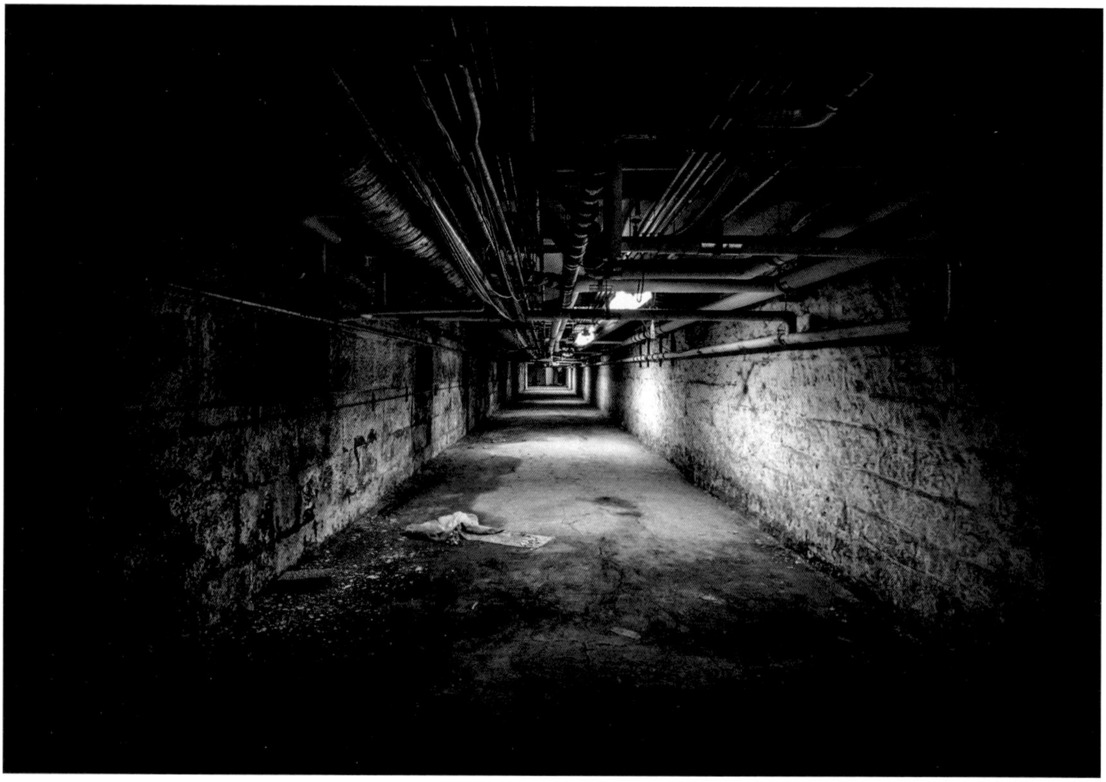

Basement Tunnel

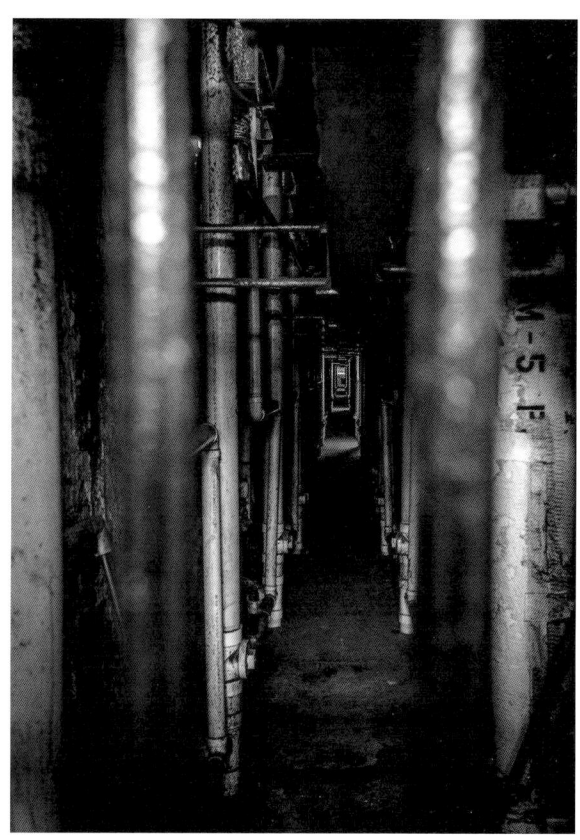

Access Tunnel

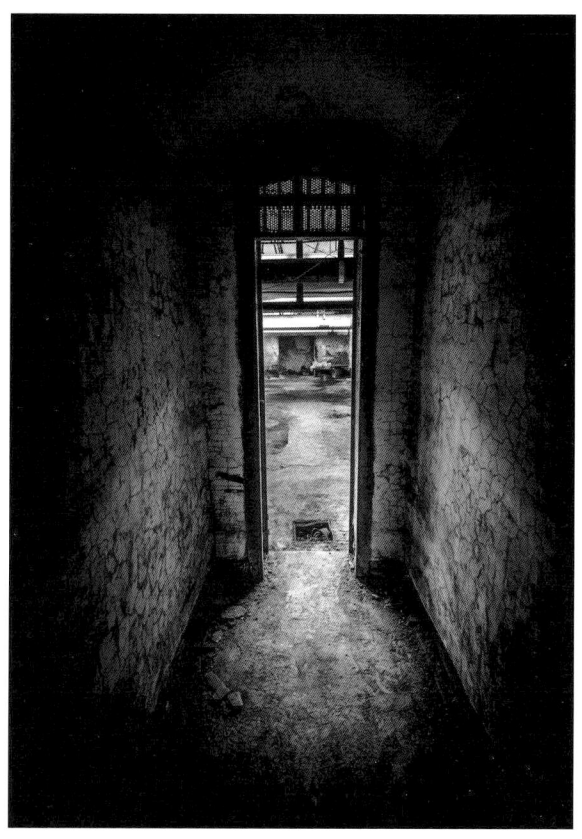

Holding Cell

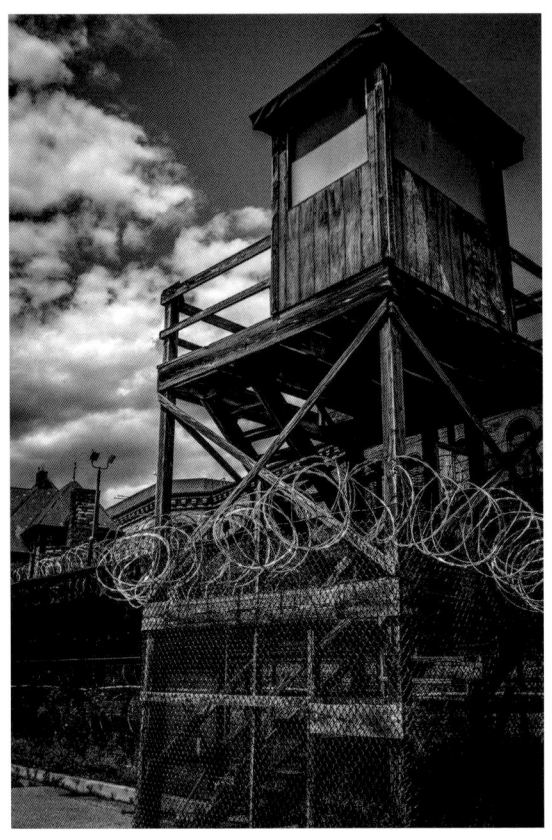

Lookout

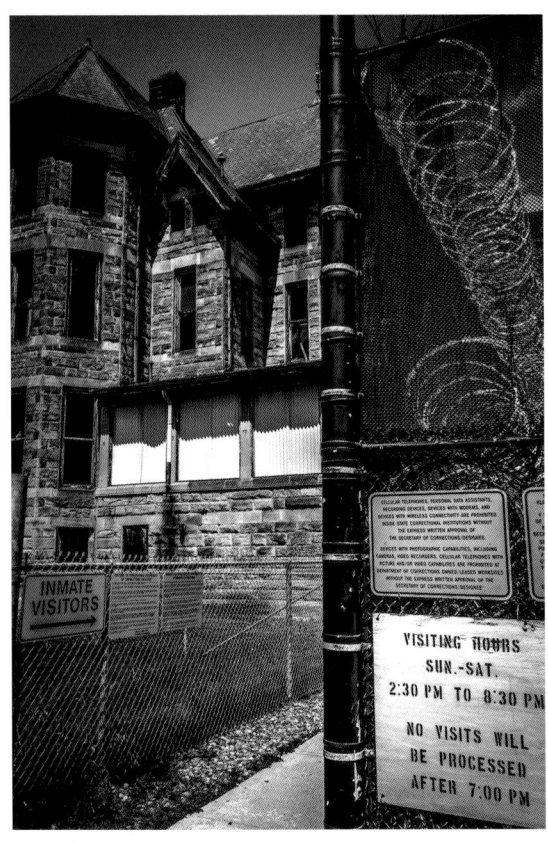

Visiting Hours

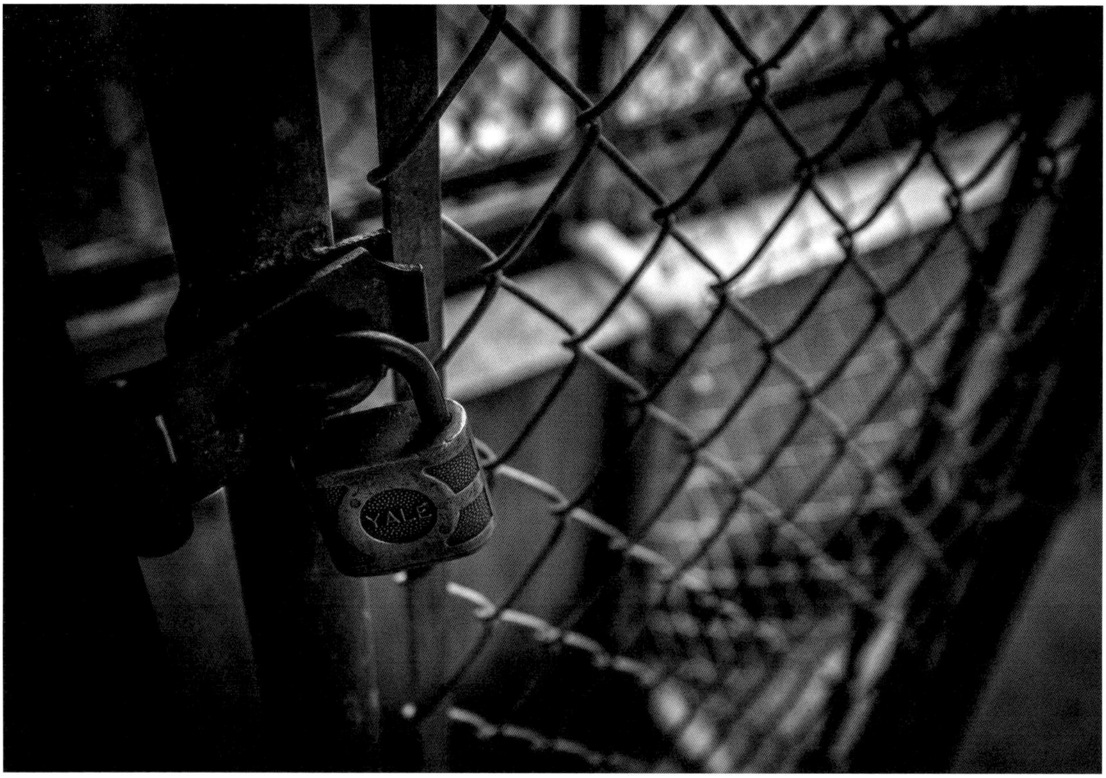

Yale Lock

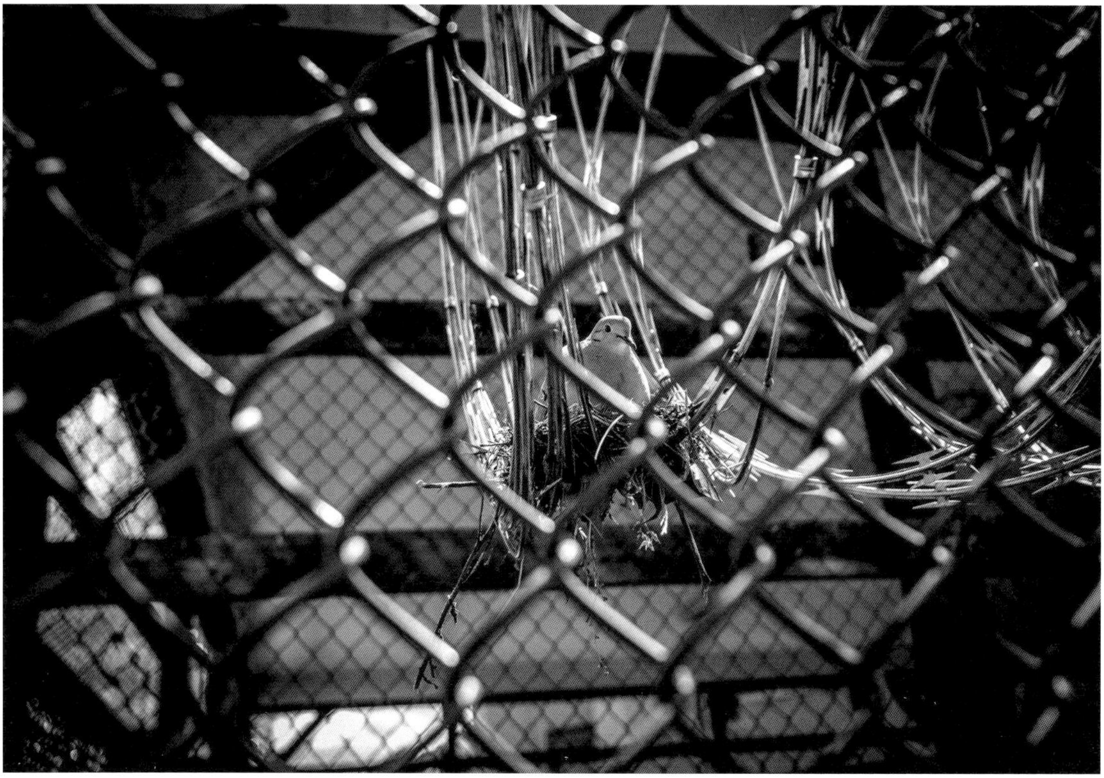

The Caged Bird

ALSO BY CHUCK BEARD

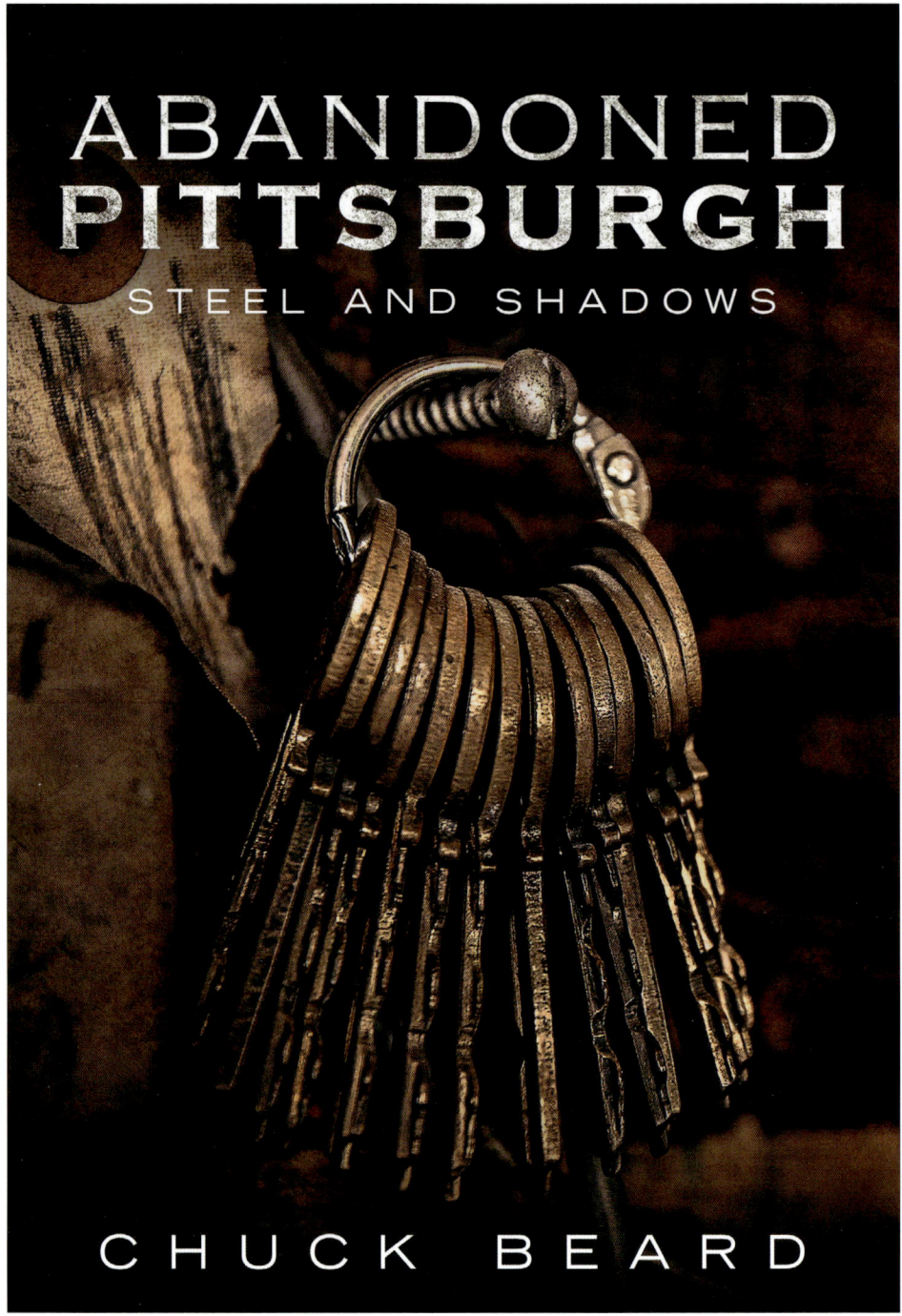

Abandoned Pittsburgh: Steel and Shadows
978-1-63499-045-5
$24.99